Everyman in Vietnam

anneen so I'll let yo
back to the TV s
right? tell Daddy 1 T
said hello and the
of the peons and b
way I have a fo
you, you know I do
worry about money so
each pay day wo
write and tell m
my allotment check
done alright, I do
whether you got
for June or not
please let me kno
reason I did not ad
letter to Mom & Da
because I thought
give you a thrill of
a letter from V

Everyman in Vietnam

A Soldier's Journey into the Quagmire

MICHAEL ADAS

JOSEPH GILCH

New York Oxford

OXFORD UNIVERSITY PRESS

To young men sent to fight in foreign wars

Oxford University Press is a department of the University of Oxford. It furthers the University's objective of excellence in research, scholarship, and education by publishing worldwide. Oxford is a registered trade mark of Oxford University Press in the UK and certain other countries.

Published in the United States of America by Oxford University Press
198 Madison Avenue, New York, NY 10016, United States of America.

For titles covered by Section 112 of the US Higher Education Opportunity Act, please visit www.oup.com/us/he for the latest information about pricing and alternate formats.

Library of Congress Cataloging-in-Publication Data

Names: Adas, Michael, 1943- author. | Gilch, Joseph J., author.
Title: Everyman in Vietnam : a soldier's journey into the quagmire / Michael Adas, Rutgers University ; Joseph Gilch, Rutgers University.
Description: New York : Oxford University Press, [2018]
Identifiers: LCCN 2017001161 | ISBN 9780190455873 (pbk.)
Subjects: LCSH: Vietnam War, 1961–1975—Campaigns. | Gilch, Jimmy, 1945–1966—Correspondence. | Soldiers—United States—Biography. | United States. Army—Biography. | Vietnam War, 1961–1975—Political aspects—United States. | Runnemede (N.J.)—Biography.
Classification: LCC DS557.7 .A435 2017 | DDC 959.704/342092 [B]—dc23
LC record available at https://lccn.loc.gov/2017001161

Table of Contents

Acknowledgements

The letters of Jimmy Gilch were the indispensable source for our account of the impact at ground level of American interventions in Vietnam. But an abundance of accessible primary sources both archival and published were essential for our efforts to frame interactions at the micro level with the broader forces that converged in one of the most costly and violent conflicts of the global cold war. The daunting abundance of often superb secondary literature on the war, which is acknowledged in footnotes for each chapter, and an equally selective list of key secondary sources, made possible our multiperspectival framing of the war at various levels, from the decisions of policymakers and military commanders to the broader historical forces in Vietnam, the United States, and the Cold War era that made for the collision of a global superpower and a small, emerging postcolonial nation.

Jimmy's friends and siblings (Maureen, Joe Sr., George Jr., Christine, Helen, Barbara, Alice, and Kathleen) shared details about Gilch family life and his growing years that was vital to the early chapters on postwar America. Special thanks to Maureen, Louise Fasulo-Cosenza, Linda Beck-Gilch, Emily Gilch, the Shields family, and members of the Runnemede, NJ VFW who provided encouragement and feedback as well as helping to locate and select relevant photos, letters, home movies, and military service records. On the other side of family support, we've sought to abide by Joel Adas's advice that we keep the book both short and engaging in order to reach students and readers beyond the academy.

Without the connections made in the seminar on "Witnessing War in the Twentieth Century," our collaboration could not have begun. The senior honors thesis that grew out of Joe's presentation was critical to our growing conviction that Jimmy's wartime experiences could provide the core of a book on the war. Thus our debt to colleagues at Rutgers University is substantial. Kathleen Hull worked tirelessly to develop the Bryne seminars, where Joe first presented material on his uncle's service in Vietnam. As careful readers for Joe's honors thesis, Professors John Chambers and Jim Masschaele provided corrections and insights that significantly influenced our approaches to the book. John Chadwick at the Rutgers news service and Reity O'Brien at the *Philadelphia Enquirer* covered both our pedagogical interactions and book in progress for the broader audience we've had in mind from the outset of the project. Chris Sherer provided invaluable support for the Masters Program in Global History at Rutgers, which made it possible to extend our collaboration, and Christopher Zarr at the National Archives and Records Administration gave us access to high definition images of the war.

From a longer-term perspective, colleagues at Rutgers and other universities, including Jochen Hellbeck, Sam Baily, David Fogelsong, Chris Jespersen, Jonathan Nashel, Gary Darden, Ben Justice, Justin Hart, Chris Fisher, Andy Buchanan, and especially Michael's longtime co-teacher and friend, Lloyd Gardner, suggested important connections and leads to useful sources. David Ekbladh, Mark Bradley, David Schmitz, David Biggs, Bill Parsons, and Fumiko Nishizaki as well as numerous Japanese respondents at conferences held at Seikei and Tokyo Universities contributed useful ideas for our work in progress. Also valuable was the feedback we received from participants in local presentations, especially Mary Jane Chambers at Triton High School, the educators and social studies teachers associated with the New York Department of Education—particularly the imaginative responses of Joseph Schmidt—and in sessions further afield at the University of Maryland, the University of Hawaii, the University of Seattle, and the State University of New York at Binghamton.

Early communications with Jimmy's platoon commander Ted Jagosz, and Randy Kethcart, the webmaster of the Fifth Mechanized Infantry Regiment's online archives, gave us indispensable insights into the day-to-day camp and combat experiences of the US infantrymen who bore the brunt of the war on the American side. The questions raised and suggestions offered by outside readers provided important corrections, and in many cases ways of enhancing arguments or the overall narrative. Our readers included Robert McMahon, Michael Hunt, Eric Bergerud, David McFadden, Christopher Laney, W. Taylor Fain, William Chafe, Allan Winkler, and most especially the late Marilyn Young who offered incisive, constructive interventions at pivotal stages of the writing process.

Special thanks go to our wise and deeply engaged editor at the Oxford University Press, Charles Cavaliere, who provided close readings of the book manuscript at several stages. Scott Bledsoe, also at the press, shepherded the book through production. Jane Adas was an insightful and thorough copy editor of the final draft of the manuscript. We cannot imagine a better editorial team.

About the Authors

Michael Adas is the Abraham E. Voorhees Professor Emeritus and Board of Governors' Chair at Rutgers University in New Brunswick, NJ. His teaching and early books focused on the comparative history of European colonialism, particularly patterns of economic and social change and peasant protest in South and Southeast Asia. Adas's more recent publications have emphasized the impact of science and technology on European and US interventions in Asia and Africa. They include *Machines as the Measure of Men: Science, Technology, and Ideologies of Western Dominance* (Ithaca, NY: Cornell University Press, 1989–1992, 2014), which received the Dexter Prize from the Society for the History of Technology and the NJ-NEH Annual Book Award, and *Dominance by Design: Technological Imperatives and America's Civilizing Mission*, which was published by the Harvard University Press in 2006 (pbk. ed, 2009). Adas's writings have been translated into seven languages, and in 2013 he was awarded the Toynbee Prize for his contributions to global history. He is currently writing a comparative history of Misbegotten Wars and the Decline of Great Powers: Britain, America, and a Century of Violence for the Harvard University Press.

Joseph Gilch is currently working to complete his graduate degree in Global and Comparative History and his Ed.M. in Social Studies Education at Rutgers University, New Brunswick. His reading and writing focus on American and global military history, and recently the history of science and technology. His undergraduate senior honor's thesis on the Vietnam War won multiple departmental prizes, and the university-wide Henry Rutgers Scholar Award. Gilch is currently working on collaborative project with Michael Adas and Joseph Schmidt for Bloomsbury's *Debates in World History* series, writing an accessible primer to the "Great Divergence" to engage high school students and undergraduates in the practice of history through analyzing and evaluating its key arguments.

"Tunnels"

Crawling down headfirst into the hole,
He kicks the air and disappears.
I feel like I'm down there
with him, moving ahead, pushed
by a river of darkness, feeling
blessed for each inch of the unknown.
Our tunnel rat is the smallest man
in the platoon, in an echo chamber
that makes his ears bleed
when he pulls the trigger.
He moves as if trying to outdo
blind fish easing toward imagined blue,
pulled by something greater than life's
ambitions. He can't think about
spiders and scorpions mending the air,
or care about bats upside down
like gods in the mole's blackness.
The damp smell goes deeper
than the stench of honey buckets.
A web of booby traps waits, ready
to spring into broken stars.
Forced onward by some need,
some urge, he knows the pulse
of mysteries & diversions
like thoughts trapped in the ground.
He questions each root.
Every cornered shadow has a life
to bargain with. Like an angel

pushed against what hurts,
his globe-shaped helmet
follows the gold ring his flashlight
casts into the void. Through silver
lice, shit, maggots, & vapor of pestilence,
he goes, the good soldier,
on hands & knees, tunneling past
death sacked into a blind corner,
loving the weight of the shotgun
that will someday dig his grave.

—Yusef Kommunyakka

"Tunnels" from *Dien Cai Dau* (Middletown, CT: Wesleyan University Press, 1988)

"They [the tunnels of Cu Chi] are something very Vietnamese, and one must understand what the relationship is between the Vietnamese peasant and the earth, *his* earth. Without that, then everything here is without real meaning. But I fear you will not understand."

—Captain Nguyen Thanh Linh,
North Vietnamese Army, as quoted in Tom Mangold and
John Penycate *The Tunnels of Cu Chi*

Prologue

In the Ho Bo Woods, June 28, 1966

One of the first things a soldier learns is never stand when he can sit and never sit when he can lie prone. Some men couldn't get low enough, and even those who did were still sometimes killed. Bad days were inevitable, but never quite predictable. Coping with them was difficult, especially when the heat burned and a raw visceral fear worked on one's nerves. This particular day began early and ended badly. It was a Tuesday. The summer monsoons had inundated the whole of the Cu Chu region. Foxholes were flooded and the rats scurried everywhere. By 0600 hours the temperature was already in the mid-eighties. The humidity in the Ho Bo Woods made it seem much hotter.

James Gilch took bites of his C-ration and traded away items he had grown tired of forcing down. He ate his meal cold. The fuel tablet took too long to heat up, and though he considered using a piece of C-4 explosive to speed up the heating process, it might be needed in the combat to come. Many GIs thought C-4 was the greatest stuff they'd ever seen. It heated their breakfast and boiled their coffee. Hooked up to a blasting cap it blew houses off their foundations. It also mangled limbs. But unlike gunshot wounds that burned, C-4 or booby-trap explosions happened so quickly that the brain didn't have time to register the pain. Shock and massive blood loss followed. One man whose leg was blown off described the feeling as "pins and needles all over."[1] Before the morphine kicked in, he felt as if his nerves had shorted out and his body had fallen asleep even though his eyes were still open. Soldiers fighting in Vietnam repressed the idea of becoming a casualty. Those killed became whole numbers on after-action report casualty lists. Some were really just bits and pieces of a number.

As a member of the Twenty-Fifth Infantry Division, Fifth Mechanized Regiment, B Company, Third Squad, James Gilch was back out in the bush to search for a Viet Cong field hospital and combat training center. "Operation Coco Palms" was his fourth trip to the densely forested Ho Bo and Boi Loi Woods. Many troops, including Jimmy Gilch, griped openly to friends that they were going—yet again—back to "that same damn area." They felt they were spending more than their fair share of time in the field. This complaint reflected a general attitude toward operations in the Hau Nghia and Binh Duong Provinces. Soldiers of the Fifth Mechanized Infantry Regiment wondered why the army had not set up a base camp in the area and stayed on, rather than of going in, "kicking ass," and then leaving, only to later return and get their "ass kicked."[2] This line of questioning persisted as the orders for "Coco Palms" made it clear that after the operation they would leave, thus allowing Charlie to rebuild his defenses and booby trap the area in anticipation of the next American assault. Search and Destroy didn't make much sense to most American grunts. Then again, not much in Vietnam did.

Before he "saddled up" and manned the point position atop his unit's armored personnel carrier (APC), Jimmy wrote a letter home while he ate his breakfast: "Well, to start off, your hero is back out again for about 6 to 10 days. I didn't wait around for mail [the other night], because I went down to see my pals to tell them I am going out into the field." His letters home increasingly downplayed the nature of the war and the carnage he had seen. Instead, he focused on the "good laughs" and beer enjoyed during a last minute visit with his friends at Company headquarters. He tried to assure his parents that all was well and that he was all right, and when he returned home, he said, he would make them proud by "showing off [his] uniform and the medals [he] had won." But his actions in the field reflected a different reality. In the last month he had grown increasingly outspoken and been reprimanded for that. In country since February, the war had taken its toll. He had become fixated on his upcoming R&R. He would rather be cleaning dishes in the mess hall or even disposing of human waste on the firebase than going out on patrol.

Around 0630 the men of B Company advanced toward the day's first objective. The rampant vegetation and tall sawgrass provided excellent cover for the Viet Cong and severely limited the visibility of their American pursuers. Jimmy's company commander had to constantly realign his platoon's firing lines. The maneuver was tedious and loud, and the noise made them prone to ambush. Just getting to the combat area was troublesome. The nearby stream had flooded and bogged down the armored personnel carriers. The mud made movement on foot slow and treacherous. When the company arrived at the target area, they found the Vietnamese had fortified a strong defensive perimeter. Eight-foot deep trenches linked bunkers to underground rooms where switchboard operators controlled command-detonated mines that were buried in the nearby open clearing. The whole area was booby trapped. Around 1030 hours the company encountered an extensive tunnel network and underground storage facility that was reinforced with steel and concrete. It held massive amounts of supplies, including surgical instruments, medicine, thousands of pounds of rice and clothing, and large weapon caches. It was by far the largest enemy complex Jimmy's unit had yet discovered, and it could easily withstand a direct aerial bombardment.

Before attempting to "flush out" the Viet Cong with tear gas and destroy the entrance to the complex using a piece of C-4, Gerald Rolf, an experienced "tunnel rat," was called in to explore the underground network. Rolf was well aware that he was undertaking one of the most dangerous tasks assigned to infantrymen in Vietnam. Small and lean, he knew that his size was critical to his ability to navigate the tunnels that stretched for miles beneath the forests of Cu Chi. The enemy engineers had purposely made the well-camouflaged entryways as small as possible to allow the shorter, slighter Vietnamese access and make entry difficult for the generally taller, bulkier Americans. The shafts down into the tunnels were also slanted in ways that would force the GIs when entering to flatten their bodies in a manner that would make them less likely to be able to defend themselves in the critical moments after their descent.

Unlike the rodent he was dubbed, his merely human vision was limited in the dark. He relied on instinct and lessons gleaned from previous underground probes. Some "rats" claimed they could sniff out the enemy, who were alleged to smell of "stale sweat and spice."[3] But the Vietnamese were aware that their food, clothing, and bodies could give off distinctive scents and tried to cover them. The Americans used German Shepherds to sniff out tunnel entrances, but the Vietnamese countered by spraying mosquito repellant around openings and left US government-issued soap and cigarettes underneath trap doors. For K-9 handlers locating the enemy was like searching for ghosts. Most of the time the dogs couldn't smell them. The Vietnamese rarely left signs of their presence, and they took great care to avoid stepping on plants along trails or discarding trash.

On the day when Rolf entered the tunnels in the Ho Bo woods, it is possible that among the guerrilla fighters waiting to ambush him was Vo Thi Mo, a fifteen-year-old girl whose home had been destroyed, family's land despoiled, and farm animals killed in an American bombing raid months earlier. Following precedents established in ancient times when Vietnamese women had commanded guerrilla bands resisting foreign invaders, Vo was a squad leader. But informal Viet Cong regulations discouraged female soldiers from engaging in hand-to-hand combat with American soldiers out of concern that they might be captured and abused. Nonetheless, Vo Thi Mo and others from her female company joined in efforts to repel or kill tunnel rats who crawled into the communist sanctuaries. Vo Thi Mo recounted how the guerrillas would lead the American intruders through the tunnels always able to keep ahead of their pursuers due to their familiarity with the system. A favorite ruse was to draw the tunnel rats into a second, lower level of the network and shoot them when they sought to push through the narrow trap doors that led back to the surface. When several tunnel rats were working their way out of the underground maze, Vo Thi Mo and her comrades would spear and wedge the lead soldier in the trap door. Having thus blocked the way out for the tunnel rats behind him, it was impossible for them to open fire on the Vietnamese defenders. She recalled the fury of the Americans when their comrades were killed in this way.[4]

Everything Rolf had learned in basic training about fighting a ground war seemed of little relevance in the tunnels. All he found was a curious and alien terrain full of holes that he had to crawl through in search of weapons, documents, or enemy soldiers. Underground nothing ever worked to the GIs' advantage. They struggled with claustrophobia and fatigue. If they encountered someone or something, the tunnel rats had to make quick decisions, weighing the consequences of using force. Firing a weapon, or the blast of a grenade could blow out eardrums and possibly collapse the tunnel. The only advantage—if one could call it that—of being a tunnel rat was sometimes when it was intolerably hot above ground, the tunnels were still cool and dank.

Rolf took off his helmet and ammo belt. He had learned from experience that they only got in his way. Other rats fitted themselves out with gas masks, miners' helmets, and attached field radios to their belts. But Rolf wore only a fatigue jacket and armed himself with a flashlight, a small-caliber pistol, and a bayonet. Before he made a full descent he waited for a fellow squad member to gear up and follow him into the tunnel. Jimmy and the men above watched as their friends dropped into the narrow entrance.

A tunnel rat never knew what he was going to encounter down below. Some found bats and dead bodies; others scorpions and snakes (said to be as much as six feet long). Rolf slowly crawled into the unknown. When he got to a ninety-degree turn, he twisted—probing with his searchlight—and suddenly froze. "Oh no," he whispered. Gunshots. Silence. A small recovery team was sent down to rescue the wounded eighteen-year-old from Cincinnati, Ohio. When reinforcements reached Rolf and his backup, they began to drag him out. But they too came under fire. Left with no other choice and desperate to save themselves, they used Rolf's body as a human shield.

A dust off was called.

Gerald Rolf was bagged, tagged, and sent home.

After the medevac flew off, Jimmy remounted the APC and continued the search.

*

Introduction

The great majority of the two generations of Americans who have come of age since the end of the Vietnam War know little about that conflict or the impassioned policy debates that it engendered. In an age dominated by soundbites and social media, few of those on either side in the political arena seeking to rouse the nation to battle or to oppose further overseas interventions have made informed use of the prodigious amount of information made available in memoirs, social science analyses, and historical narratives. Retired generals, political pundits, and academics have periodically engaged in often-acrimonious controversies concerning the fateful decisions made by civilian and military leaders in the 1960s and early 1970s. But these exchanges have been mainly confined to the academic and policymaking elite. Prominent politicians, most vigorously Ronald Reagan, have challenged the widespread conviction that Vietnam was a bad war. The specter of the so-called "Vietnam syndrome" was resurrected in 1990 by both the advocates of Desert Storm, who insisted that they had devised a very different strategy, and those who warned that another quagmire was in the offing. Although in the aftermath of the first US–Iraq War President George H.W. Bush had famously declared that the nation had "kicked [the syndrome] behind" it, the debate surged again in the months before a second conflict with Iraq in 2003. But neither the second Bush administration's sloganeers, who promoted the overthrow of the Ba'athist regime, nor the protesters who opposed the invasion and military occupation, seriously interrogated the very relevant questions raised by the Vietnam debacle or demonstrated reliable knowledge about that earlier conflict.

Misremembering America's military interventions in Vietnam in fragmented, often misleading ways has been pervasive despite the often-superb, interdisciplinary scholarship that has been published on the conflict.[1] Memoirs and semiautobiographical fictional accounts by those who fought in the war are often assigned for US history survey courses at the secondary and college levels. Though many of these make for compelling reading and provide personalized accounts of the traumatic conditions endured by Americans engaged in combat, they offer little understanding of the Vietnamese side of the conflict. More general historical narratives that predominate in upper-level college courses on the war tend to focus on American policymaking, diplomacy, and overall military strategy with rather episodic treatment of combat situations. Though numerous, books that provide extensive coverage of US military operations are intended for select audiences. The best of these narratives make some attempt to include Vietnamese perspectives,[2] but they are seldom assigned in secondary school or college-level courses, and are not readily available to a broader readership.

Thus, aside from veterans and families of soldiers who served in Vietnam, scholars specializing in various aspects of the conflict, and upper-level college students who take their courses, most Americans have little sense of who the Vietnamese are, or even where their country is located. Only a tiny minority of Americans have any in-depth knowledge of Vietnamese history and culture, the forces that divided Vietnamese resistance to colonial domination, or how the communists were able to win the allegiance of the majority of the Vietnamese people. Even more troubling is the fact that, despite frequent allusions to precedents based on the Vietnam conflict in controversies generated by recent US military interventions in the Middle East, very few Americans have even a rudimentary understanding of the motivations of the leaders and the decision-making processes that drove the nation into the Southeast Asian quagmire. In contrast to many of the fine scholars specializing in the history of the war, remarkably few political pundits or public intellectuals have addressed the reasons why, for example, the nation that Lyndon Johnson dismissed as a "dammed little piss-ant country" and Henry Kissinger deemed at best a "fourth-rate" adversary, was able to defeat a global superpower. Reflecting on the hubris and ignorance that led to America's misbegotten war in Vietnam might well have prompted our leaders and policymakers to proceed with greater caution in launching subsequent overseas interventions.

These trends suggest that there is clearly the need for an accessible and multidimensional way to convey an understanding of the nature and enduring significance of the Vietnam conflict for students and a broader reading public. Over decades of teaching (and in recent years writing) about the war, I have experimented with approaches that bring together the multiple perspectives of the adversaries, and the different levels of engagement—from policymakers in Washington and Hanoi to the soldiers and civilians struggling to survive in the borderless combat zones. What turned out to be an enabling response to these challenges emerged several years ago from an unexpected source. A moving presentation by Joseph Gilch in a seminar I was leading at Rutgers University on "Witnessing War in the Twentieth Century" suggested a number of highly revealing connections between the personal account of his uncle Jimmy Gilch's time in Vietnam, the criteria by which young Americans were selected to go into battle, and the nature of the war that made it such a harrowing ordeal for combatants on all sides as well as for Vietnamese civilians. In the semesters that followed, I mentored Joseph's work on what proved to be a prizewinning honors thesis based on a much-expanded version of his earlier presentation. Working on that project made us both aware of the exceptional nature of the collection of letters Jimmy had written to his parents and best friend during his tour of duty.

The backstory of how the letters were nearly destroyed and then saved was something of a saga in itself. During the summer of 2000, at the age of eleven, I spent Fridays with my grandmother in Runnemede, New Jersey. Growing up in the suburbs of the nearby town, it was difficult to play sports without getting into trouble with the neighbors, so my grandmother's house became a refuge. She had several acres of land, a basketball court, and for a short while even a baseball diamond. My Uncle George, who had bought the house from her in the late 1970s but allowed her stay on, farmed portions of the backfield, and I helped him pick tomatoes, squash, and pumpkins. There was also a blackberry bush on the edge of the property. When the fruit was ripe, I took the berries to my grandmother, Catherine, who prepared them in a bowl of warm milk and sugar for us to enjoy while we watched reruns of Matlock. I soon lost interest in the TV shows, but was intrigued by the picture above the television. I had been curious for sometime about the man in the photo. He was dressed in army khaki, and medals and unit citations were displayed on either side of the frame. I soon found out that the soldier was my uncle James, or "Jimmy."

My persistent questioning about my uncle led my grandmother to share with me the nearly eighty letters that he wrote to her and my grandfather during his tour of duty in Vietnam. Discussions during my Friday visits were mostly about family history during a period of time and a war that I knew almost nothing about. As we read the letters, my grandmother explained the family interactions that framed certain jokes, and told me what she knew about the war and the people Jimmy mentioned. When we finished reading several letters, we packed the whole set in the old shoebox where she kept them, and put them away in her closet—or so I thought. Unbeknown to me, Catherine would continue to read the letters after I went home. Some of her children felt that the letters had trapped her in the past, and because she was often seen crying while reading them, they insisted they be destroyed. To ensure they would not be, my grandmother gave them to me along with his military service records, notepads, and other memorabilia that I stored in my bedroom closet at home.

I did not seriously study the Vietnam War until I took Michael Adas's seminar. In order to understand Jimmy's experiences, I soon found that I needed to master the broader historical context of the war he was sent to fight. The core primary sources I used for my senior honors thesis included Jimmy's letters to his parents and best friend during his six months in combat service. I supplemented these with additional letters from his best friend, and with factual clarifications, home movies and photos, and memories generously provided by Jimmy's siblings. For his months in the military, I used after action reports compiled by the United States Army to track his day-by-day service in the Fifth Mechanized Infantry in Vietnam. I also made use of the unit's official history and online recollections and personal communications provided by several of the officers in charge of his platoon.

Responses to the thesis on the part of fellow students and Rutgers history department colleagues prompted the two of us to read and discuss the letters together the following summer. We were soon convinced that they could provide the basis for a broader history of the Vietnam War. Our ability to draw out the deeper meanings of Jimmy's often abbreviated references to his combat missions and the impact of those operations was subsequently informed by additional reading of a number of fine collections of soldiers' correspondence and oral interviews. Similar to letters from other combatants, many of Jimmy's were preoccupied with questions about how his family was faring back in New Jersey and rather banal comments about camp routines and army regulations. Jimmy's letters abound in grammatical errors, particularly those written at the beginning of his tour of duty. Though we frequently quote directly from his correspondence, in order not to lose his voice, we have refrained from editing stylistic errors except in passages where it was necessary to clarify his meaning. As he came to accept the need to take charge of his life, he asked his parents to send him a dictionary. He wanted to improve his writing so that he could better share intense moments in combat as well as his growing interest in Vietnam and its people, whom he initially dismissed as appallingly backward.

Similar to most of the other American soldiers in combat in Vietnam who shared Jimmy's loss of a sense of purpose in the conflict and his dismay with its brutality, he was not sufficiently educated or connected to aspire to someday publish an account of his wartime experiences. He sought instead to create his own, alternative mission in Vietnam. This involved reaching out to some of the Vietnamese he encountered, and though he continued to be a dependable soldier on combat missions, whenever possible he contrived ways to avoid them. Jimmy's increasing distress about fighting a war that seemed mainly to victimize Vietnamese civilians—including large numbers of children—rather than defeating the elusive guerrillas, epitomized the responses expressed in the letters and interviews of many of the "ordinary" soldiers who fought in Vietnam. But Jimmy went to great lengths to escape the search and destroy missions that he and so many who served in Vietnam realized were ill-conceived, and ultimately futile.

Aside from his M-16 rifle, mail was quite possibly the most important thing in Jimmy's life as a soldier. His letters home were filled with comments about little things: mundane details of daily life, apologies for past mistakes, conversations with foxhole buddies, combat stories and anxieties, and plans for his future after military service. Similar to other soldiers, the mail he eagerly awaited was also a crucial coping mechanism. In contrast to memoirs and oral testimony published or narrated after the war, Jimmy's letters were written in "the here and now." They are raw, unscripted, deeply personal, and honest. They relate immediate feelings and responses that are often overlooked or differ significantly from those in accounts written or recorded after the war. Because he was inducted into the military in the fall of 1965, the antiwar protest movement at home and the dissent that spread in the ranks of combatants in subsequent years only marginally affected his growing doubts about the war. Taken together, his letters build a narrative of the conflict that viscerally conveys its carnage and confusion, the weariness and constant strain of the soldiers engaged, the excitement of battle and boring routine of camp life, and his obsession with the ever-present possibility of death.

Because Jimmy wrote home regularly when he was not out on a mission, we have been able to base the personal perspectives that anchor our narrative of the war on his account of his experiences in combat and military service more generally. The regular and comprehensive nature of Jimmy's correspondence allows us to track his evolving reactions to the kind of war he and his comrades were ordered to fight. One unexpected revelation in this regard is how early in the conflict both line officers and Jimmy's fellow infantrymen had begun to doubt that the American intervention would be successful. His letters also address a range of reactions and concerns, including his evolving attitudes toward the Vietnamese and their culture, and race relations and class differences among the military personnel sent to Vietnam. His encounters with individual Vietnamese and nonconfrontational attempts to withdraw from a conflict that had lost purpose for him exemplify a process of disillusionment that increasingly sapped the morale of many of the infantrymen who bore the brunt of the war on the American side.

The personal experiences of American soldiers who fought in Vietnam have, of course, been vividly captured in the numerous novels, short stories, poems, and memoirs that, together with cinematic portrayals, have proved to be the most influential artistic representations of the conflict. The best of these—including Philip Caputo's *Rumor of War*, Tim O'Brien's *The Things They Carried*, Karl Marlantes' *Matterhorn*, Ron Kovic's *Born On the Fourth of July*, and Michael Herr's *Dispatches*—are emotionally powerful soldiers' stories that reveal the traumatic nature of counterinsurgency operations. But their authors are not mainly concerned with the larger historical context of the war. Their purpose is not to describe the sociopolitical forces that led to the war or examine its impact on the policymakers and generals or soldiers and their families, whose lives were transformed by the Vietnam tragedy. With regard to its victims, little attention has been given by American writers, with the exception of expatriate Vietnamese,[3] to the devastation visited on the Vietnamese people and their country. Nonetheless, these highly personal accounts have been rightly considered some of the definitive works on the Vietnam War, and in some cases their modest length has made them widely accessible for American students. But none of these memoirs or fictional narratives explores the history of the multinational and global processes that led to the US interventions, the political calculations on opposing sides that shaped successive decisions for military escalation, or Vietnamese perspectives on the conflict in any depth.[4]

Our close reading of Jimmy's letters led us to realize the many ways his personal experiences mirrored in microcosm key themes and events in the broader post–World War II history of the United States, and later became enmeshed in the very different history of Vietnam in the same era. These trajectories were in turn shaped by global cold war confrontations, particularly those arising from superpower rivalries, decolonization, and the emergence of developing nations. The challenge of bringing together these complex connections in a coherent and concise narrative was, we believe, surmounted by our rediscovery of John Steinbeck's *Grapes of Wrath.* His alternation of chapters relating the struggles of the Joad family to survive the impoverishment and displacement brought on by the Dust Bowl with overviews of the origins and impact of the Great Depression on the nation as a whole provided a prototype for a book of modest length that could integrate American, Vietnamese, and global narratives. Rather than alternating different perspectives by chapter, however, we decided to intersperse accounts of Jimmy's growing years and wartime experiences *within* chapters among accounts of divergent post-World War II histories, postwar cross-cultural interactions, and eventual conflict between the United States and Vietnam. This approach made it possible for us to compare the contrasting sociocultural and geopolitical factors that led to successive—and increasingly violent—American interventions with those that enabled the successful resistance of the Vietnamese to efforts to subvert their long quest for liberation and national unity.

For chapter segments on relevant events and patterns in American, Vietnamese, and global history, we have used a mix of primary and secondary sources. Primary source materials include the Pentagon Papers, memoirs of key policymakers, published collections of soldiers' letters, and compilations of oral interviews, which were particularly important for understanding Vietnamese civilian and combatant perspectives. Secondary materials include a substantial slice of the now voluminous scholarly literature that has appeared in the half century since the war, as well as books and articles intended for a broader readership. Novels, poetry, photography, diaries, and artifacts—from propaganda leaflets to "the things [soldiers] carried"—were essential to our efforts to capture the ordeal of both Americans and Vietnamese who fought in the war and Vietnamese civilians who were caught in the middle of it. We have kept back notes to a minimum, citing them mainly to document statistics, to quote passages from primary sources and published works, and to back up potentially controversial assertions. We have also included books and articles that we found especially informative on specific aspects of the war and the converging forces that led to or sustained it. We have included a bibliography of select sources divided into each of the major themes we explore in our narrative of the war and the broader history of Vietnam, the United States, and the world in the first three-quarters of the twentieth century.

The sections devoted to key developments in post–World War II America in the first two chapters serve to contextualize Jimmy Gilch's family background, growing years, and coming of age. These narratives are interspersed with sections dealing with the Vietnamese revolution and struggle to gain national independence from French colonial rule. Each of the early chapters also includes analysis of the ever-shifting rationales for the increasing involvement of the United States in Indochina from the administration of Harry S. Truman through John F. Kennedy.

These chapter sections also deal with American policymakers' steadily increasing hostility to the communist-led Viet Minh, which had taken the lead in the war of liberation against the French. Accounts of Jimmy Gilch's early life and willingness to be inducted into the U.S. Army provide both a human dimension to these larger confrontations and a means of weaving together the alternating historical perspectives covered in the opening chapters and those that follow.

Chapters 3 and 4 begin with analyses of the tense deliberations and anxiety-ridden decisions that by the summer of 1965 led Lyndon Johnson and his advisors to escalate American military interventions in Vietnam's civil war. In chapter three, Jimmy's boot camp experience is contrasted with the organization and training of the guerrilla forces of the NLF (National Liberation Front) in South Vietnam and the Peoples Liberation Army (NVA) of the Democratic Republic of Vietnam north of the 17th parallel. Coverage of the entry of American ground troops into the Vietnam quagmire begins in chapter 4, which focuses on Jimmy's arrival and US operations in the Cu Chi District, where he and his mechanized unit of the Twenty-Fifth Infantry Division would spend their tour of duty. With its extensive underground network of shelters and tunnels, the Cu Chi region in southern Vietnam had for decades been a stronghold of communist-dominated guerrilla resistance, first to the French colonizers and later the autocratic Diem regime.

In chapter 5, American approaches to what soon became a massive military intervention in Vietnam are framed by an account of the battle of Ia Drang in early November 1965. The prior decision of the US commander William Westmoreland and his staff to fight a conventional war stressing massive firepower appeared to be confirmed by what they claimed was a major victory over numerically superior communist forces. Several sections in chapters 5 and 6 focus on the methods subsequently adopted by the North Vietnamese and their NLF guerrilla allies to counter the high-tech weapons and mobile tactics deployed by the American superpower. These chapters are interspersed with segments that trace the arc of Jimmy's evolution from a reliable, committed soldier to a disillusioned and reluctant participant in what was becoming a war against Vietnamese civilians rather than guerrilla insurgents or NVA regulars. In discussions of the incessant warfare that devastated most of South *and* North Vietnam, we also seek to gauge its impact on American and Vietnamese combatants more generally, as well as the peasant population of Vietnam that became a major target of a seemingly never-ending conflict.

The epilogue focuses on an assessment of the aftermath of the war from both US and Vietnamese national perspectives and its survivors at various sociopolitical levels, from Jimmy's family and Vietnamese civilians to soldiers on all sides of the conflict. It also surveys the enduring legacy of the Vietnam debacle in terms of its repercussions for American and Vietnamese politics and society, which persist in important ways into the early decades of the twenty-first century. We end with reflections on the lessons from the war that were heeded or ignored by subsequent leaders and remain relevant for future American military interventions and nation-building projects in the postcolonial world.

Each of the chapters is prefaced by epigraphs and images intended to foreshadow the perspectives, themes, and events covered therein. Discussions of varying perspectives and the involvement of participants at different political and socioeconomic levels are also linked by recurrent themes. These include the contrasts in wealth, resources, and power that set highly industrialized, affluent America apart from Vietnam—a peasant-based, war-ravaged, postcolonial society and divided nation. Asymmetry in terms of material abundance was also manifested in the high-tech, massive firepower unleashed by the US military in a failed effort to defeat both guerrilla-based resistance to the regime in South Vietnam and regular communist forces from the North.

Obviously no one individual can represent the diverse range of American soldiers who served in Vietnam. But Jimmy Gilch shared a good deal with a majority of those who actually engaged in combat in terms of family and class background, religious affiliation, level of education, generational cohort, reasons for willingness to serve, and reactions to the conflict that engulfed him.[5] The nature of the Selective Service System and the composition of local draft boards ensured that young working class males with a high school education or less were disproportionately inducted for compulsory military service. Although he was not officially included in the lists of "dropouts" and other disadvantaged youths who made up Robert McNamara's "one hundred thousand" young American males who were targeted for combat duty in Vietnam, Jimmy only slightly exceeded their overall profile.[6] He had the misfortune to be in his early twenties when the escalation of the US military commitment to the Saigon regime accelerated in the summer of 1965. He was from a working class family that was financially and materially moving into the lower middle strata of American society. But he had quit high school before graduation and had no plans to go to college, which at that time would have earned him a deferment. As was fitting for an American Everyman in the early post-World War II decades, Jimmy was raised a Christian and instilled with a sense of duty. Though he gradually became quite independent-minded when it came to Catholic doctrines, he took seriously the Church's mandate to care for those in need. Following his father's example, he also sought to live up to some of the best of American values, including fair play, respect for women and the elderly, and the necessity for hard work and self-improvement.

Similar to most Americans at the time, Jimmy viewed Communism as a threat to the United States and the way of life to which he was accustomed. Also like most of his fellow citizens, he had only a superficial knowledge of Soviet Russia, Communist China, and the cold war—and knew little about Vietnam beyond occasional reports of guerrilla assaults and coups in Saigon on the evening news. Though patriotism may have been important for some young men who served in the military in the early stages of the US buildup, it was not a significant motive for Jimmy's willingness to be drafted and sent to war. He believed that military service would give him purpose in what had become a rather aimless life, and provide career opportunities far more appealing than those available to him in Runnemede, New Jersey, where he grew up. He also felt that wearing a uniform would garner him respect in a society in which the military was still widely admired for its victories in World War II. Although undereducated, Jimmy was intelligent, self-conscious, and reflective—hence able to assess the counterproductive nature of the devastation US interventions were inflicting on Vietnamese society. He also came to recognize what Robert Jay Lifton has termed the "moral inversions" inherent in the kind of war he was sent to fight.[7]

Everyman in Vietnam

A tale of two very different countries: a surfeit of automobiles and stores filled with consumer goods in 1950s America underscores the contrasts with an abandoned street in Hanoi awaiting occupation by Viet Minh Troops.

CHAPTER 1

Divergent Trajectories: America and Vietnam after World War II

"So seven per cent of the earth's surface and population was wealthier, by itself, than the rest of the world put together. As monetary proof of this wealth, sixty per cent of the gold and precious metals of the whole world lay in the vaults of the Federal Reserve Bank. The result was that, despite its proliferation, the dollar was the only real gold currency in the world . . ."

—HENRI MICHEL, *The Second World War* (New York: Praeger, 1974)

In the sleep of the innocents, gunfire sounds like lightning
Incoherent dreams
Awake with a start
The specter of the enemy torments the lips of the young
Our rage will not subside
This land will note their crimes

—HONG CAM, "Ben Kia Song Duong" [On the Other Side of the Doung River], translated by Kim N.B. Ninh, (1948)

"The old imperialism—exploitation for foreign profit—
has no place in our plans. What we envisage is a program
of development based on the concept of democratic
fair-dealing."

—HARRY TRUMAN, Point Four Program (1949)

It was early May 1945. The rain continued to fall. There was an uncommon silence in the house, but it was temporary and contented him. He walked from his room through the living room into the kitchen, cracked a few eggs—fried, never scrambled—then waited for the coffee to perk. Wartime rationing had accustomed him to drink it black, a taste he had come to enjoy. He circled a piece of stale bread around the plate to sop up the yolk. Nothing was to be wasted. Kate usually made breakfast, but she was still in the hospital. He placed the dishes in the sink, made for the door, and walked to the barn to feed the livestock. Finished, he glanced at his watch. He had a few extra minutes to spare. If he stopped by his parents' house where his two older children were spending the night, his restful mood would be spoiled. He wanted to relish what was left of the morning's gray softness.

He lit his pipe and began his morning commute. Driving through the farmland surrounding Runnemede, he passed Saint Teresa's. Built on land donated by his father-in-law, the boxy structure looked more like a factory than a church. He headed up the Black Horse Pike en route to the New York Shipbuilding Corporation in Camden. George's skills as a welder and mechanic had exempted him from the draft. He had also taken on part-time work at a lumber mill and sold real estate on the side. He hoped when the war ended to have saved enough money to open his own business.

George knew Kate was okay. But he was still anxious, and he smoked more as the day wore on. He was typically a man of few words, but he couldn't wait to tell his fellow workers that his wife had just given birth to his second son, Jimmy. He told them that the drive to hospital was hell, but everything went fine. The men continued to talk, and could have for a lot longer, but work was what paid the bills.

The Promise of Prosperity in Postwar America

By August 1945, World War II was finally over. Local papers wrote about the "holiday spirit that prevailed" as towns along the Black Horse Pike celebrated the Japanese surrender.[1] Cars of every description appeared on the streets and drivers drove aimlessly, their hands pumping the horns. America had exited the war the only true victor. Hard times were coming to an end, and the worst of the rationing was lifted. Returning GIs cashed in on government aid, allowing many to finally return to school, which meant a chance for a better job. Others went right to work, marrying their sweethearts and starting families. Near the end of the decade, over one million babies were born. The postwar decade soon became a high for American consumerism, and there was no material thing the average American male wanted more than a new car. By the mid-40s, there were twenty-four million passenger cars in the United States. It was estimated that fifteen million new buyers were in the market, ten million looking for new cars and five million for used. Factories in Detroit managed to turn out over two million new automobiles in 1946, but because the country was still retooling from the war, that was millions short of consumer demand. A half-decade later the demand was finally met.[2] Cars were becoming the quintessential symbol of American power, advancement, and material wealth.

George Gilch also profited from the boom. He rented two empty lots along the Pike, and opened a small auto repair shop and gas station. When cars broke down, he fixed them. When they needed gas, he pumped it. His was a perfect business for an affluent time. He was able to take home more in a week then he ever had, and he too was in the market for a fine automobile. At thirty-five

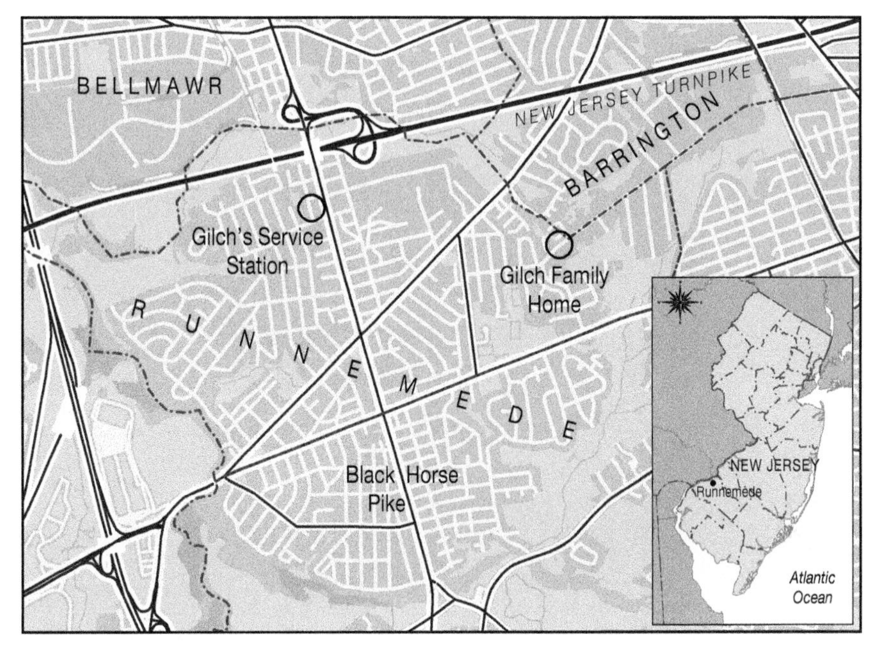

Runnemede, New Jersey

George was doing well, servicing America's surging passion for automobiles. His business was nothing extravagant, but for a family that would grow to nine children it was a livelihood that paid well. The work was hard, and its demands often made for sleepless nights. But he had to do it, and he had to make sure it was done right—an attitude common for a man who had come of age in the Great Depression. It was one that he would pass on to his children. From the first day of operation, George had done everything himself. His own stubbornness was partly to blame for the lack of employees. But mostly he could not afford them. His health was excellent. There was no way his business could go under. George saw a good future for his family. He was not alone.

With the rise in auto sales, factory workers on assembly lines saw a 15 percent wage increase. By the early 1950s, buyers jokingly remembered that they once bought anything they could get in an automobile, but now they had become far choosier. As Americans began to move out of the cities into the suburbs, the number of registered motor vehicles tripled and auto mileage went up one thousand percent. But driving was dangerous. Thousands of fatal accidents occurred each year due to roads that lacked proper traffic signs and signals. As more and more Americans got behind the wheel, the Eisenhower administration initiated the building of a nationwide interstate highway system. Roads were designed, paved, widened and rewidened to accommodate the increase in traffic and to improve driving conditions.

For decades Henry Ford had insisted that what the public needed was basic transportation. In 1954 Chrysler Corporation executives, following Ford's

Linking New York and Philadelphia, the New Jersey Turnpike was one of the most heavily traveled stretches of the highway system built across America in the postwar era.

assumption, allowed their engineers to talk them into producing a short, sturdy, sensible black car. They watched sales of their New Yorker model drop by half. The bosses sent the engineers back to the designing boards. The next year Chrysler introduced the Imperial, which was three inches lower, sixteen inches longer, and available in three colors. It was said to have tailfins higher than the sides of a B-29 bomber.[3] The Company's sales rocketed and the design changed incrementally each year—most of the time "change" amounted to just adding more chrome. These superfluous but costly add-ons sustained a booming market for automobiles and prodded George Gilch to expand his business and add a towing service. His family was leaving the working class behind, holding on to their basic values but striving to secure a position in the middle class. He bought land from his brother, and built a station a few hundred yards from the New Jersey Turnpike. George contracted to market a wide variety of automotive accessories supplied at cut rates by the Tydol Flying-A Oil Company.

Complete with an advertising campaign in the local Runnemede press, and giveaways of free samples for customers and their children, George's renovated towing and service station opened in July 1953. Colored pennants were strung from the building to the "twenty-six cents-a-gallon" signs atop the iron gasoline

They Came To Look,

Stayed To Buy . . .

And Service Keeps Them Coming Back

Tape-cutting ceremony at Dealer George Gilch's station is shown at left. From left to right are F. A. Guerin, Philadelphia District Sales Supervisor; C. H. Blackburn, Middle Atlantic Dept. Sales Training and Promotion Manager; George Gilch; William Elliott, Camden County Freeholder; S. K. Jones, real estate representative; John P. Julian, Runnemede Chief of Police; J. G. Jimenez, Middle Atlantic Dept. Automotive Products Sales Manager; and L. McGlincy, salesman.

TYDOL FLYING-A-DEALER George Gilch has only recently joined the Tydol Flying-A-Dealer Team. In fact, George opened his Runnemede, N. J. Flying-A-Station on July 30, 1953.

It was a big opening . . . complete with local advertising, both in the newspaper and by direct mail . . . distribution of giveaways to customers and their children . . . all climaxed with a tape-cutting ceremony presided over by Camden County Freeholder William Elliott, and Runnemede Chief of Police John P. Julian.

Gilch's Tydol Service Station was opened with a bang! Lots of people came to look, but stayed to buy . . . and are still coming back for all their car needs. These motorists keep coming back because George Gilch features a complete line of Tide Water Associated's auto accessories. They keep coming back because George keeps Runnemede's new Tydol Flying-A-Station looking like new. But more than all of these, people like to take their business to Gilch's Service Station, because they like the way George Gilch does business.

Read the excerpts from the two following letters . . . letters that George Gilch has received from two of his many satisfied customers. Reading these excerpts make it easy to understand why people like to do business with George Gilch.

"Dear George:

. . . Providence above surely arranged for that bearing to let go at a point convenient to Gilch's Station, where the term 'Service' means something more than I have ever experienced before . . .

"I tell you frankly, George, that I have never come in contact with a finer guy than you . . .

"Again our most sincere thanks . . .

Yours,
Gordon Urner"

"Dear Mr. Gilch:

"Through this note, I would like to convey my sincerest thanks for your many kind services . . .

"I would also like to congratulate you on running one of the most cheerful and friendly service stations I've ever encountered in my travels . . .

Sincerely yours,
John J. McManus"

Sure, a Grand Opening is fine when it comes to getting a service station off to a successful start. A Grand Opening invites people to do business with you. But the example set by George Gilch proves that it takes service . . . friendly service . . . to keep that business coming back.

This beautiful new Tydol Flying-A-Station got off to a good start. And under George Gilch's direction, promises to become one of the finest stations in Tide Water Associated's Middle-Atlantic Department.

Shown above is the forceful newspaper ad Dealer George Gilch ran in conjunction with the Grand Opening ceremonies at his Tydol Flying-A-Service Station

George Gilch (third from left) at the tape-cutting ceremony for his service station with the Tydol sales managers and local officials.

pumps, and a swirling poster was cleverly positioned along the street to entice passing motorists. How could they resist:

> GILCH'S SERVICE STATION: We have a full stock of TYDOL FLYING-A-ACCESSORIES, FEDERAL FLYING-A-SAFTI-RIDE tires and SAFTI-SEAL tubes and PREST-O-LITE HI-LEVEL batteries, VEEDOL HIGH-DETERGENCY motor oil and TYDOL motor oil in gallon pails, QUALITY HYDRAULIC brake-fluid and HOUSEHOLD OIL!

Among the witnesses to this small town spectacle was George's eight-year-old son. Jimmy was dazzled by the sleek cars driven by many of the visitors, but he found nothing more exciting than the station's brand new red tow trucks. It was their size and power that enthralled him. He couldn't wait to drive one.

The Struggle to Liberate a Shattered Land 1945–1954

By late November 1946, it was abundantly clear to most observers that the fragile peace between the governments of the Democratic Republic of Vietnam and the French Fourth Republic—both of which had been established in the last months of the Second World War—would not hold. Tensions between the newly independent Vietnamese and their former colonizers had erupted into violent clashes. These included a fierce French assault on the port of Haiphong and simultaneous operations to cut the road and railway linkages from the capital at Hanoi to the borders of China. A month later full-scale war broke out as the French forcibly occupied Hanoi despite determined and costly Vietnamese resistance. The retreat of the main Vietnamese military forces of the Viet Minh coalition into the countryside and mountainous terrain of northern Vietnam set the stage for the First Indochina War. It would rage for nearly a decade until 1954.

As was the case in much of the rest of the post-1945 world, for the people of Vietnam the end of the greatest conflict in human history brought little respite. After nearly a century of subjugation and plunder as one of France's premier "colonies of extraction," and post–World War I decades punctuated by brutally repressed popular risings, the Vietnamese struggled in the years of the Pacific War to resist the rapacious demands of what Ho Chi Minh, the leader of the resistance, aptly termed a "double yoke" of colonization. Beginning in September of 1940, Japanese military forces occupied strategic locations throughout Indochina, but left French officials in charge of day-to-day administration. Because these officials sided with the Vichy regime that collaborated with the Nazis in occupied France, the Japanese allowed them to continue their arrests, imprisonment, and often executions of suspected Vietnamese nationalists—especially those who were members of the Indochinese Communist Party. In exchange for Japanese acquiescence to their continuing control of the colony, the Vichy-oriented bureaucrats oversaw the forced collection and transportation of rice, rubber, and other commodities the Japanese needed to sustain their home islands and overextended empire. As Allied forces fought their way across the Pacific, surviving communist operatives radically altered their mode of resistance, mounting a war of liberation against both the French and Japanese colonizers.

In September 1939, after more than a decade of failed insurrections and French repression, the remaining members of the Central Committee of the Indochinese Communist Party (ICP) reversed their longstanding emphasis on international political priorities and domestic class conflict with a call for unity among the diverse political parties who vied to lead the movement for Vietnamese independence. Following another failed revolt a year later, the Party mandated a complete overhaul of its political strategy at a May 1941 meeting in a cave in the

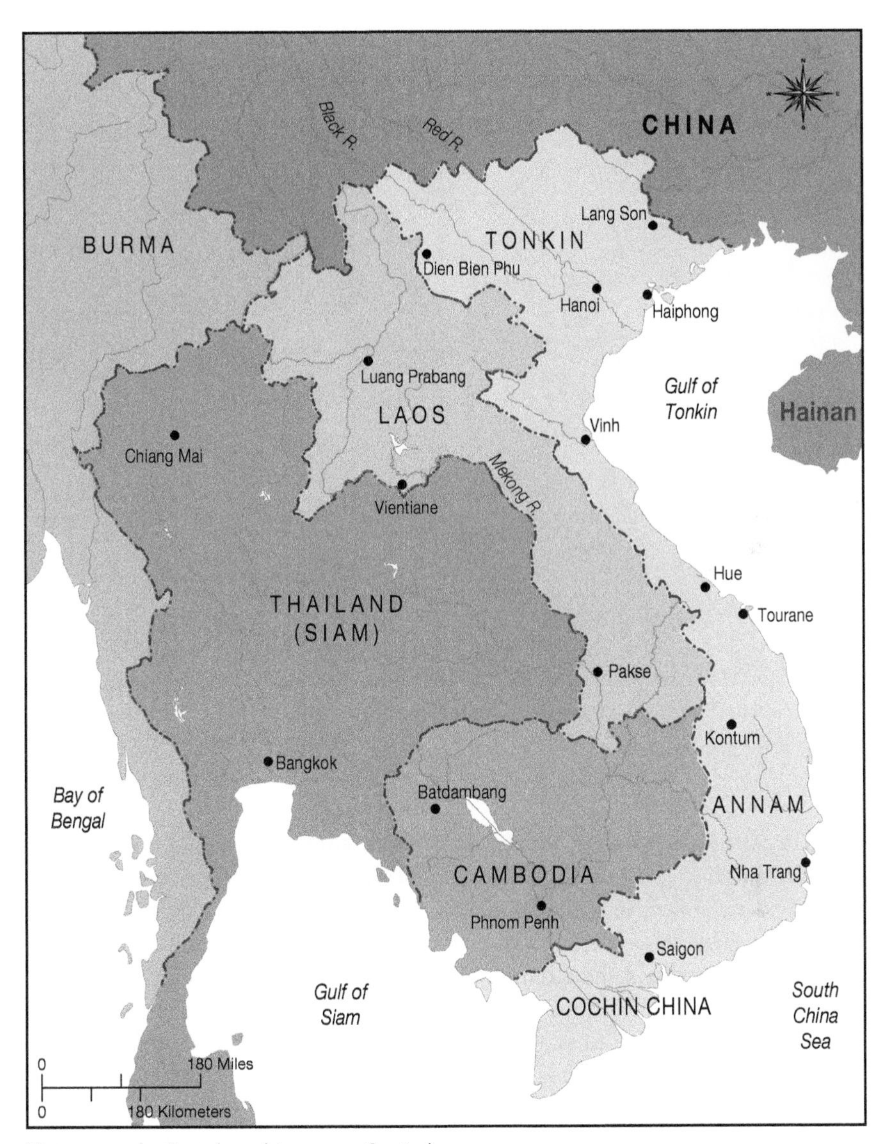

Vietnam under French and Japanese Control

remote northern mountains near the Chinese border. Ho Chi Minh, who had just returned from three decades of exile, led the conclave. The much-depleted membership present stressed the need to create a united front that included the ethnic minority peoples who dominated the highlands throughout Vietnam, rival nationalist parties, students, the urban-based intelligentsia, and women. By the last years of the war, the Viet Minh Front—the sometimes-fractious alliance that emerged from the disparate forces attending the May meeting—had become the standard bearer for the nationalist cause.

Ho Chi Minh (left) and Vo Nguyen Giap (center), the chief architects of the Vietnamese revolution and wars of independence.

After the Japanese took direct control of the administration of French Indochina in March 1945, the Viet Minh prepared for a full-scale war of national liberation. Under a collective leadership increasingly dominated by Ho Chi Minh and Vo Nguyen Giap, who was to become the organization's chief military strategist, the Viet Minh bases in the mountainous north that had been established in the years of Vichy French rule were consolidated and expanded. With the assistance of Chinese Communist advisors, Giap and other Viet Minh leaders had been training volunteers how to wage Maoist guerrilla warfare since the early 1940s. Though poorly equipped in the early stages of the fighting, Vietnamese guerrilla units raided French arsenals or captured most of their weapons after clashes with colonial forces. In preparing for a colony-wide insurrection against the Japanese, special military squads had also been organized to spread pro-liberation propaganda among the civilian population and mobilize them for the coming armed struggle.

In the months leading up to full-scale warfare, mass support for the Viet Minh, and especially the communist revolutionaries within that uneasy coalition, increased dramatically as a devastating famine spread across the villages of the Red River Delta and down the north-central coastal plain of Vietnam. The famine was manmade. It resulted in part from allied naval attacks on shipping in the Gulf of Tonkin and South China Sea. These led to a sharp reduction in rice and other foodstuffs that had for decades been transported from the paddy fields and plantations of southern Vietnam to the densely populated northern

Vietnamese Famine of 1945

provinces. But perhaps even more critical were the continuing requisitions, perversely extracted in the north, by both the French and Japanese of rice raised by the Vietnamese peasantry.

Hoarding on the part of Vietnamese landlords and merchants also exacerbated food shortages.[4] Viet Minh volunteers not only seized granaries and distributed rice to destitute villagers, they organized peasant resistance to government tax collectors and raids on French plantations and storage facilities. When set against the callous indifference of the French and Japanese occupiers to the widespread suffering and death by starvation of perhaps a million Vietnamese, the Viet Minh's aggressive efforts to provide famine relief bolstered its efforts to win the fervent support of a growing majority of the colonized peoples. That support would persist despite the conflict and appalling devastation to Vietnam and its peoples in the decades to come.

With the end of the war in the Pacific, the Vietnamese were left with the task of negotiating the withdrawal of the troops stranded after the precipitate collapse of the Japanese empire in August 1945. They also had to deal with the Guomindang (Nationalist) Chinese forces that invaded the northern portions of Vietnam as well as British troops who occupied Saigon and portions of the south—ostensibly to hold them for the return of the French. In defiance of these maneuvers on the part of the victorious allies to restore French rule in Indochina, Ho Chi Minh proclaimed the independence of the Democratic Republic of Vietnam before a massive crowd that packed Ba Dinh Square in Hanoi on September 2, 1945.

Ho began his brief but stirring address with a quotation from the American Declaration of Independence. Abbreviating what he termed an "immortal statement" from that earlier call to armed resistance against colonial tyranny, he declared: "All men are created equal. They are endowed by their Creator with certain unalienable Rights, that among these are Life, Liberty, and the pursuit of Happiness." Ho's decision to begin the Vietnamese Declaration of Independence with the most resonant passage from the preamble of the American one can be seen as cruelly ironic in view of subsequent history. His choice of American precedents was almost certainly in recognition of the cooperation—and the deep, mutual respect it engendered—between Vietnamese guerrilla fighters and the American Office of Strategic Services (O.S.S.) in the final stages of the war against the Japanese. It was also a wary acknowledgement of the ascendance of the United States as the paramount global power and the key to the Allied victory in the Pacific War. Ho was reaching out to President Truman and his advisors in the hope that they would continue to provide the material assistance and military supplies that Franklin Roosevelt had approved. Roosevelt's harsh appraisal of French rule in Indochina had provided rhetorical backing for the Viet Minh cause. But the fact that Ho went on to extend the American rebels' declaration of fundamental human rights to "all the peoples on the earth," suggests that he was moved above all by the promise of freedom proclaimed by another band of beleaguered revolutionaries in 1776.[5]

Similar to its American predecessor, the declaration of Vietnamese independence was essentially a detailed indictment of the oppression and abuses visited on the Vietnamese by their European overlords. At the top of the list of charges against the French was the occupiers' political division of what had been a people united by a common language and a strong sense of ethnic identity. The Vietnamese had experienced two millennia of shared history, and cultural norms that differed significantly from those of the powerful Chinese empires to the north and neighboring ethnic groups of mainland Southeast Asia. Particularly galling was the fact that the Vietnamese, but not the French, were required to carry the equivalent of passports to travel between three separately administered colonies: Tonkin, Annam, and Cochin China. The French had carved these rather arbitrarily out of the Nguyen kingdom, which after centuries of warfare between rival dynastic houses had in 1802 reunited the Vietnamese from the Red River Valley in the north to the upper Mekong Delta far to the south.

Ho Chi Minh then turned to French economic policies that he charged "had reduced our people, especially our peasantry, to a state of extreme poverty." For well over half a century French officials had overseen the depletion of Vietnam's natural resources by foreign companies. French colonizers had turned vast tracts of cultivable land over to foreign investors for plantation development, and imposed onerous taxes and periodic stints of forced labor on the peasants. Although port facilities had been improved and road, railway, and canal construction promoted in order to facilitate expansion of the market economy, French and other foreign investors had reaped most of the profits. The sharp drop in the average annual per capita consumption of rice from 576 pounds in 1900 to 411 pounds in 1937 starkly revealed the deteriorating condition of the peasantry, which made up the great majority of Indochina's population.[6]

VIỆT-NAM DÂN CHỦ CỘNG HÒA
CHÍNH PHỦ LÂM THỜI
BO NGOAI GIAO
*

YKB-3739-1

HANOI FEBRUARY 28 1946

MAR 11 RECD

TELEGRAM

PRESIDENT HOCHIMINH VIETNAM DEMOCRATIC REPUBLIC HANOI
TO THE PRESIDENT OF THE UNITED STATES OF AMERICA WASHINGTON D.C.

ON BEHALF OF VIETNAM GOVERNMENT AND PEOPLE I BEG TO INFORM YOU THAT IN COURSE OF CONVERSATIONS BETWEEN VIETNAM GOVERNMENT AND FRENCH REPRESENTATIVES THE LATTER REQUIRE THE SECESSION OF COCHINCHINA AND THE RETURN OF FRENCH TROOPS IN HANOI STOP MEANWHILE FRENCH POPULATION AND TROOPS ARE MAKING ACTIVE PREPARATIONS FOR A COUP DE MAIN IN HANOI AND FOR MILITARY AGGRESSION STOP I THEREFORE MOST EARNESTLY APPEAL TO YOU PERSONALLY AND TO THE AMERICAN PEOPLE TO INTERFERE URGENTLY IN SUPPORT OF OUR INDEPENDENCE AND HELP MAKING THE NEGOTIATIONS MORE IN KEEPING WITH THE PRINCIPLES OF THE ATLANTIC AND SAN FRANCISCO CHARTERS

RESPECTFULLY

HOCHIMINH

Hochiminh

This telegram was sent from Hanoi by Ho Chi Minh to President Harry S. Truman on February 28, 1946, in which Ho requests the assistance of the United States government in the peace negotiations with France.

The colonizers' disregard for their subject population's welfare was underscored by the fact that the steady reduction in the consumption of the peasants' staple food was occurring while Vietnam became one of the world's largest exporters of rice. State-enforced quotas for the sale of opium and alcohol that were applied to village communities throughout the colony even more blatantly demonstrated French indifference to the plight of the colonized. In the view of colonial officialdom, the potentially pernicious effects of the state's forced promotion of these debilitating substances were offset by the taxes the state was able to levy on them—and perhaps because they were seen by some to provide a literal opiate for the increasingly impoverished masses.

During the half decade of the Pacific War the condition of Vietnam worsened significantly. The descent from mass hunger to starvation in many areas during the famine years confirmed the conviction of Viet Minh cadres and the ever more influential nationalist leaders that the revolution could not wait. The growing strength of the Maoist movement in China (despite escalating US support for its Guomindang rivals), the American occupation of a Japan in ruins, and moves to restore British colonial dominance in Malaya and Burma also made it clear that the time for radical action could not be delayed. French duplicity and intransigence, particularly on the part of officials in Indochina itself, made a mockery of ongoing negotiations with Ho and other nationalist leaders. Rising violence across the makeshift barricades and roadblocks that demarcated liberated and recolonized areas of Vietnam pushed the two sides, seemingly inexorably, to war in the last months of 1946.

All pretense of a negotiated settlement was abandoned as the French military sought to recoup the lost honor and *gloire* of France by crushing the communist-led insurgency and putting an end to the recently founded Democratic Republic of Vietnam. As the postwar rivalry between the Soviet Union and the United States expanded into a prolonged cold war, and France's importance to America's alliance system in western Europe became ever more obvious, the Truman administration began to back away from Roosevelt's earlier support of Vietnamese nationalist aspirations. In the decade that followed, the United States would provide critical funding and military resources to ensure the success of the French effort to crush the communist-led insurgency and to recolonize Vietnam.

Early US Interventions in Indochina

Whatever Franklin Roosevelt's plans for Indochina were at any given moment, it was clear that—similar to most policymakers and virtually all of the American public—he knew very little about Vietnam or its diverse peoples and their long history. He apparently did not know who Ho Chi Minh was, and probably had no serious understanding of what the Viet Minh stood for and why it had come to represent most of the Vietnamese. At a private meeting with Joseph Stalin during the Yalta Conference in early February 1945, Roosevelt had dismissed the Vietnamese as "small [of] stature" and "not very warlike."[7] Compared to the size of FDR's fellow citizens, the first observation was on average true, but bulk was later to prove a serious liability for many American GIs, especially those battling communist guerrilla fighters in the tunnels of Cu Chi. The second stereotype was clearly at odds with ample evidence of hard-fought Vietnamese resistance struggles that punctuated a millennium of Chinese rule, turned Mongol invasions in 1284 and 1287 into costly disasters, and frustrated the efforts of the newly installed

Ming Dynasty to recolonize Vietnam in the early 1400s. The piecemeal conquest of the Nguyen domains by the French beginning in the late 1850s was met from the outset by localized guerrilla warfare that inaugurated a century of periodic uprisings and at times widespread rebellions against France's colonial rule.

The long history of Vietnamese resistance struggles against their powerful Chinese neighbors and Mongol, French, and Japanese expansionists ought to have given Franklin Roosevelt and future American policymakers pause for serious concern. But neither Roosevelt nor virtually any of the major politicians or military commanders who shaped US approaches to Vietnam in the early decades of the cold war were aware of this tradition of defiance and independent-mindedness. Though Vietnam and Indochina more generally were intermittently on Roosevelt's mind during the Pacific War, they were hardly priority concerns. His vision for the future of these French colonial enclaves was abstract at best, and often vague, idealistic, and mercurial. It was shaped in large part by an animus towards the French as repressive and exploitative colonizers, a view that was shared by a number of the prominent East Asian experts in the military and at the State Department.

Roosevelt's policies regarding the postwar disposition of Indochina were also informed by his broader conviction that the era of European colonial dominance was coming to an end. He felt that America should use its growing global preeminence and vast resources to promote decolonization and nation building throughout East and Southeast Asia. Despite the tension and uncertainty that these all too often openly expressed views aroused on the part of the French and British, the president insisted that Indochina should not be returned to France. He felt that it should be placed in trusteeship until its peoples "matured" sufficiently to govern sovereign states of their own. In tandem with the rapidly changing geopolitical situation in Asia in the last years of the war, FDR's choice of trustee shifted over time. As the option of Nationalist China faded with the eclipse of the Guomindang by the Communists, Roosevelt came to favor a coalition of the United States and the soon-to-be established United Nations as co-trustees.

There is some evidence that near the end of his life in the spring of 1945, Roosevelt relented somewhat in his opposition to the French determination to recolonize Vietnam. But he continued to insist that if they were granted trusteeship, the colony had to be governed in ways that would promote national independence. In part because the French did little to assuage his doubts about their intentions in this regard, in the months before his death he refused to share US signal intelligence relating to the impending Japanese seizure of power in Indochina. He also instructed his ambassadors and military commanders in East and Southeast Asia to supply French and British units only if the aid were to be used to fight the Japanese and not be deployed to suppress local resistance forces.

Harry Truman, who was soon—and abruptly—to become Roosevelt's successor, knew little about these machinations or even Roosevelt's intentions with regard to the postwar fate of Vietnam. Truman had been given little access to FDR's inner circle of advisors and played almost no part in wartime policymaking. Remarkably, until the day he was sworn in as president on April 12, 1945, he was not even informed about the Manhattan Project to develop an atomic bomb. Truman's inexperience and meager access to military planning and diplomatic maneuvers left ample openings for far better informed officials, especially in the Department of State, to take the lead in shaping policy in Indochina and the Pacific region more generally. In the last months of the war, long-standing rivalries intensified between those policymakers who sought to prioritize European concerns and a minority who viewed East Asia as the key to the postwar global order. In the years that followed, the "Europe-firsters" steadily gained the upper hand. As their influence grew, Roosevelt's vision of a decolonized and independent Vietnam faded. It had been subverted by cold war imperatives to restore the power of France and Britain, and frustrated by real and imagined communist designs for the future of Indochina.

By June 1945, the Allies' Southeast Asian Command was rearming French forces in Vietnam, and State Department spokespersons had begun to distance the Truman administration from FDR's proposals to establish a trusteeship for Indochina under United Nations auspices. Military plans for American landings along the Indochina coast were shelved in favor of leaving the Japanese military—once defeated—in control until British and French forces could occupy Vietnam in anticipation of its return to French colonial rule. As the importance of France in the struggle to preserve western Europe from Soviet domination became a fixture of American geopolitical thinking about the cold war, the necessity of France's retention of its colonial empire came to be assumed as a given by Truman and his more influential advisors. Indochina's raw materials, rice exports, and rubber plantations, and a projected abundance of opportunities for investment and commercial development, gave credence to the insistence of French premiers and diplomats that Vietnam would be an essential colony in their restored empire. Though Secretary of State George C. Marshall still criticized the French as late as 1947 for their refusal to accept the realities of the postcolonial world, he concurred with the decision to recognize France as the sovereign power in Indochina. As French counter-insurgency warfare against the Viet Minh guerrillas escalated and Vietnamese resistance stiffened, American financial and military assistance grew, and its role as a counterrevolutionary superpower became ever more evident.

Within months of Mao Zedong's proclamation on the first of October 1949 of the People's Republic of China, the new communist regime formally recognized the Viet Minh as the legitimate government of Vietnam. The Soviet Union and its eastern European satellite states soon followed suit. To counter the perceived expansion of the communist sphere, the Truman administration acknowledged the legitimacy of the government in southern Vietnam led by Bao Dai, the last of the Nguyen dynasts to collaborate with the French colonizers. These diplomatic machinations also marked the endgame of the transformation of the contest for control of Indochina from one centered on the fate of Europe's much-diminished colonial empires into what was to become one of the more fateful battlegrounds of the cold war. Partly in response to British pressure and repeated French threats to withdraw from Vietnam, the United States steadily shifted its support wholly to the French during the late 1940s. American backing for French efforts to recolonize Vietnam was seen as essential to holding the line against the advance of Communism, not only in Indochina but in all of Southeast Asia.

In the postwar years, a consensus emerged among the political and military leaders of the allied nations of the "Free World" that Southeast Asia was vital to the recovery of the economies of the British and French metropoles. The region was also seen as essential to American efforts to rebuild occupied Japan to offset the "loss" of China to the communist bloc. By the last years of the Truman administration, supporting Japanese economic growth and ostracizing the People's Republic of China had become major priorities. These imperatives of East Asian policy took on a new urgency for US policymakers with the emergence of Joseph McCarthy in early 1950. His sensationalist allegations that China's "loss" to Communism was due to the policies promoted by leftist East Asian experts in the State Department transformed the hitherto little-noticed senator from Wisconsin into a national spokesperson to be reckoned with. Prodded by extensive and often unreliable press coverage of McCarthy's bogus charges, politicians and an increasingly vocal segment of the American public came to associate the Maoists and China's peasant warfare with the communist-dominated Viet Minh and their surprisingly resilient struggle to end French control in Indochina. By the end of 1950, the United States was backing the French counterinsurgency with over a hundred million dollars worth of funding for arms and supplies.

With the election of Dwight Eisenhower and the installation of his circle of advisors, disdain for the ability of the French to take control of the situation in Indochina became ever more apparent to all parties in the Euro-American alliance system. Cajoled incessantly by his overbearing Secretary of State, John Foster Dulles, and caught up in his own personal commitment to the cold war crusade against Communism, Eisenhower came to accept the French as an unreliable but necessary proxy in America's campaign to prevent communist advances in East and Southeast Asia. Over the course of his first term in office, Eisenhower oversaw a major escalation of support for the faltering French efforts to defeat the Viet Minh insurgency. American aid totaled more than 150,000 tons of equipment including 15,000 vehicles, 2,500 artillery pieces, and 100,000 small arms and automatic weapons. The Air Force also provided France with over 200 fighter jets and light bombers, along with massive amounts of spare parts, and bombs. By 1954 the cost of the war had soared to three billion dollars, of which Americans were paying 80% of the annual cost of the French military campaign to sweep Ho Chi Minh and his supporters into the "dustbin of history." The futility, even folly, of these ever-increasing expenditures was underscored by the fact that portions of the aid were funneled into the four-million-dollar stipend that the French paid annually to the puppet emperor, Bao Dai, so that he would rubber stamp the colonizers' war against his people and the continuing occupation of Indochina. That total was four times the amount spent on land reform, which was desperately needed by the great majority of the peasantry and promised by the Viet Minh once Vietnam was fully liberated.[8]

Nearing the end of Truman's presidency, Dean Acheson, then the Secretary of State, had cautioned Eisenhower about the dangers of expanding American commitments to the French recolonizing enterprise. He worried that the French counterinsurgency was beginning to look like a "lost cause." Despite Acheson's misgivings, which were shared by other leading policymakers, involvement in the Indochina conflict increased substantially in the Eisenhower era. Both the president and Dulles were convinced that a communist takeover of Vietnam would prove a significant setback for the United States in the cold war. Yet, they were beginning to doubt whether Indochina was the best place to test the effectiveness of their "New Look" approach to American security.

Ike and leading members of his policy team had both moral and pragmatic qualms about continuing the containment strategy that had shaped the Truman administration's efforts to counter the real and imagined advance of Communism in Europe and Asia. They viewed their predecessors' approach as reprehensible because they believed it left peoples who had come to be ruled by communist regimes unwilling subjects of brutal police states that denied them basic human freedoms and the prospect of a decent standard of living. The policy of containment was also at odds with the premium placed by the Eisenhower administration on balancing the national budget because it meant massive spending to support military personnel, high-priced bases, and formidable naval fleets across Eurasia.

The "New Look"[9] makeover of US strategy for waging the cold war that the Eisenhower administration sought to implement was centered on nuclear deterrence and the threat of massive retaliation to prevent Soviet expansionism within Europe and throughout the developing world. This major shift in global strategy was also premised on the conviction that it was essential to roll back rather than merely contain Communism. It entailed a commitment to back leaders and movements resisting the imposition of communist control from without or seeking to undermine communist regimes from within. The latter imperative provided the main rationale for funding the French in Indochina. Whatever qualms American political and military leaders had about abetting French schemes to restore their colonies, they continually pressured their French counterparts to refuse negotiations with the Vietnamese that would result in a Viet Minh takeover of part or all of Vietnam. Fear of a Viet Minh victory also explains the Eisenhower administration's willingness to put up with the French fiction that Bao Dai was the legitimate representative of the Vietnamese people. Direct support for the French counterinsurgency in the form of American military advisors, which increased from 125 in 1952 to 250 in 1954, also marked a major shift in the US approach to the war. More ominously, the possibility of

Viet Minh hoist the flag of victory over the ruins of the French fortress at Dien Bien Phu.

deploying American air power or committing American troops to bolster the wavering French was seriously considered on a number of occasions, particularly in the final stages of the conflict.

Because Eisenhower was opposed to sending in American troops—at least without British military support—the possibility of resorting to the nuclear option loomed ever larger. In the spring of 1954, when a final French miscalculation resulted in their humiliation at Dien Bien Phu, Ike's policy team seriously considered deploying atomic weaponry. After nearly eight years of indecisive firefights and failed offensives, and confronted by increasing opposition in France to the long war, General Henri Navarre had come up with a plan that he argued would yield a decisive French victory. Navarre sought to draw the Viet Minh guerrilla forces into a conventional, set-piece battle by building what he boasted would be an impregnable fortress in the remote mountainous northwest corner of what would soon become North Vietnam. Vo Nguyen Giap, who had become the Viet Minh's top military strategist, appeared to have taken the bait. But it was soon clear that the French had trapped themselves. Surrounded by forest-covered hills that provided ample cover for the very substantial guerrilla forces that Giap could by then deploy, and incessantly pounded by Vietnamese artillery on the high ground, the ill-fated fortress was soon isolated except for erratic supplies delivered by air. With their fortified positions soon reduced to rubble by enemy artillery fire and repeated Vietnamese assaults, what was left of the beleaguered garrison surrendered in early May 1954.[10]

In the months before the fall of the fortress, Eisenhower and his advisors shifted from proposals to deploy American bombers to the possibility of using tactical nuclear weapons. Eisenhower mused that the latter ought to be seen as standard ordnance in the conventional arsenal that would (presumably) annihilate the Viet Minh cadres. But he was concerned that direct American military assistance of this magnitude would very likely trigger massive Chinese interventions; hence, another land war in Asia comparable to the one in Korea where he had only recently managed to negotiate an uneasy ceasefire. Combined with the president's understandable reluctance to plunge the United States into another major conflict, the refusal of French leaders to contemplate the use of nuclear weapons put an end to American schemes to salvage at least a standoff, if not defeat the Viet Minh.

Nonetheless, the collapse of an ally that the United States had backed with so much treasure raised new alarms about the spread of Communism throughout Southeast Asia, and elevated Vietnam (and Indochina more broadly) to the ill-starred status of grave concern for US policymakers. Hundreds of American advisors were already in country, and American politicians and diplomats were scrambling to find a leader who could save South Vietnam for the free world. Little thought had been given to the toll bombing raids, much less nuclear

Gilch family home after additions.

weapons, would have taken on the already poverty-stricken and war-devastated peoples and societies of the region, or the fact that Vietnam would now become a major military target in the cold war.

Exemplar of Modernity

By the end of the 1950s Americans were moving out of the cities in increasing numbers to take advantage of cheap housing in suburban areas. Their exodus created a rapidly growing real estate market that drove prices down as houses went up. George watched the countryside disappear under houses and a local high school. His town, Runnemede, had a population of 2,835 in 1940. In the next decade it nearly doubled, and by 1960 it was home to nearly 9,000 people. Within the same span the total US population increased from 140 million to 180 million, while the rural population declined by nearly ten million.[11] In addition to managing his business, George cleared his land for farming, and had the town's first in-ground swimming pool installed for his kids. He planted pine trees along the fences to hide the suburban sprawl that soon surrounded his patch of property. Holding to his conservative values, George wanted to shield his land and livestock from the public eye. His twelve-year-old son sensed his father's unease with the rapid development that threatened to engulf what was left of the family farm.

Jimmy was shedding the soft contours of childhood. He was average in height and build. Though he slouched, he had not yet been made awkward by adolescence. He was assertive and, similar to most children, he lived in the here and now. His enthusiasm for adventure was often associated with troublemaking. But combined with an outspoken personality, Jimmy proved to be popular with his fellow seventh graders at Saint Teresa's Catholic School.

Jimmy's room was in an upstairs corner of the house. Half of the area belonged to his older brother Georgie, and to make more space, the two pushed their beds against the bare walls. The ceiling was low, making entrance into the room awkward for their tall father. Darkened from years of use, the hardwood floors absorbed most of the light from the far window that overlooked the fields on the side of the house. Another room adjacent to theirs with a similar layout belonged to two of Jimmy's sisters. At the end of the hallway the rest of his six sisters shared two more rooms. The stairwell ran down to the living room and their parents' bedroom, which was in the front of the house. On the opposite side of the ground floor there was a dining area and a small kitchen. In 1960, George built an addition to the house. Two more second floor bedrooms, a bathroom, and a large wood-paneled den were added. The thick oak mantle over the stone fireplace was crowded with pictures of family and friends, and on the sidewall several ducks were displayed—forever frozen in flight.

As an adolescent Jimmy took special pleasure in something he thought would never grow old, something almost all American kids at the time enjoyed: televised cartoons. TV was yet another technological marvel of the era and what the mass media offered was overwhelmingly popular entertainment, as W.H. Auden quipped, "intended to be consumed like food, forgotten, and replaced by a new dish."[12] During the 50s an entire industry built from scratch took hold of the nation. The first telecasts offered little beyond bland news programs and "Howdy Doody." But by the mid-1950s the broadcast industry was booming. Within a ten year-span from 1949 to 1959, the number of household television sets increased from 940,000 to 44,000,000.[13] With a growing family, George, similar to all self-respecting middle class American fathers, saw a television as another essential possession. He bought an RCA set with a twelve-inch screen and placed it in the den near the radio and record player.

Watching the TV became a family affair in the evening. In 1957, five of the top-ten-rated television programs were quiz shows, most famously *The $64,000 Question* and *What's My Line.* Inexpensive to produce and sponsored by corporations eager to attract consumers, game shows awarded lavish prizes to successful contestants. Even participants who failed to collect the jackpot on *The $64,000 Question* were compensated with a Cadillac. Other networks popularized American's second most watched genre, comedy. CBS featured rising stars, including Lucille Ball and Jack Benny. Jackie Gleason became so popular that his salary rose from $8,000 to $11 million within a couple of years, and his show's budget averaged $120,000 per program.[14] Television crossed generations by condensing entertainment and news into one source for adults, while pandering to postwar fads and cultural crazes. Vance Packard claimed in his bestselling exposé, *The Hidden Persuaders*, that the attitudes and consumer choices of TV viewers like Jimmy were unwittingly being manipulated by subliminal messages flashed on the screen.[15]

After school Jimmy would often race home and sit on the red carpet in the den watching television to avoid his schoolwork. He watched cartoons and teen-targeted programs, such as *Tom Terrific* and *Spin & Marty.* His favorite was *Tennessee Tuxedo.* He also witnessed the emergence of the civil rights movement, but like most middle-class youths in 1957 he was far more attentive to Elvis Presley's third and final appearance on the Ed Sullivan show.[16] Previously, Sullivan had announced that he would never allow Presley to perform on his family-oriented program. But Elvis generated high ratings, so CBS paid him $50,000 for his three appearances. Those performances, particularly the first, captured over eighty-three percent of the viewing audience. Elvis and other music idols gave rise to new genres for American entertainers and teenagers—Pop and Rock 'n' Roll.[17] These new sensations replaced the Big Band craze of the World War II generation and gave birth to a new era in popular entertainment. Jimmy and his family also watched newscasts covering the successful launching of the Russian *Sputnik* satellite. Similar to the majority of Americans, the Gilches found the Soviet Union's newfound technological superiority a threat to American democracy and the Christian values that were especially important to Jimmy's mother, Kate.

After World War II there was an unexpected rise in church membership in the United States. By the 1950s the number of Americans regularly attending religious services nearly doubled over what it had been in the war years.[18]

Many families who joined religious congregations were influenced by President Dwight Eisenhower's call to the American public to seek out a religious community. In a speech at the 1952 Freedoms Foundation in New York City, Eisenhower declared that, "Our government makes no sense unless it is founded in a deeply felt religious faith,"[19] a sentiment that further enhanced the President's status as one of the most influential political and spiritual leaders of his time. For Ike, politics was an extension of Christian values. Many families answered the call to worship. George had converted to Catholicism in order to marry Kate, and the couple took their children to St. Teresa's. Kate attended Mass regularly, and sought to impress upon her children the importance of the Church's moral teachings, especially the obligation to care for the poor and needy. Many devout Catholics were convinced that their Church and their country were forces for good in a world threatened by the evils of Communism. Whether it was alleviating famine or bettering the lives of children in impoverished societies, the Church instructed the faithful to embrace its mission to uplift humanity.[20]

Raised to take his religious responsibilities seriously, Jimmy took Holy Communion regularly, and chose Francis Xavier as his patron saint for confirmation. He added "Xavier" as his middle name, which proved intriguing since it was far from popular. As an active member of Saint Teresa's congregation, he bonded with older residents of Runnemede, and Gilch home movies make clear his protective attitude toward his younger sisters. Spending time at his father's gas station, Jimmy learned the importance of hard work and achievement. But eventually he came to question some of his religious commitments, and like many adolescents he relied on God only in times of need.

Attending school at Saint Teresa's, Jimmy found himself rebelling against the rote recitation of daily prayers and the boredom of Monsignor Jess's long-winded homilies at Sunday Mass. He became a school rebel whose disdain for middle-class conformity rankled his teachers and some town elders. On one occasion, one of the nuns who sought to persuade her charges that scrubbing classroom floors was a privilege ordered Jimmy to do it. He refused, arguing: "My dad says that's what the janitor is for." In the eighth grade he decided to sport a D.A.-styled haircut. He greased his hair, combed it high on the top, and slicked it back around the sides of his head to form a part in the back that ran down to the top of his neck. The D.A. fad, popularized by Elvis Presley and James Dean, had become a stereotypical feature of self-styled rebellious youths in the 1950s. The nuns could not stand what they viewed as a tauntingly obscene haircut, especially when Jimmy admitted it was meant to resemble a "Duck's Ass."

He was suspended from school and sent home. But to the surprise of school administrators and teachers, the students refused their lessons and posted makeshift signs protesting how unfair they thought it was to censor Jimmy. He returned to St. Teresa's the next day with his haircut intact, and found himself something of a school hero. Jimmy graduated that spring, and was soon wandering the halls of Triton High School in search of a future.

American teens enjoying a night at a drive-in movie

Viet Minh troops burn the French base at Dien Bien Phu after the end of the 115 day siege

CHAPTER 2

Cold War Convergences

"Our objective is clear: to transpose to the field of Vietnamese domestic politics the quarrel that we have with the Viet Minh, and to involve ourselves as little as possible in the campaign and reprisals which ought to be the work of the native adversaries of that party."

—LÉON PIGNON, *L'Echo du Viet Nam*, 6 June 1949

"Mr. Diem who has been absent from Viet Nam for too long, returned to us with the point of view of a mandarin, with ideas either twenty years out of date or imported directly from abroad . . . [though] he takes nothing for himself, he always considers corruption as the best means of government and he distributes jobs among his family. He has no popular support, except for a section of the Catholics . . . "

—GENERAL NGUYEN VAN HINH, *France Soir*, 27 November 1954

"A remarkable hubris permeated these times."

—DAVID HALBERSTAM, *The Best and Brightest*

The crushing defeat that the Viet Minh dealt the elite forces of the French military at Dien Bien Phu raised expectations among the Vietnamese people that their colonial ordeal was at last coming to an end. Weeks before the surrender of the ill-fated fortress on May 8, 1954, an international conference had been convened in Geneva to reach agreement on a broad range of pressing issues. By mid-May the main agenda of the Geneva gathering had been narrowed to ending the conflict in Indochina. Having lost the confidence of their American backers, and demoralized by defeats on the battlefields of Vietnam and intense political divisions at home, the French were anxious to secure an armistice that would open the way for an orderly retreat from Southeast Asia. Even though the First Indochina War had resulted in widespread destruction throughout Vietnam, and inflicted heavy losses on resistance fighters and civilians alike, national unification appeared to have been secured at last. Both of these goals, however, were to be imperiled by the machinations of the great powers during and after the Geneva gathering. The Viet Minh's stunning victory should have given them the upper hand in the ongoing negotiations, but due to pressure from the ostensibly nonparticipatory American and British delegations, and prodding from their putative Soviet and Chinese communist allies, the Viet Minh were forced to settle for half a country. They very reluctantly agreed to delay unification, but only after it was explicitly stated in the accords—and witnessed by the parties attending the conference—that the final status of the whole of Vietnam would be determined by nation-wide elections to be held within two years under the auspices of an international commission.

Flawed Settlement at Geneva and a Nation Divided

Having been "double-crossed" by their communist allies, as Pham Van Dong, the head Vietnamese negotiator at Geneva, muttered after a difficult negotiating session,[1] it is not surprising that the Viet Minh leadership put little trust in the elections that were promised within two years of the settlement. Their skepticism was reflected in the determination of the newly installed communist government in Hanoi, the capital of the northern half of the bifurcated nation, to unify Vietnam by force if necessary should the great powers seek to renege on the pledges made at Geneva and fabricate a separate state in the southern half of the former colony. Their resolve was all the more remarkable given the devastation wrought by the expulsion of the Japanese and especially the war of liberation against the French. After eight years of brutal conflict, France's premier, non-settlement colony was in ruins. The counterinsurgent campaigns waged by French-led forces against the Viet Minh guerrillas made a shambles of much of the road and railway infrastructure built in the colonial era. The scorched earth strategy waged by both sides, which Ho had foreseen, was also evident in the ravaged state of the extensive canal and irrigation systems that the colonial regime had introduced, especially in the Mekong Delta region.

These impressive displays of French engineering and Vietnamese labor were intended both to expand the colony's production of lucrative export crops, such as rice and rubber, and to open new lands in the south that could be settled by migrant peasants from the overcrowded north. During the war they became major targets of Viet Minh guerrilla forces seeking to disrupt the water routes that the French often relied upon for military operations. Hundreds, perhaps thousands, of villages had been destroyed or decimated by French offensives, Viet Minh guerrilla raids, and fierce infighting among the many political and religious factions that had emerged in the long struggle for independence. Nearly a decade of warfare and reprisals on all sides had also severely damaged sections of major urban centers, especially Hanoi and its port at Haiphong in the north, and the city of Saigon in the Mekong region far to the south.

Despite the outcome of the Geneva conference, even the most fervently anti-communist observers had to admit that the Viet Minh had emerged from the war against the French and the negotiations that ended it as the most potent political force in Vietnam. Most American leaders—including Dwight Eisenhower—conceded that an overwhelming majority of the Vietnamese would have voted for Ho Chi Minh and the Viet Minh had the elections been held as scheduled.[2] But few of the American military advisors and policymakers at the time, and scarcely any in the decades that followed, understood that independence and national unity—and not the spread of international Communism—had been the primary concerns of most of the young dissidents. In addition to Ho Chi Minh, revolutionaries who privileged patriotism included many Marxists, who went on to become pivotal leaders of the Viet Minh coalition during World War II.

Although Marxist-Leninist thinking was clearly a key component of the Vietnamese Revolutionary Youth Association that Ho Chi Minh (at the time using the alias Nguyen Ai Quoc or "Nguyen Who Loves His Country") founded in 1925, patriotism was the driving force and liberation from French colonial rule the central aim of the short-lived organization. Ho's interest in Communism was deepened by his travels to New York, London, and Paris where, working as a dishwasher and busboy, he shared the experience of menial laborers. His attraction to Communism was further intensified by his humiliating failure in 1919 to gain a hearing from Woodrow Wilson regarding his petition for the right of the Vietnamese people to self-determination. As Ho recalled decades later, the appeal of Communism had mainly to do with his "love and admiration" for Lenin. Even though Ho admitted he had not yet read Lenin's books, he viewed the Russian leader as a great patriot and champion of oppressed peoples. As the Youth Association gradually morphed into the Indochinese Communist Party, the study of Marxist theory and Leninist revolutionary strategy became major preoccupations for Ho and the mostly younger contingent of activists who gathered around him. But until the end of the 1920s, Vietnam's independence was at the top of his and the Youth Association's revolutionary agenda.[3]

During the decades of the Great Depression and World War II, the Soviet-dominated, internationalist Comintern favored policies that privileged doctrinaire Communism and worldwide, working-class revolution. In the early 1930s and mid-1940s, orthodox Marxist-Leninist prescriptions, which often had little to do with the nature and condition of Vietnamese society, provided the rationale for violent rebellions against the French colonial regime. All of these ended in defeats and fierce repression that nearly proved disastrous for the Indochinese Communist Party. Nonetheless, party members who doggedly pursued these failed policies dominated for over a decade, and dismissed Ho along with other members of the Youth Association as "petit-bourgeois, fraudulent revolutionaries."[4] But despite Ho's virtual ostracism from the party and his exile in China through most of the 1930s, patriotism and the independence of Vietnam remained central to his quest for a broader sociopolitical revolution the rest of his life. His steadfast adherence to the Vietnamese nationalist cause was perhaps most strikingly confirmed by the Americans who supplied and fought with the Viet Minh against the Japanese in the last year of World War II. A clear consensus emerges from their official correspondence and memoirs that Ho Chi Minh and his compatriots were fighting mainly to liberate their country, not to advance

Viet Minh leaders with members of the American O.S.S., including Ho Chi Minh (standing third from left) and Vo Nguyen Giap (standing fifth from right), during training at Tan Trao in August 1945.

the cause of world Communism. As Abbot Low Moffat, who was the head of the Department of State's Southeast Asia division observed, "I have never met an American, be he military, O.S.S., diplomat, or journalist, who did not reach the same belief: that Ho Chi Minh was first and foremost a Vietnamese nationalist."[5]

Similar to many of the thousands of Vietnamese youths who joined various strands of the anti-colonial movement in the early decades of the twentieth century, Ho Chi Minh came from a family of some prominence. Born in 1890, and somewhat older than most of the students who became involved in the increasingly radicalized nationalist agitation of the 1920s, from his teenage years he shared an intense sense of national identity. Ho and many of his compatriots were willing to give up a life of relative comfort and the promise of a professional career in order to join the struggle for independence. Unlike others with whom he would later compete for political leadership, Ho's family was known for its open hostility to the French colonizers, whom his superbly educated father had refused to serve.

Ho's upbringing contrasted sharply, for example, with that of Truong Nhu Tang, whose life trajectory was perhaps more typical of the educated youths who joined the nationalist movement. Truong's family was not only considerably more affluent than Ho's, but it had profited greatly from collaboration with the French colonial regime. Truong's father held both an administrative position in the Saigon area and a professorship at the elite Lycée Chasseloup Laubat. The family also owned several houses and drew income from a rubber plantation and a printing house. Like many of the other leaders of the various nationalist parties, the five Truong brothers were educated in the finest French-language schools in both Vietnam and Paris. Each boy was immersed in classical European music, Francophone culture, and professional training that ensured they would have lucrative careers. Also similar to many other Vietnamese youths, soon after arriving in Paris, Truong Nhu Tang abandoned the engineering career chosen for him by his father in order to immerse himself in the student political movements of the late 1940s.

Although Ho Chi Minh and Truong Nhu Tang followed rather different routes to careers in revolutionary politics, both would become leaders of the anti-French resistance and the communist-led opposition to the American interventions that followed. They and thousands of other educated activists chose to join the Viet Minh rather than one of the many other nationalist parties. Despite setbacks, the communist-led coalition built a broad and diverse base of support. Having survived successive waves of French repression, it emerged from its reverses stronger, better organized, and more skilled at coping with its powerful adversaries. Extensive clandestine networks and international connections ensured that Viet Minh cells were better positioned to evade French roundups than the more exposed offices, living quarters, and gathering places of their political rivals. The political and military hierarchical party system that developed meant that communist operatives were less likely to yield critical information about the overall organization if captured and interrogated.

From the mid-1940s the Viet Minh leadership—often overriding the vocal objections of doctrinaire Marxists in the coalition—was able to implement revolutionary social programs that focused on addressing the needs of the impoverished peasants who made up the great majority of Vietnam's population. During the 1944–1945 famine and the years of the war against the French, sheer survival was the main concern for most Vietnamese. Though the party's resources were stretched thin by the ongoing warfare, the Viet Minh alone offered emergency relief for the short-term crisis. Throughout the decade of conflict that followed the Second World War, its cadres provided food, fuel, and shelter, and even (often rudimentary) medical care, for a sizable portion of the population. More ambitious revolutionary aspirations had to be put on hold for the foreseeable future. Nonetheless, even in highly contested combat zones, teachers were trained, and students—including large numbers of illiterate adults—were educated, and local tribunals were established. The Viet Minh also made serious efforts to reduce discrepancies in living standards between the affluent landlord and merchant classes and the hard-pressed tenants and laborers.

Like the Maoists in China, the Viet Minh defied doctrinaire Marxism by anchoring their movement in the support of the peasantry rather than the urban working classes. Though the Viet Minh's scorched earth tactics against the French reduced significantly the cultivable acreage in some regions, particularly the Mekong Delta, their operatives carried out radical social transformations in communist-controlled zones. Large estates were divided up among smallholding peasants, tenants' rents were reduced, wages for laborers rose, and in some areas there were significant increases in crop yields. Particularly in the south, Vietnamese who collaborated with the colonial regime were frequent targets of Viet Minh reprisals. But in the North, the communists opted for an overall revolutionary strategy that united the different Vietnamese classes and included cooperation with large and medium-size landowners, merchants, and non-Marxist intellectuals. As a result, until the 1950s, landlords and other "undesirable petty bourgeois" social groups were spared the mass killings that have often been defining features of other twentieth-century revolutions.

In the aftermath of the Geneva settlement, the Viet Minh were unquestionably the best-organized and most popular political force in both halves of the divided polity that the Vietnamese people yearned to unify as a sovereign nation. But the communist leaders, who officially controlled only the northern half, were confronted with seemingly insurmountable obstacles to fulfilling their revolutionary commitments. Their central aim of carrying through social and political reforms vital to the creation of a society in which the great majority of the population would be able to attain a reasonable standard of living seemed a pipe dream given the war-torn and impoverished state of the ex-colony. Equally daunting was the need to establish a strong government that transcended the deep political divisions that had emerged and intensified during the decades of anticolonial resistance. The two religious sects, the Cao Đài and Hóa Hảo, for example, that had sporadically supported the French were generally hostile to communist operatives in the vicinity of Saigon and the upper Mekong Delta region. Relations between the Viet Minh and the Buddhists, who at least formally professed the religion of most of the Vietnamese, had been maintained in a state of uneasy coexistence through the periods of Japanese and French occupation. By contrast, the substantial Catholic minority—a legacy of both early French incursions and the colonial era—was openly opposed to the communists, and in many instances actively supported French recolonization. Their opposition was dramatically expressed by the mass exodus in 1954–1955 of over 800,000 Catholics from territories designated as part of North Vietnam by the Geneva accords to the southern provinces, whose ultimate fate was yet to be decided.

In the North at least, the concerted efforts of the Viet Minh to address the major ethnic divide in the emerging Vietnamese state between the polyglot constellation of hill peoples, who were usually shifting cultivators, and the lowland-dwelling Vietnamese majority had met with considerable success. This was demonstrated by the fact that from the early 1940s the mountainous regions of the north and northwest proved to be among the most secure areas of refuge and operation for Viet Minh guerrilla forces. Before and during the battle of Dien Bien Phu, for example, hill peoples in the vicinity provided Giap's forces with critical intelligence and logistical support. Longstanding divisions among the nationalist parties also persisted, though the writers and activists who sought to revive Confucianism and restore the monarchy had lost what little popular support they had garnered in the early decades of agitation against the French. Even within the Communist Party serious divisions remained between the collective leadership of the Viet Minh and intellectuals who continued to espouse Leon Trotsky's alternatives to the Leninist formula for revolution. The potential for disruption on the part of splinter groups within the communist movement was most apparent in southern Vietnam, where they remained influential in areas that the Geneva Accords had left in political limbo and beyond direct Viet Minh control.

Within months of the agreements reached at Geneva in 1954, it had become clear that the Americans, who had witnessed the accords but refused to sign or abide by them, would work to intensify the fragmentation of Vietnam. Alarmed by the Viet Minh's victory in the struggle for independence, President Eisenhower's top policymakers scrambled to find a strongman who could forge in the South a viable political alternative to the unification of all of Vietnam under the communists. Driven by the consummate cold warrior, Secretary of State John Foster Dulles, development specialists and military advisors set out to identify an effective leader to head up a rival Vietnamese nation that would serve as a bulwark against the spread of Soviet and Maoist influence in Southeast Asia. A small circle of influential Americans had been impressed by the anti-communist, anticolonialist, and very articulate Ngo Dinh Diem. But after quarreling with Bao Dai, whom the French had reinstalled to head up the quasi-colonial enclave in the south after Geneva, Diem fled Vietnam due to the very real threats to his life from political foes. Though in exile at a seminary in Lakewood, New Jersey, he remained determined to return to Vietnam to build a viable, anti-communist state. To that end, he networked tirelessly among the Catholic clergy in New York and the Washington political elite.[6]

During his years in exile Diem's younger brothers, especially Ngo Dinh Nhu and Ngo Dinh Can, worked to build a support network in Vietnam that would rally to Diem on his return. Nhu's contributions in this regard were critical. The secretive Can Lao (Revolutionary Personalist Workers Party) that he founded and directed would provide the political and military backing that Diem needed to gain control over the well-armed political factions that vied for power in Saigon and south and central Vietnam. In the summer of 1954, soon after Diem feigned to be won over by the urgent pleas of Bao Dai to become the Prime Minister of the newly formed Government of the Republic of Vietnam (GVN), he flew to Saigon where Nhu had arranged a well-choreographed welcome and installation. Diem's precarious position as the effective head of a newly created government with little power was soon bolstered by American financial assistance and arms shipments that were redirected from the retreating French forces to the GVN's rapidly expanding police force and army. Massive shipments of bulldozers, tractors, and other construction equipment followed, accompanied by a growing contingent of development specialists and counterinsurgency advisors. With far less fanfare, Edward Lansdale slipped into the new nation in the South. The CIA operative acclaimed in Washington for saving the Philippines from a communist takeover had been dispatched to Saigon to ensure that Diem would become a worthy rival to Ho Chi Minh and the "father" of a separate nation in South Vietnam strong enough to ward off the communist threat from the Democratic Republic of Vietnam in the North.

Coming of Age in Cold War America

Inundated by an ever-expanding advertising industry, Americans had come to consider thrift unpatriotic. Rapid postwar economic growth left the average citizen with an unprecedented amount of cash to spend. Consumption had become both a personal virtue and a civic obligation. Driven by commercial advertising, mass consumer demand helped secure a reign of prosperity that was longer lasting and more socially pervasive than any in human history. This culture of abundance needed to be defended. Military spending rose from $4.7 billion in 1949 to over $145 billion by the mid-1950s.[7] But downturns were inevitable. Unsettled by a deepening recession in 1958, President Eisenhower insisted that the best remedy for the slump was for millions of Americans to go shopping. Ike committed the federal government to combatting the recession by lowering interest rates and investing in public works.

By the late 1950s, government subsidies and strong unions made for a more equal distribution of material goods, including household appliances. Expendable income along with low mortgage rates broadened the potential for home ownership. Prosperity made poverty less visible. As Michael Harrington, a prominent social commentator, observed at the time: "America had the best-dressed poverty the world has ever known. For a variety of reasons, the benefits of mass production have been spread much more evenly in this area than in many others."[8] President Eisenhower affirmed his commitment to enhancing the social mobility of the laboring classes in his address to the first joint AFL-CIO convention in 1955. Ike maintained that the "Class Struggle Doctrine of Marx was the invention of a lonely refugee scribbling in the dark recess of the British Museum. He [Marx] abhorred and detested the middle class. He did not foresee that, in America, labor, respected and prosperous, would constitute—with the farmer and the businessman—his hated middle class."[9] The distribution of superior American consumer products was helping to beat the Soviets at their own game of creating a classless society—and came to be seen as a major factor in securing the victory of capitalism over Communism.

Most Americans shared the Gilchs' view of Russian society as materially backward. Social commentators and political pundits routinely contrasted the relatively low cost and widespread availability of consumer goods in the United States with the shoddy quality, high prices, and scarcity of even basic material amenities in communist societies. The contrast between their own opulence and the abysmal standard of living they had come to associate with repressive totalitarian states led the American citizenry to embrace projects for the economic uplift of the peoples in the "third" or "underdeveloped" world. When George Gilch watched the televised version of the famous "kitchen debate" between Vice President Richard Nixon and Russian Premier Nikita Khrushchev in 1959, he sensed

Vice President Nixon and Premier Khrushchev debate the merits of communism versus capitalism in terms of opportunities for material improvement at the height of the cold war.

that America had left the humiliation of the *Sputnik* episode behind. He felt a rush of pride as Nixon pointed to the modern technologies that filled the model American home at the Moscow exhibition, and he heard the vice president exclaim: "This is what freedom means."

A year later, Eisenhower added consumerism to freedom and democracy as America's trump cards in the cold war competition between the superpowers. He challenged the Soviets "in the peaceful field of trade" and insisted that a free market society would "protect freedom and . . . promote rising levels of well being in all nations wishing to be independent and free."[10] As both the president and vice president's responses exemplified: America had become the ultimate consumer society. According to John Kenneth Galbraith's calculations, though the American people were only ten percent of the world's population, their consumption of raw materials since World War I had "exceeded that of all mankind through all history."[11]

As Eisenhower's comments suggest, the meanings of consumerism and social mobility were often misread. During the late 1950s the economic woes that intermittently afflicted "the affluent society" had not been resolved. Although human necessities seemed a less urgent concern in America than in communist or developing countries, gender and racial inequalities were still pervasive. For example, reductions were made in female college admissions to make way for aspiring young men exiting the military after WWII. Not until a decade later were wives of deceased combatants able to receive benefits for education along with loans for homes and businesses. Whether or not the husband was financially dependent on his wife, until the 1970s only he could be the legal credit card holder. As credit cards increasingly became the preferred method of payment, women shoppers were given easier access to their husbands' earnings, but remained economically dependent on their spouse's financial standing. By the late 1950s suburban developers and enterprising retailers alleged that shopping in the city centers had become inconvenient for mothers of growing families. Catering to the white middle-class flight to the suburbs, the American mall was born.[12] Initially, suburban stores were highly feminized. As women gradually got behind the wheels of their own automobiles, parking spaces were widened to accommodate their presumably inferior driving skills. In order to enhance women's "insatiable" need to consume, teams of male marketers devised flashy advertisements. Because of the close proximity of malls to suburban neighborhoods, husbands began playing a larger role in family shopping, so department stores increasingly catered to males by selling hardware and sporting goods.

Consistent with then current notions of what it meant to be a proper American male, George prided himself on being the sole breadwinner in his growing household. Thus, it seemed perfectly reasonable for him to expect that his new wife Kate would become a full-time homemaker, despite the fact that she was an honors graduate of the Pierce School of Business in Philadelphia. She had recently begun a career as an accountant at the American Can Company, and she dreamed of becoming a schoolteacher. But her father considered the profession too dominated by women—and thus not highly respected. He believed that teaching would never allow her to earn enough money to help support a family. By 1960, with her career clearly on hold, she had given birth to nine children. She prayed nightly and dressed modestly, but her glasses were always of the latest fashion. Nonetheless, her tax expertise and good bookkeeping proved critical to the success of her husband's towing company. She also did all the grocery shopping—once having to leave some of her children as collateral until she retrieved her wallet from home. She cleaned the house, took care of the cows and the horse, and washed and ironed the clothes. With eleven mouths to feed, Kate strove to become a good cook. She learned to can vegetables and improvise on cookbook recipes. She had come to accept that the place of the new middle-class woman was in the home—cleaning, shopping, taking the kids to school, and preparing meals for the family.

It was no coincidence that the "kitchen debate" focused on household technologies and contrasting approaches to gendering modernity. The centerpiece

Kate Gich (on the left) and children—Kathleen, Georgie, and Jimmy

of America's new suburban lifestyle was the mother. Representing a new type of republican motherhood, the postwar housewife was said to be a "specialist in consumption" who "nurtured a spirit of togetherness" in the family and the local community.[13] Drawing attention to the lowly washing machine, Nixon boasted that affordable consumer goods and technological development had advanced the lives of American housewives, clearly implying an invidious comparison with Soviet women. His claim was bolstered and likely prompted by early cold war exhibits and popular magazines in the United States that showcased the abundance of American women's appliances, lavish beauty products, high fashion, and sleek automobiles that made suburban living and shopping possible. But these comforts often had detrimental effects on the environment and the human body. The emergence of environmentalism and public health concerns were reactions to new postwar inventions that—driven by scientific prowess—also provided America with ever more powerful instruments of destruction.

During the 1950s, Congress sought to protect the American public from atomic radiation, chemical pesticides, defoliants, carcinogenic make-ups, cobalt salts (mostly used to stabilize beer foam), and synthetic food additives. Special attention was given to artificial sweeteners due to their long-term health effects, especially saccharin and sodium cyclamate, both of which were later banned. But regardless of human health hazards and ecological degradation, the American women's stylish lives as homemakers and ladies of leisure were contrasted in the US media with the drudgery that dominated the lives of women under Communism. While American women were depicted as well educated and engaged in high-profile professions, despite the fact most were not, Russian women were portrayed as field or factory workers—little more than domestic slaves.[14]

America was unsettled not only by the challenges Communism posed. Racism left much of the African American population with limited opportunities to advance in social status or share the benefits of the postwar prosperity. The GI Bill made it possible for mostly white men to continue the college education that many had begun before the war, as well as to borrow funds to start businesses and to obtain low-cost mortgages to become homeowners. The bill, however, offered limited funding to working-class males who often opted for two-year vocational schools because they lacked the finances required for a university degree. Educational options for blacks were even more marginal. Because postwar social programs were mostly administered locally and did not contain antidiscriminatory provisions, a majority of blacks—especially those living in the South—were usually confined to underfunded and segregated institutions. Few southern black veterans of WWII had access to training for skilled employment, and discrimination also reduced their access to fair-paying jobs. Some families who managed to escape poverty did so due to employment in government services or opportunities available in the military. But a majority of black families, given their lack of assets, could not afford to borrow funds to purchase homes in middle-class suburbs, so they were forced to buy older houses in the inner cities—if they could even afford them. The scarcity of unskilled jobs and widespread poverty brought about by racial bias and lack of opportunity forced many young blacks to join the ranks of the U.S. Army.

As the white middle class moved away from the city centers, businesses and factories followed them to the suburbs. Downtown areas became ghettos for poor whites and impoverished minorities. Once crowded with shoppers and workers, inner cities gradually mutated into concrete battlefields where racial conflict periodically erupted. Not far from Jimmy's town, the city of Camden saw a large influx of blacks in search of service jobs available in the urban centers. When Jimmy was an adolescent, New Jersey had the largest population of African Americans in the northern states, and South Jersey, which had many affinities with the Jim Crow South, was popularly dubbed "the Georgia of the North." When the 1960 census was taken, nearly six million Americans—mainly black adults living in northern cities—were not even counted. As Michael Harrington concluded, "Their lives were so marginal—no permanent address, no mail, no phone number, no regular job—that they did not even achieve the dignity of being a statistic."[15] That same year Camden was ranked one of the poorest cities in the United States.

George's work often took him to the nearby cites of Camden and Philadelphia where he saw run-down row houses of these once prosperous cities as evidence that blacks and poor people in general didn't mind living in poverty. He assumed blacks were lazy and not troubled by being out of work. He was not alone in mocking "niggers with Cadillacs," whom he assumed drove about in luxury vehicles despite the fact that they had bad credit ratings and lived in slum dwellings. His ambivalence toward the growing assertiveness of African Americans led him to support George Wallace's presidential bids because he felt the US government was doing too much for blacks. He was also convinced that liberal politicians were destroying the traditional American values he cherished.

George's prejudices, which were pervasive in white American society, were products of his upbringing and working-class environment. But despite George's bigotry, he never refused to service African Americans in need. On more than one occasion, if a black family could not afford to pay their towing bill, he waived the fee. And though he had a quick temper, he was a decent man. In his late forties, he began to go bald and he grew stout. He covered his head with a tan fedora, which he nicknamed his "thinking cap," and attributed being overweight to Kate's home-cooked meals and cold beer. He usually returned home right after work, and spent the evenings with his wife and children.

The upward mobility of working-class families in the 1950s was neither abrupt nor totally transformative. Even though many now lived in suburban neighborhoods, they retained much of their working-class culture and lifestyle. There was, of course, economic stagnation, with layoffs and rising unemployment, but the wages and purchasing power of those who held onto their jobs were increasing steadily to keep pace with inflation. Even though George Gilch had to tighten his belt during the 1958 recession—and continued to find his daily work routine arduous—he and his family sought fulfillment and satisfaction through consumption. As long as there was plenty of food on the table, the house was well furnished, and a decent car was in the garage, workers could take pride in being part of an expanding American middle class. Children of this upwardly mobile working-class generation—as exemplified by Jimmy Gilch and his siblings—were among the main beneficiaries of the convergence of the skilled working and lower middle classes in postwar America.

The Invention of South Vietnam

There was some truth to the contention of a number of American notables in the early 1950s that Ngo Dinh Diem was the ideal leader to oversee the building of a new nation in South Vietnam. Archbishop Francis Spellman of New York and other prominent church prelates championed him as a devote Catholic from one of Vietnam's most distinguished families. Supreme Court Justice

William O. Douglass admired his personal integrity for which, Douglass opined, Diem was "revered" by the Vietnamese people. More internationally minded Democratic leaders, including Hubert Humphrey and Mike Mansfield, stressed his anti-French and anti-communist credentials. The former appeared to be confirmed by his much-publicized resignation in 1933 as the Minister of the Interior in one of a succession of French puppet governments led by Bao Dai. The French periodically trotted out the perennial emperor-in-waiting to legitimize their colonial rule, and after World War II to bolster their beleaguered control over Indochina. Diem's anti-Communism was as intense as his antipathy to the French. After the Viet Minh captured Hanoi in 1945, they arrested Diem's elder brother, who had served as a French provincial governor in the early 1940s and had plotted with the Japanese to wipe out the Viet Minh high command. The Viet Minh later buried his brother and his nephew alive. The next year, while a prisoner, Diem was asked by Ho Chi Minh to join the communist-dominated coalition government he had formed to defend the infant Vietnamese nation against the return of the French colonizers. Diem demanded to be a full partner with Ho, and when his rather audacious condition was refused, Diem went into hiding in a Hanoi monastery.

Whatever his merits, even before the Americans decided to support Diem's bid to force Bao Dai out and declare himself president in June 1954, knowledgeable observers, including most persistently General Lawton Collins, the first US ambassador to the Saigon regime, were raising serious doubts about his ability to

President of the Republic of Vietnam Ngo Dinh Diem (center) confers with an advisor as his brother Ngo Dinh Nhu looks on approvingly, Saigon, Vietnam, May 1956.

govern South Vietnam. Diem's credentials looked impressive to some, but given the political and religious divisions in southern Vietnam, his ideological rigidity, autocratic leadership style, and unscrupulous close advisors were all serious liabilities. Though appealing to his Catholic supporters, Diem's commitment to celibacy and asceticism, and the bishops and priests who frequently joined his entourage, proved offensive to the Buddhist majority he sought to govern. Resentment of the patronage that he lavished on his extended family and other loyal supporters among the Catholic minority was exacerbated by the fact that many of them had fled from the North to escape the communist regime. Hostility to Diem and his inner circle of confidants was compounded by the regime's at times brutal repression of nonviolent Buddhist protests, which gravely weakened Diem's ability to rally both widespread domestic support and international sympathy during his decade in power.

The mix of Confucianism and Catholicism and the elitist familial cocoon in which Diem grew up nurtured personal traits that were bound to alienate rather than bring together the many political factions and splinter sects in the South. In his youth, he had earned a reputation as a studious, hardworking, and basically honest individual. But when combined with his deeply held religious convictions, these qualities made for a highly opinionated and overly self-confident person. Diem lectured rather than listened, and he had little regard for the advice—much less the criticism—of even the most experienced and influential of would-be counselors, including all but the most compliant of the American emissaries stationed in Saigon. Confident that he would always choose the right course to follow, and guided by the conviction that he personally could serve as a paragon of morality for the Vietnamese people, Diem governed as if he were a Confucian autocrat. He refused to compromise with potential Vietnamese allies, and eschewed negotiating with religious leaders who were adept at mobilizing vociferous mass protest or military commanders with potent backing in the army or air force.

Diem's elite upbringing and years in exile meant that he had a rather skewed understanding of the social inequities, misery, and devastation that a century of colonial rule and decades of civil strife, war, and rebellion had inflicted on the Vietnamese people. Although he styled himself as a reformist and pushed for programs that he had conceived and was convinced would improve the lives of the peasantry, more often than not his initiatives increased the burdens and discontent of the rural population.[16] His first year in office was mainly devoted to destroying the Binh Xuyen, a quasi-criminal organization that had come to dominate Saigon and nearby Cholon, where its gambling and racketeering operations were centered. Once the capital was secured, Diem and his allies concentrated on coopting or disbanding the militias that had empowered the Cao Dai and Hoa Hao sectarian fiefdoms south of the city. Having impressed only the most gullible observers with his popular appeal by staging a rigged landslide victory in an election that pitted him against the discredited Bao Dai, Diem turned his attention to leaders and political factions linked to the Viet Minh.

The maneuvers to win over the sects and crush the Binh Xuyen and communists relied heavily on police and military forces that had been organized and overseen by Ngo Dinh Nhu.

Corrupt and prone to violent responses to enemies and perceived rivals, Nhu fully supported Diem's determination to marginalize opposition parties and discredit alternative political viewpoints. Nhu figured importantly in Diem's decision to privilege Catholic refugees from the North, most egregiously by providing them with land, housing, and US-funded government stipends (however meager) in the Mekong delta that might have gone to poverty-stricken local tenants and landless laborers. Nhu concurred with Diem's persistent refusal to heed American advice that land redistribution, education, and other measures to improve the sorry condition of the peasantry and check the exploitation of the planter and landlord classes were essential to counter communist reform programs and enhance the legitimacy of the Saigon government. As both brothers were acutely aware, ambitious and effective improvement programs that targeted the mass of the peasantry and the urban poor could well undermine their very narrow base of support among the landlord and commercial classes as well as fellow Catholics. Nhu's "reformist" alternatives were mainly resettlement programs: first "agrovilles," and when those had clearly failed, "strategic hamlets." Both programs resulted in tens of thousands of peasants being herded from their rice paddies and ancestral villages into sterile, sun-baked mini-prisons, where they were heavily dependent on American-supplied provisions. These included surplus artificial sugar-substitutes called cyclamates that were under investigation in the United States (and later banned) because they were believed to cause cancer.[17]

The Ngo brothers' ability to coopt or suppress potential rivals enhanced the number and enthusiasm of the American powerbrokers who were convinced that they were the leaders who could bring together South Vietnam's fractious sects and political factions to build a viable, anti-communist nation. Among the prominent Americans who backed Diem, several—most notably Senator Mike Mansfield—were widely thought to be "Asian experts." But none (including Mansfield) knew very much about Vietnamese history, and very few were willing to listen to the advice of departing (and often far more knowledgable) French officials and journalists regarding the perils of the Indochina quagmire. Most presidential advisors in Washington and development specialists in country were well aware of Diem's self-esteem and truculence. Few thought him ideal, and some were prescient in their assessment of the personal flaws and deeply held policy convictions that would over time alienate key segments of the population he needed to support his ambitious nation-building agenda. But with the deadline for the elections agreed upon at Geneva approaching, there appeared to be few other serious candidates who were able and willing to take on the daunting challenges that Diem was confident he could surmount.

Given his shortcomings, and the mediocrity of the string of generals who succeeded him, it is remarkable that the state officially designated as the Republic of Vietnam lasted as long as it did. Through the late 1950s, Diem's hold on power owed much to the divided and disorganized internal opposition to his autocratic rule. But from the outset, South Vietnam's survival depended heavily on ever increasing amounts of American financial, developmental, and technical assistance. By the mid-1960s, direct and massive military interventions first supplemented and soon eclipsed earlier American strategies for averting the collapse of the Saigon regime and the unification of all of Vietnam under a communist government.

The growing commitment of the Eisenhower administration to Diem's survival was inextricably linked to previous setbacks and outcomes elsewhere in East Asia and their repercussions in the United States. Rather than events in Vietnam, broader cold war concerns were initially the main forces driving US involvement in Indochina. Preventing Laos and Vietnam from slipping into the communist sphere became a key component of the containment strategy embraced by Eisenhower, Dulles, and others who shaped cold war responses to the Soviets. The adoption of the containment option, and the falling domino analogy that became its much-cited corollary, owed a great deal to the "loss" of China to Mao Zedong's revolutionary armies. The opportunistic manipulation of these perceived threats to American security by Joseph McCarthy and his allies in the anti-communist crusade of the early 1950s heightened the sense of urgency that administration policymakers placed on the need to check the expansion of Communism. The uneasy truce based on the division of Korea into two states negotiated by the Eisenhower administration suggested that a similar north/south division of Vietnam could solve the dilemmas posed for American policymakers by the Geneva settlement.

Eisenhower and his closest advisors were prone to militant anti-communist pronouncements. But hardline posturing was often rhetorical and intended mainly for domestic political consumption. Dulles's relentless and much-publicized brokering of the formation of the Southeast Asian Treaty Organization (SEATO) was in large part intended to lend legitimacy to US interventions in the region. But it also served to demonstrate that the administration was responding aggressively to communist infiltration. Although by the end of Eisenhower's two terms in office there were over 1,500 Americans in South Vietnam, US support for the Saigon regime was overwhelmingly financial and material. The war-ravaged infrastructure and impoverished landscape of the region were selectively transformed by large-scale construction projects, but beyond the capital the American presence was sparse, and the Saigon government's control was increasingly contested by insurgent forces.

Between 1955 and the end of the Eisenhower era in 1960, American economic aid and military assistance to South Vietnam soared to over 1.6 billion dollars. A significant portion of the development funds that flowed into the South's severely underdeveloped society served to cover chronic trade deficits

Vietnam Divided

that owed a great deal to imported consumer goods that mainly benefitted the Saigon elites and Diem's political and commercial cronies. The influx of American funding was also essential for efforts to offset the rampant inflation that would have alienated what little popular support the regime had been able to muster beyond its Catholic base. A parallel stream of military assistance made possible the arming of a rapidly expanding police force and the Army of South Vietnam (ARVN). The former were deployed mainly to crush civilian dissent; the latter already exhibited an inclination to avoid combat with armed insurgent forces. Despite rampant corruption and misappropriation of US funding, Senate leader Mike Mansfield insisted that if Diem were overthrown, American assistance should be completely cut off.[18]

The Mounting Costs of Containment

It is likely that we will never know with certainty whether John F. Kennedy intended to cut back or escalate American military commitments in Vietnam if he had lived and been elected to a second term as president. It is clear that his anti-communist rhetoric was a good deal more vociferous and openly expressed than Eisenhower's in campaign speeches, inaugural and Congressional addresses, and other public venues. But having been convinced by Robert McNamara that massive nuclear retaliation, which was the centerpiece of the Eisenhower administration's strategic approach to the Soviet Union, was self-defeating—hence untenable—Kennedy and his inner circle of advisors explored other options for containing Communism. Nonetheless, lingering fears of a massive Chinese offensive ensured that tactical nuclear retaliation remained for some policymakers a credible response, and in the first year of Kennedy's short term in office, Laos rather than Vietnam was the focus of efforts to counter communist advances. Once the crisis in Laos was defused by an uneasy Soviet-US compromise, South Vietnam emerged as the primary testing ground for American counterinsurgent alternatives to peasant-backed "peoples wars" that had engulfed many regions of the developing world.

As his handling of the Laotian standoff made clear, Kennedy was more inclined to negotiate than wage war. In contrast to Dulles, he was also more accepting of neutralist leaders. But the increase in guerrilla resistance to the Saigon regime, and Eisenhower's parting insistence that a communist takeover in South Vietnam must be thwarted, appeared to constrict the young president's room for maneuver. Above all, Kennedy's evolving approach to Vietnam was shaped by Nikita Khrushchev's declaration in January 1961 that guerrilla insurgency could be used to circumvent the nuclear stalemate that had developed between the cold war superpowers in order to continue the spread of Communism throughout the postcolonial world. Guerrilla war had after all been pivotal to the success of communist-led revolutionary movements in China, Cuba, and—in view of the growing US commitment to create a counterforce in Vietnam—most tellingly against the French in Indochina.

Khrushchev's challenge more or less coincided with the growing interest on the part of Kennedy and some of his advisors in the potential of counterinsurgency. The president himself visited training facilities devoted to developing tactics and weaponry specifically designed to defeat guerrilla warfare. He and his policy team also read the iconic works of Mao and (perhaps less attentively) Vo Nguyen Giap, and pondered ways to deny guerrilla operatives access to their peasant base.

Kennedy's enthusiasm for counterinsurgency was often at odds with his steadily diminishing confidence in President Diem and deep ambivalence about the increased levels of commitment to South Vietnam that some of his most prominent military and civilian advisors were urging him to sanction. The computer analyses of the course of the ever-expanding civil war and the alleged successes of American-sponsored development projects in South Vietnam that McNamara and his "whiz kids" in the Pentagon churned out did not fully allay Kennedy's anxieties. But they emboldened the Chiefs of Staff, and General Paul Harkins, who headed up the U.S. Military Assistance Command in South Vietnam (USMACV), to press ahead with the buildup of Saigon's military forces and repressive police apparatus. The faith McNamara's team invested in America's technological capacity to surmount all obstacles gave credence to the irrepressible optimism of key Kennedy advisors, particularly the increasingly influential W.W. Rostow. One of a number of Ivy League academics included among Kennedy's inner circle, Rostow was convinced that the prototype for America's nation-building mission in the developing world could be successfully fashioned in Vietnam. Drawing on the celebrity he had achieved as one of the foremost proponents of modernization theory, Rostow relentlessly pushed for the free-trading, democratic makeovers that he was convinced were the best antidote to communist expansionism. Despite Kennedy's misgivings, economic aid and military assistance for Diem's regime in Vietnam spiked in the last two years of his administration, reaching nearly 472 million dollars in 1963. Equally troubling, in 1962 and 1963 military expenditures exceeded civilian aid for the first time. The gap between the two would grow dramatically in the years that followed.

Efforts by American advisors, including Ambassador Frederick Nolting in Saigon, to leverage the buildup of US military assistance to prod Diem and Nhu to initiate meaningful reforms to shore up their corrupt regime proved embarrassingly feeble. Ambassador Nolting and most of the American military officers assigned to assist the Army of the Republic of Vietnam's (ARVN's) efforts to crush a rapidly spreading insurgency, proved to be supporters of the Saigon government. But as Lieutenant-Colonel John Paul Van and a handful of Diem's critics discovered to their dismay, few of ARVNs often forcibly recruited rank and file and almost none of its officers were eager to engage the Viet Cong. American civilians working with Vietnamese officials to expand the Strategic Hamlet Program were equally disillusioned by the false claims of the Saigon regime, and some of its American backers, that defections to the Viet Cong were steadily decreasing in most of the southern provinces.

The upbeat assessments of progress made on both the military and civilian prongs of the counterinsurgency were based largely on fudged or completely imaginary statistics that consistently overestimated Viet Cong casualties and minimized ARVN losses. The number of strategic hamlets established in most combat zones was routinely inflated, and many of those actually set up were far from secure. In fact the bleak "secure" settlements were very often fertile recruiting grounds for guerrilla units. A portion of US aid was earmarked for compensation to villagers forcibly resettled in strategic hamlets. But each family was allotted only twenty-one dollars, and government officials often held up payment of even that risible sum to ensure that the relocated peasants would not try to return to their destroyed former homes. American funds for building schools and clinics were often funneled into the coffers of local notables, Saigon bureaucrats, or the Vietnamese Special Forces that mainly served as Nhu's enforcers. Weapons intended to arm hamlet defense units were seldom distributed, in large part because the government feared that they would be passed on to the Viet Cong or turned against the regime by the villagers who received them.

Until the months before the traumatic end of Kennedy's presidency on November 22, 1963, when he was assassinated in Dallas, Vietnam was seldom the major focus of his administration's foreign policy deliberations. Center stage was occupied by the ongoing cold war rivalry with the Soviets that spawned successive crises in Cuba—the second of which nearly triggered a global nuclear war. That brush with planetary catastrophe led Kennedy to moderate his anti-communist rhetoric and pursue—among other overtures for rapprochement—an atmospheric test ban treaty with the Soviet Union. But when mass protests led by Buddhist monks against Diem's increasingly isolated and repressive regime suddenly erupted in August 1963—and were met with tear gas and brutal beatings on the part of the police and Nhu's Special Forces—the deteriorating situation in South Vietnam became for the first time the preeminent concern for the American media and US policymakers. It would command that level of attention for most of the decade that followed.

As the Diem regime imploded, the divisions among Kennedy's advisors made a muddle of American efforts to avert its collapse or promote more viable alternatives. The Joint Chiefs, McNamara, and Harkins favored continuing support for Diem, even if it meant allowing Nhu to remain the main power broker in Saigon. The Joint Chiefs also pressed Kennedy to deploy American air power to interdict the supplies and soldiers that were increasingly infiltrating from North Vietnam to bolster the Viet Cong insurgency. Opposition to those who urged that there was no leader of Diem's stature to replace him was candidly provided by the newly appointed Republican Ambassador to South Vietnam, Henry Cabot Lodge, who was backed by a small cluster of Kennedy's less prominent civilian advisors and several development specialists. The latter were the only participants with first-hand knowledge of the situation at the local level in the Vietnamese countryside who were (irregularly) invited to participate in the increasingly heated debate.

These lower-level dissenters risked their careers by bluntly recommending that Kennedy either actively support a nascent military coup to overthrow Diem and Nhu or at the very least stand aside and let the ARVN generals decide the fate of the floundering regime.

Although Kennedy vacillated in the face of the fractious disagreements among his advisors, he insisted that if a successful coup occurred, American officials should not be directly involved and Diem should not be harmed. The president also grew more and more skeptical about the accuracy of the statistics that Harkins, Nolting, and the "fact finders," whom he periodically sent to assess firsthand the situation in South Vietnam, had been providing the administration. These were, of course, the same estimates that McNamara's whiz kids were feeding into Pentagon computers to come up with "hard facts" to counter the arguments of Diem's critics. The critics' assessments and recommendations were strongly supported by an intrepid band of reporters in country, whose press releases and editorials left little doubt that the Saigon regime had lost the support of the people and army, and that the Viet Cong was steadily gaining control of the peasant majority of the population. In the last weeks of his administration, Kennedy continued to insist that the United States could not abandon South Vietnam to the communists and to fret about falling dominos. But he made it clear in public pronouncements and two nationally televised interviews that he would continue to restrict US involvement to noncombatant operations, and that he still did not count the fate of Vietnam among America's vital global interests. His indecision persisted, and perhaps even an inclination to retreat was evidenced by the fact that he let stand McNamara's recommendation that at least a thousand American troops would be withdrawn by the end of the year.

The shock of John F. Kennedy's assassination and the turmoil and intense national mourning that followed supplanted for a time the deteriorating situation in Vietnam as front-page news. The low-key transition to the Lyndon Johnson presidency assuaged somewhat popular anxieties, especially since he made it clear that his priorities would be domestic and not foreign policy. Difficult decisions about the extent and nature of America's commitment to what had become a military regime in South Vietnam would—if possible—be put on hold until after the 1964 elections. Although as vice president, Johnson had made a much-publicized fact-finding trip to Vietnam and Southeast Asia in May 1961, Kennedy and his inner circle of advisors had largely marginalized his role in shaping decisions relating to foreign affairs. Unlike Harry Truman, however, who had been similarly excluded from Roosevelt's policymaking team, there were no secrets for Johnson to grapple with comparable to the atomic bomb or tasks of the magnitude of overseeing the endgame of the war in the Pacific. The approach of the Roosevelt administration to American interventions in the postcolonial world was much better defined. Roosevelt's policies were far less divisive and more consistently articulated than the vacillating, embattled, and uncertain course of action that Kennedy and his advisors had pursued in Vietnam. When consulted, Johnson had tended to side with the hardliners who insisted that the outcome of Vietnam's civil war should be considered vital to United States security. But he had not given much time or thought to the issues involved—a posture that, much to his regret, would dramatically change in the months following the abrupt onset of his presidency.

Rebel Without a Cause

Runnemede residents took pride in the well-stocked shops that lined the Black Horse Pike. Though travelers sometimes stopped, they seldom stayed. They fueled their cars at George's service station, and drove along the treeless roadway through the small, unremarkable town. Behind the stretch of weathered buildings, a network of freshly asphalted avenues framed rows of standard ranch-style dwellings. Built on concrete slabs and lined up like dominoes, they formed a neighborhood of white middle-class families. Mirroring his town, Jimmy was ordinary. In some respects he was less than average. At eighteen, he had matured into a slender youth. He had light blue eyes and brown hair. His ears were asymmetrical, but his teeth were straight. He was personable and upbeat. But he was without a clear sense of direction and unable to find a satisfactory career to pursue. Similar to most American teenagers, he struggled to maintain a balance between what was expected of him by his parents and the pull of his friends.

Jimmy claimed he was not interested in what others thought of him. He did not need their approval or guidance, but he was concerned with his image. A little vain, he spent a lot of time in front of the mirror combing his hair and practicing his smile. He saw Elvis as his ideal, sported a leather jacket, and popped its collar. He enjoyed rock and roll, and Western or action films. Like so many Americans in the postwar decades, he was an ardent fan of John Wayne. Jimmy was willing to conform, but he craved independence. A driver's license and a car allowed him to escape briefly the suburban sprawl. He bought an old green truck with a big engine and a heavy frame. It had a broken passenger door, smelled of gasoline, and had little in the way of chrome fittings. When he drove his sisters to school, he kept the windows up because he wanted people to believe the truck had air conditioning. Jimmy drove the truck like a hot rod—hard and fast. It wasn't long before he got into an accident. He claimed someone had backed up the highway ramp, hit him, and driven off. The whole side panel of the truck was dented. Despite the accident, when he got a chance he liked to race. It wasn't beyond him to "borrow" his brother's 1955 Chevy. He blew out the engine. His father gave him hell, and he and his brother Georgie got into a fight.

When they were kids, Georgie and Jimmy were close. They listened to the radio together and talked late into the night. They played baseball in the yard; had rock fights that ended in bloody noses; and built snow forts in winter and soap box derby cars in the spring. When one got in trouble, the other was supportive. On one occasion, while the town baker was making deliveries, he stopped to have a beer with their father. Determined to drive the bread truck, Georgie turned on the ignition and released the emergency break. The engine stalled, and the truck rolled down the street. When confronted by their angry father and the distressed baker, Georgie protested his innocence. Jimmy supported his alibi. They had "no idea who could have done it."

As the boys grew older, it became clear Georgie was more introverted and organized; Jimmy was more outgoing and messy. They hid their *Playboy* calendars under Jimmy's clutter. Reacting to the conformity that fashion promoted, many youths in the sixties came to value clothes as a way of expressing generational difference. Georgie mostly wore collared shirts and had a well-trimmed beard. Jimmy preferred white t-shirts and blue jeans. As teenagers, they were often at odds and seldom together. But both shared a protective attitude toward their younger sisters. Ironically, Jimmy was sterner with them. If he didn't like the way one of his sisters was dressed to go out on a date, he refused to drive her. When the sibling in question found herself without a ride, Georgie started his car. While Georgie enrolled in college and continued to work regularly at his father's station, Jimmy thought about dropping out of high school. He worked sporadically at the garage, and took a second job on the night shift at Morton's Hosiery Mill.

Like so many teenagers of his generation, Jimmy worked hard to make sure he had a disposable income of his own. He would spend most weekends with Gerry Shields. The two had been best friends since childhood, and shared the same tastes in music and movies. In the summer they drove to the Jersey shore where they chatted up women on the boardwalk, and tried to convince them to go on boat rides. They also went on double dates to nearby drive-in theaters. Hoping to avoid anyone who might know him, Jimmy always insisted on the one located a few towns away. Because parking his truck in town would attract the attention of friends, police—or worse, his father—Jimmy often drove back to the station after the movie and made use of the towed cars. He was never one to brag about his sexual exploits. He felt a loyalty toward the women he dated, and even refused to share details with Gerry. If word got out that one of his girlfriends was talking about what had happened on their date, he would break off the relationship. The day Jimmy took Louise, his first steady girlfriend, to visit his family, he allowed her to talk only to his younger brother. Joey was five years old.

Jimmy got on especially well with elderly adults. Gerry's grandmother—a Scottish-born, "prim and proper" lady who rarely cracked a smile—thought Jimmy charming and polite. His frequent visits to Gerry's house often led to conversations about sports, and once Jimmy unsettled the older woman by asking in a serious tone, "Do you think sex will ever replace baseball?" Though she found the query inappropriate, she remained fond of him. Gerry's mother and sisters also found Jimmy courteous and funny. Wrapped up in his local social life, he showed little interest in the world beyond his town, family, and friends. The assassination of John F. Kennedy shocked and saddened those around him, but Jimmy appeared little affected by the tragedy. He was not interested in politics or foreign affairs, and he was too young to vote in the 1964 Presidential election that Lyndon Johnson won with an overwhelming majority.

With the civil rights movement gaining momentum and growing anxiety about America's policy in Vietnam mounting in the early 1960s, growing numbers of young people across the country began to break away from the mainstream. They got caught up in alternative lifestyles, and openly challenged the authority of their parents, teachers, and political leaders.[19] Jimmy's rebelliousness was directed against his parents and school administrators, but his audacious pushbacks never amounted to more than vague, short-lived gestures. He was never caught up in the counterculture. Though he drank alcohol occasionally, he didn't smoke cigarettes or use drugs. He was a good Catholic kid and a patriotic American. But he hated school. One morning, his brother Georgie woke to a loud crashing sound. Jimmy had thrown himself down the stairs in the hopes of breaking a bone in order to stay home from school. He also got into fights and deliberately cut class to get suspended. Though he could be quite thoughtful, he had difficultly articulating his thoughts and feelings. His grammar was poor. He failed math, and his teachers made little effort to inspire him. When he attended school, he wandered the halls purposelessly. He slouched in class and paid little attention. He was a jokester, who deflected authority with humor, and enjoyed the attention his pranks attracted. His athletic ability was typical of kids his age, but he never tried out for sports. He preferred pick-up games at the town's baseball fields, and occasionally attended school football games. But he found them uninteresting.

Jimmy did excel in some areas. In shop class his skillsets and ambition were impressive. He learned to weld. His manual dexterity and sense of design were evident in the cedar boxes he made for keepsakes, and the carved duck decoys that he used on hunting trips with this father. Because he began to work more regularly at the station, his confidence in his practical aptitude grew noticeably. As his commitment to skilled labor and earning a decent salary increased, school seemed an impediment to what might become a worthy career. Jimmy let his schoolwork go, and officially dropped out at the start of his junior year. His mother was deeply dismayed. But his father's growing confidence in Jimmy's capacity for hard work allayed her concerns. George realized that trying to convince Jimmy to stay in school was futile and counterproductive. Rather than see Jimmy fail, he gave him a place to go to work, thus securing a future for his business—and his son.

At roughly the same time that Jimmy was struggling to find purpose in attending school, James B. Conant—former president of Harvard University and ex-chairman of the National Defense Research Committee that was responsible for the development of the atomic bomb—was conducting a study to measure the quality and rigor of the American education system. In the 1960s, the U.S. Department of Education reported that 700,000 high school students, mainly from the working and middle classes, dropped out every year. President Kennedy saw the underfunded educational system as a major problem for American society and argued:

> The human mind is our fundamental resource. A balanced Federal program must go well beyond incentives for investment in plant and equipment. It must include equally determined measures to invest in human beings—both in their basic education and training and in their more advanced preparation for professional work. Without such measures, the Federal Government will not be carrying out its responsibilities for expanding the base of our economic and military strength.[20]

But many reformers, including Conant, felt that both the general and specialized aspects of education would be better served if left under the control of "noneducationists." They believed that too many high school youths favored leisure over learning, and that American students were not being adequately challenged and trained to assume leadership roles in an emerging technically dominated world. "Every person should make the most of himself," Conant wrote, "and it is the responsibility of a democracy to help in this endeavor through education at public expense." According to Conant this was the ideal way to foster the "necessary bonds and common ground" among Americans in the "technological age." Thus, he recommended that secondary school administrators encourage students to take foreign languages, and that more advanced mathematics and science courses be added to curricula. Persuaded by Conant's findings, many political pundits argued that education was the "best defense against the communist menace."[21]

In line with the cold war propaganda that fed Americans' fears of Communism, the educational programs proposed by Conant and other experts were explicitly designed to strengthen democracy in its struggle with the Soviet Union and China. Though one of Conant's goals was to get the layman to "behave scientifically in social environments very different from the one in which science actually proceeds,"[22] his way of institutionalizing education did little to develop the learning capacity of America's youths as a whole. Ultimately, his reforms did little to ensure that students from impoverished backgrounds finished high school. Consequently, only the "right kids"—white, upper-middle-class boys—would be groomed for prestigious colleges and high-profile careers. Because Conant believed that only fifteen percent of high school students had the mental capacity to excel in mathematics, science, and foreign language courses, he instructed school counselors to speak frankly with "overambitious parents" that their children were not "academically talented." As for a great majority of students who struggled with math and science, which would include Jimmy, Conant considered them irresponsible citizens because they failed to comprehend the complexities of technology—and were not worth the investment. He was privately convinced that the "deadwood" must be encouraged to quit school at the first opportunity.

Contrasting Cold War Councils:
Ho Chi Minh dines with Russian Premier Nikita Khrushchev and Chairman Mao Zedong in Beijing, China, and below LBJ consults with South Vietnamese Prime Minister Nguyen Cao Ky and Robert McNamara chats with President Nguyen Van Thieu at the Honolulu International Airport, February 6, 1966.

CHAPTER 3

The Making of a Quagmire

"[The Army] gave me a pair of size-twelve jungle boots and I wear a size-ten. My foot slid in it. I tried stuffing it with paper, but part of the problem is how you walk. . . . So the left side of my foot developed a blister, then a callous, and then a planter's wart. That's the kind of shit we got. Size-twelve boot, and a size-ten war."

—JAMES HEBRON, Twenty-Sixth Marines, quoted in Al Santoli, *Everything We Had* (New York: Random House, 1981).

"Those who touched bottom carried the fetus of their breakdown through the gates of Fort Dix . . . "

—MICHAEL HERR, "Fort Dix: The New Army Game," 1966.

"Generally speaking, I found the VC and NVA soldier to be tough, courageous, well-motivated, dedicated and competent . . . Units were well led, well trained, reliable . . . the VC and NVA demonstrated convincingly their ability to withstand the physical and psychological hardships of campaigning 'for the duration' in an environment of uncommon severity and danger."

—General W. B. Rosson (six years of service in Vietnam)

As the U.S. Postal Service expanded its carrier routes in July 1965 to incorporate the recently built homes in Runnemede, Davis Road was designated "rural," and thus outside the regular delivery area. Residents on the rural routes were required to pick up their letters and packages directly from the town's small post office. It was a minor inconvenience. George Gilch often sent one of his daughters, but after the Pollard's son was drafted, he went to get the mail. George was worried about his sons, especially when he learned President Johnson had decided to rely on the draft to provide enough able bodies to meet conscription quotas. If a notice came, George wanted to see it first. He was strong-willed, and in tight spots he was inclined to take charge. He disliked surprises and felt that the drive home from the post office would at least give him time to think about what to do. He would have been a good deal more worried had he known that eighty percent of the men chosen by Selective Service Boards had no more than a high school education, and dropouts were three times more likely to experience heavy combat.[1] Jimmy was clearly "draft-bait." By late summer 1965, the military's overall rejection rate of draftees had fallen significantly (from fifty to thirty-four percent). Thirty-five thousand men were drafted monthly, and the average age of a conscript was nineteen. Seventy percent of the members appointed to the four thousand local draft boards were white professionals or public officials over the age of fifty. Each of the panels met only 120 times from 1964 to 1973, and in that timespan they would select over two million men for military service. Had it not been for the war, George—similar to Jimmy and so many other Americans—might have gone all his life knowing next to nothing about Vietnam. But all that changed when the draft notice came for George's younger son.

Draft Decisions

Jimmy's refusal to find ways to avoid being drafted into the regular army was neither carefully thought out nor fully planned. It was based on a strong sense that he needed to prove his worth. He realized that the rebel image neighborhood kids associated with him was not going to last forever. Many times he felt misunderstood. Friends failed to see his serious side. His high school teachers allowed him to settle for less than what he felt he could achieve. Joining the military would free him from the shame of lost chances, and give him a sense of purpose and a steady income. He felt that in return for his service in the army, the training and discipline he gained would provide a better future. He could escape the arduous work at the station, and when he returned home—presumably whole and undamaged—he would be respected for the hardships endured in combat. Because Jimmy knew nothing but security, comfort, and peace, he hungered for the danger and challenges of war. He wanted to be drafted.

The glorification of military service also contributed to his decision. His grandfather had fought in the Spanish-American War, and Jimmy had grown up listening to stories about World War II, and how some family members bent the rules to get into the army. Romantic images of decorated soldiers and battlefield heroics, pervasive in American popular culture, shaped his attitudes towards combat. But patriotism had little do with his resolve. He hardly questioned the rationales American leaders had given for going to war. He seldom watched Lyndon Johnson's televised speeches in which the president tirelessly asserted that it was in the vital interest of the United States to defend South Vietnam from communist aggression. Beyond being convinced that the advance of Communism needed to be checked, and that US military intervention would bring democracy to South Vietnam, the meaning of

America's role in Southeast Asia did not play a significant part in his refusal to avoid the draft. He had little knowledge about the war he was going to fight, and was not in the least concerned about the commitments his country had made to South Vietnam. Like most Americans in the early 1960s, he assumed that the United States was always on the right side of any conflict.

Just weeks before he received his draft notice in early August, his dad watched the end of Walter Cronkite and Morley Safer's special broadcast from the village of Cam Ne in South Vietnam. With the sound of gunfire in the background, Safer described the panic of the peasants while his Vietnamese cameraman panned to US soldiers of the First Battalion Ninth Marines crossing a flooded rice paddy in Armored Personnel Carriers. He reported that the Marines—in retaliation for a burst of light weapons fire from the nearby village—were ordered to level every house in the hamlet. No Vietnamese translators were attached to the American units. When one soldier was told to burn a thatched hut, Safer's cameraman, Ha Thuc Can, who had overheard the villagers' screams, put his equipment down and yelled, "Don't do it! Don't do it!" In the house, six people, including a newborn child were huddled in an underground dugout where rice was stored. One trooper later said of burning down the houses: "When [you're told to] level a village, you don't use torches. It's not like the 1800s. You use a Zippo. That's why people bought Zippos. Everybody had a Zippo. It was for burning shit down."[2] At the end of the broadcast Safer told viewers that the Marines had systematically demolished 150 houses, wounded three Vietnamese women, and killed a newborn child. They also took four prisoners. But no weapons cache was found.

When senior officers at the Marine Corps Headquarters read Safer's telex, they denied his findings and countered with very different versions of the operation. According to Lt. Col. Verle Ludwig's after action report (AAR), US infantrymen reported encountering hostile fire from thirty-three Viet Cong (VC) soldiers. The discovery of multiple trails of blood led him to guess that five Viet Cong guerrillas had been killed, despite the fact that no bodies were found. On orders from the colonel, an additional report detailing the "lessons learned," written by a Major Hatch, reported malfunctioning radios had cut off communications between ground troops and helicopter squadrons, which meant costly delays in the evacuation of the wounded personnel. He added that inaccurate maps positioned artillery range finders off by three-hundred to five-hundred meters, and caused "multiple puncture wounds to the right arm, neck and face" of one Marine. Of the five soldiers wounded in the operation, four were likely victims of friendly fire as indicated by the location of their injuries. Hatch concluded that the company's inability to accurately locate positions on a map while maintaining visual contact in the flooded, densely wooded terrain slowed its advance to a rate of seventy-five meters (246 feet) per hour.[3] The absurdity of the situation was captured in Morley Safer's closing interview. As the

Destroying villages in which peasants were suspected of cooperating with NLF guerrillas became standard procedure for Americans troops on search and destroy missions.

confusion and disorder escalated and the village burned, the telecast concluded with a rather uninterested soldier replying to Safer's questions between intermittent chews on a wad of bubblegum. Safer concluded that the raid on the village was "what Vietnam was all about."[4]

The following morning Frank Stanton, the president of CBS, received an unexpected phone call from a friend. "Frank," the voice yelled. "You tryin' to fuck me?" It was Lyndon Johnson. "Yesterday, your boys shat on the American flag!"[5] After the incident, Johnson insisted Safer was working for the Soviets, and he urged the FBI and CIA to open an investigation. Secretary Dean Rusk was also deeply unsettled by the broadcast. He believed the CBS footage had mistakenly recorded a training exercise in a remote, abandoned Vietnamese village, which Safer had treated as an official operation. Safer would discover years later that Cam Ne had been destroyed only because a provincial chief, angered by the villagers' refusal to pay taxes, misled US officials into believing that the hamlet was a base for "fifteen to twenty Viet Cong sympathizers." Like many Americans who saw the newscast, the Gilches were deeply upset by Safer's revelations. George swore he was going to find ways to protect his son.

In the pine-paneled room in the back of the house, George leaned back in his chair. His work shoes were still on. The August heat had begun to subside. As he waited for Jimmy, he talked a little to himself and stared at the deer heads mounted on the wall. So far he had failed at every attempt to persuade his son not to go to war. He had even lobbied his political connections to get Jimmy admitted into the National Guard, which already had a waiting list in the tens of thousands due to President Johnson's steadfast refusal to activate reserve units. In 1966 a Pentagon study found that 71 percent of all reservists were draft-motivated, which led many on active duty to label guardsmen as "Sergeant Bilkos," who "try to look brave while making sure that someone else does the fighting."[6] Though it was difficult for members of the working and middle classes to gain an appointment to the Guard, Kate's cousin was Atlantic City solicitor Murray Fredericks. Fredericks was the law partner and long-time friend of Senator Frank S. "Hap" Farley, who had assumed control of New Jersey's Republican Party after its previous boss, Enoch "Nucky" Johnson, was convicted of racketeering and sent to prison. In the decades that followed, Farley's influence quickly grew. He became "the most powerful politician in the state legislature's history."[7] George was sure he could secure the deferment, but Jimmy had insisted on serving in the regular army.

With only a few days remaining until his son entered boot camp, George had decided that he was going to make one final attempt to convince Jimmy to avoid the draft. He was even open to driving his son to Canada. George hadn't waited long before the green truck came down the driveway. Jimmy entered through the back door holding a box of defective nylon stockings that his boss had allowed him to take home to his mother. He was tired. He anticipated that his father might confront him yet again about his refusal to take advantage of the family's political connections. So he tried to go directly upstairs. Anyone who had overheard the argument they had a couple days earlier would have expected them to come to blows. On this occasion, however, George's tone was more of a plea than a demand. He spoke in a low voice and was careful not to lose his temper. But Jimmy was unconvinced, and made clear his annoyance that his father continued to press the issue. He told his dad that even if he really didn't want to go to Vietnam, he couldn't be a draft dodger—especially since his sister Kathleen had just enlisted in the Air Force. With nothing left to say, Jimmy quietly marched up the steps. He turned away from his brother, undressed, and slipped into bed.

Lyndon Johnson's Dilemmas

Despite his father's premonitions, Jimmy Gilch did not assume that being drafted in the summer of 1965 meant that he would be sent to fight in Vietnam. Even though, after much vacillation, President Johnson had just approved a $700,000,000 defense appropriation, and an increase of US forces stationed in

Vietnam from 75,000 to 125,000, it was difficult for most Americans to imagine that nearly a half a million servicemen would be in country two years later. Similar to most young Americans who were concerned with communist expansionism, Jimmy assumed that if direct intervention proved necessary, America's unparalleled military power would rout the enemy in short order. As late as mid-1965, many draftees' complacency about the chances of actually being sent into battle was also shaped by Lyndon Johnson's deliberate policy of concealing the accelerating commitment of military forces to Vietnam. When he was vice president, Johnson had openly differed with Kennedy's repeated assertion that the fate of South Vietnam was *not* a vital security issue for the United States. Once he was in command, Johnson became even more determined than Kennedy had been to keep reports about the deteriorating condition of the Saigon regime out of the headlines.

In the months after his abrupt assumption of presidential powers in late 1963, Johnson's main concerns were taking charge of his own administration, laying the groundwork for the civil rights legislation he planned to introduce, and tackling the chronic poverty that remained widespread in the world's wealthiest nation. By late spring 1964, however, yet another election cycle compelled Johnson and his advisors to find ways to prevent the collapse of the Saigon regime and a communist takeover in South Vietnam. The Republicans' nomination of the hawkish Senator Barry Goldwater as their presidential candidate intensified the pressure on Johnson to respond forcefully to the National Liberation Front's steadily expanding control of the South Vietnamese countryside and North Vietnam's increasing support for their guerrilla insurrection. When George Wallace challenged Johnson in the presidential primaries, LBJ's determination to be a strong decisive leader began to be increasingly fixed on finding a way to resolve the standoff in Vietnam. In contrast to Kennedy, who mistrusted and often disregarded the advice of the Joint Chiefs of Staff, Johnson consistently valued their council—even when it was clearly out of sync with the information emanating from American officials in South Vietnam.

Although Johnson was a masterful politician who had long been a dominant force in Congress, he was a far less secure individual than either Eisenhower or JFK. Johnson was voluble and prone to regale his congressional colleagues, and later White House advisors, with often ribald anecdotes calculated to shore up the support of wavering allies or discomfit those who opposed his legislative initiatives. Despite his remarkable achievements, he was hypersensitive about the way he was perceived by the military brass, conservative Republicans, and especially his fellow Southern Democrats. Having grown up in poverty, Johnson was ill at ease in the presence of the well-born, elite-educated Kennedys and their inner circle of "egghead" advisors. In dealing with Vietnam, and foreign affairs more generally, his anxieties were heightened due to his marginalization by JFK and White House staffers while he was vice president. Kennedy's growing ambivalence in dealing with the unraveling of the Saigon regime provided little guidance for a successor abruptly thrust into the role of commander in chief and confronted with a growing international crisis. Johnson's predicament goes far

In the Vice President's Office, Lyndon Johnson (center) sits with his inner circle of advisors: (from left to right) Ambassador Henry Cabot Lodge, Secretary of State Dean Rusk, Secretary of Defense Robert McNamara, and Under Secretary of State George Ball.

to explain his decision to retain most of JFK's team of advisors, with the major exception of Bobby Kennedy, with whom an intensely adversarial relationship had developed.

In large part because resistance by the National Liberation Front did not appear strong enough to topple the Diem regime until the last year of the abbreviated Kennedy presidency, Johnson's predecessors had managed to contain American involvement in Vietnam's civil war and above all limit military commitments. Soon after Johnson was elected in his own right, he was forced to confront the possibility that the post-Diem regime would collapse. A succession of coups, fierce Buddhist opposition to the predominance of Catholics in Saigon politics, and growing support from North Vietnam for the NLF insurgency, left little doubt that Vietnam would remain a major challenge for American policymakers. The fate of Vietnam also had the potential to become a defining measure of LBJ's presidential legacy. Cautious at first and relying heavily on the recommendations of Robert McNamara and McGeorge Bundy, Johnson sought to stabilize the South Vietnamese government with assurances of continuing financial support and material assistance. He also pondered ways of demonstrating America's resolve to force the NLF and North Vietnamese to cease their ever expanding efforts to incorporate the South into an undivided nation.

From the outset Lyndon Johnson approached the Vietnam quagmire with uncertainty and forebodings of the setbacks to come. He shared his misgivings in private conversations with long-standing friends and allies from his congressional days. But in public and in sessions with his advisors, he concealed his hesitations with tough questions and increasingly, ridicule for those counseling limits to US involvement or a staged withdrawal. He overrode objections to each escalation with dismissals of the Vietnamese adversary and their "piddling, damn little piss-ant country."[8] Denigration of the enemy was often interposed with hubristic assessments of the vast superiority of American resources, technological acumen, and military might. The president could also rely on Robert McNamara and his team of computer whizzes to come up with statistics to counter anecdotal warnings from American officials in South Vietnam or the prognoses of George Ball and less influential advisors based on their personal experience. In addition to fears of being perceived as weak by Southern conservatives and hawkish generals, Johnson was also caught up in cold war concerns regarding where to stand firm against perceived communist advances. He claimed that abandoning South Vietnam would significantly diminish US credibility with its allies and the leadership of emerging, postcolonial nations, despite the fact that Britain and France refused to back American interventions and the leaders of the nonaligned bloc consistently condemned them. His resolve to accelerate military commitments was also bolstered by his sense that he had proved himself a winner; a leader whose will to prevail would ultimately force concessions from the Vietnamese communist leaders just as it had his congressional colleagues.

Despite Johnson's frequent disavowals that he was planning to put American "boots on the ground" in South Vietnam, he had begun to escalate US military involvement in the Vietnam civil war even before his election victory. He approved the intensification of covert operations along the coast of North Vietnam in midsummer 1964, which fed the tensions that resulted in the Gulf of Tonkin incidents in August. Johnson knew that deliberate Vietnamese attacks on American warships had not actually occurred. In fact, within days of the alleged attack, he remarked to an aide, "Hell, those dumb, stupid sailors were just shooting at flying fish!"[9] Duplicitously, he seized on what he knew to be false intelligence to justify his decision to launch air raids against the North. He also parlayed the alleged Gulf of Tonkin attacks into a resolution in which Congress surrendered its responsibility for taking America into war to the president and his advisors. Over the course of the year that followed, Johnson sought to conceal from the American people the buildup of American forces and their increasing involvement in combat operations in both South and North Vietnam. When confronted by reporters with evidence of US military escalation, he insisted that

As Lyndon Johnson led America into full-scale war with the Democratic Republic of Vietnam, he increasingly realized that the country's nuclear arsenal was unusable and its conventional forces were ill-prepared to fight a guerrilla war.

he was "staying the course" set by previous administrations. He claimed that he had no intention of putting American "boys"—especially "his Texas boys"—in harm's way.

Johnson and his spokesmen continued to deny that there was any significant change in the US approach to Vietnam all throughout the early months of 1965. His assurances were clearly belied by major increases in bombing operations against the North, code-named Rolling Thunder. In March, two Marine

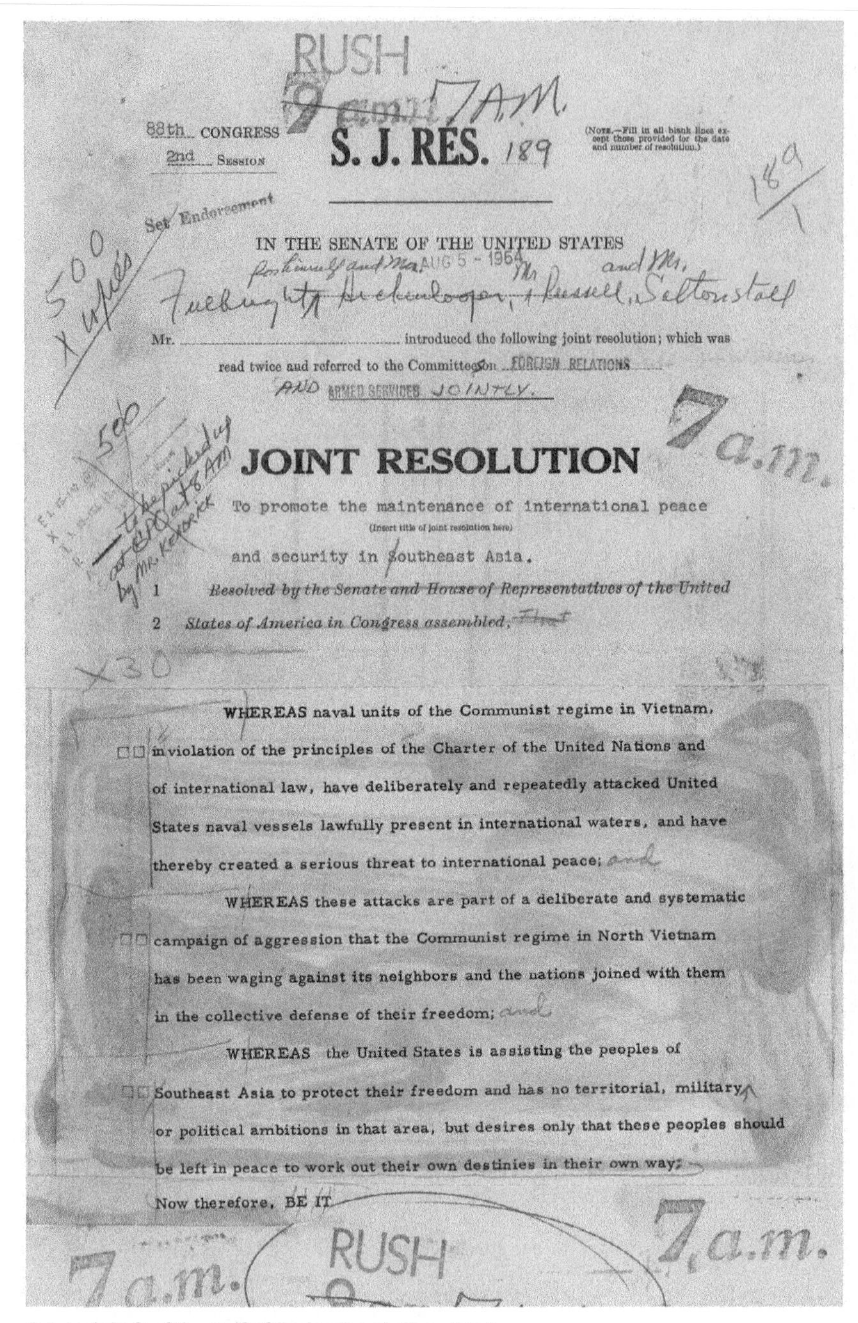

RUSH

88th CONGRESS
2nd SESSION

S. J. RES. 189

(NOTE.—Fill in all blank lines except those provided for the date and number of resolution.)

IN THE SENATE OF THE UNITED STATES

AUG 5 - 1964

Mr. .... introduced the following joint resolution; which was read twice and referred to the Committee on FOREIGN RELATIONS AND ARMED SERVICES JOINTLY.

JOINT RESOLUTION

To promote the maintenance of international peace

(Insert title of joint resolution here)

and security in southeast Asia.

1 *Resolved by the Senate and House of Representatives of the United*

2 *States of America in Congress assembled,*

WHEREAS naval units of the Communist regime in Vietnam, in violation of the principles of the Charter of the United Nations and of international law, have deliberately and repeatedly attacked United States naval vessels lawfully present in international waters, and have thereby created a serious threat to international peace; and

WHEREAS these attacks are part of a deliberate and systematic campaign of aggression that the Communist regime in North Vietnam has been waging against its neighbors and the nations joined with them in the collective defense of their freedom; and

WHEREAS the United States is assisting the peoples of Southeast Asia to protect their freedom and has no territorial, military or political ambitions in that area, but desires only that these peoples should be left in peace to work out their own destinies in their own way: Now therefore, BE IT

7 a.m.

RUSH

Original draft of the Gulf of Tonkin Resolution, 1964.

battalions waded ashore at Da Nang to a comic-opera welcome on the beach by young Vietnamese women bearing leis. Despite administration assurances that Marines were sent to guard US airbases, the arrival of large combat units made it all too apparent that Johnson was contemplating committing substantial numbers of American soldiers to preserve the Saigon regime. That possibility gave renewed resonance to the somber warnings raised by General Douglas MacArthur in 1961 about the dangers of US involvement in land wars in Asia, based on earlier American interventions in the Korean civil war.

In an attempt to allay stirrings of antiwar protests at several major universities by moderating his increasingly hawkish approach to the Vietnam quandary, in early April 1965 Lyndon Johnson offered the prospect of a massive development project that would span the Mekong River watershed. Modeled on the Tennessee Valley Authority that had transformed a large swath of the American South during the Great Depression, the scheme would encompass Laos, Cambodia, and the two Vietnams. Similar to the TVA, it would focus on building dams, improving riverine transport systems, and electrification. If implemented, the Mekong development scheme might well have become an engine for economic growth and improved living standards throughout much of mainland Southeast Asia. It would also have provided the basis for realizing Ho Chi Minh's post–World War II vision of Americans working with the Vietnamese people to overcome the poverty and devastation inflicted by a century of colonialism. But the credibility of Johnson's proposal in his nationally televised speech at Johns Hopkins University was nullified by his insistence that the provision of development assistance was dependent on the North Vietnamese and the NLF putting an end to their struggle to unite North and South Vietnam in a single, communist-led nation. Whether or not the offer was sincere or merely a ploy to regain the moral high ground that had been lost at home and abroad due to American aggression and high levels of Vietnamese civilian casualties, it was all but ignored by the leadership in Hanoi and the NLF in South Vietnam.

By June 1965, LBJ's decision to approve major increases in American combat forces signaled that the United States was taking over the war to save the nation that it had struggled for over a decade to create in South Vietnam. The government in Saigon remained divided and unstable. ARVN forces continued to retreat in the face of NLF advances and cede control of the countryside and the peasantry that both sides realized was pivotal to the outcome of the civil war. Increasingly attributing these reverses to the expanding infiltration of fighters, arms, and supplies along the Ho Chi Minh trail from the North, the Joint Chiefs pressed Johnson to broaden and intensify the air assault on the North and commit ever-larger numbers of troops. The convergence of these trends made it clear to the president that he was confronted by a true dilemma. He realized that the often-iterated insistence that the Saigon government must develop the capacity to defend itself was illusory. Despite prodigious injections of military, financial, and material assistance, the regime remained divided, vulnerable, and reluctant to engage NLF and NVA (North Vietnamese Army) forces. Johnson and his advisors feared that without significant reinforcement by American combat troops, the South would soon be absorbed into the Democratic Republic of Vietnam, and the rest of Southeast Asia would be threatened by a surging tide of communist expansionism.

The alternative, however, was equally fraught. The costs of escalating the direct involvement of US military forces to ward off a communist victory would both reduce the funding and weaken congressional support for domestic programs, particularly the War on Poverty. Because LBJ considered these social initiatives the centerpiece of his presidency, and hoped they would be the defining measure of his legacy as a leader, their diminution or demise was a source of intense anxiety. Nonetheless, in the months that followed, LBJ and his top civilian advisors steadily relinquished control over the pace, scale, and the very nature of American interventions in the Vietnam civil war to the Joint Chiefs of Staff and military commanders, most especially General Westmoreland in South Vietnam. Rather than working around the quagmire that had been enmeshing Indochina for over a half a century, Johnson and McNamara gave the military the go-ahead to plunge in.

Basic Training: Fort Dix, New Jersey
September 1965

When the buses arrived at the reception center, the drill sergeants promptly directed the new recruits into a concrete building. Each man was ordered to stand at attention when called upon, raise his right hand, and repeat the affirmation of enlistment in which he swore to protect the "Constitution of the United States against all enemies," and obey the "President of the United States and the orders of the officers appointed over him." After the oath, Jimmy's transformation into a soldier began swiftly and efficiently, and within seventy-two hours the induction process would be completed.[10]

As a prelude to discarding his civilian identity, he was first ordered to strip. A barber then sheared his hair down to his scalp—it took less than a minute. While showering he was careful not to look down the line. He must have felt uneasy. The ordeal of the medical examination came next. It was an assembly-line procedure where physicians weighed him and measured his height, looked for flat feet, counted his teeth, listened to his heart and lungs, stuck needles in his arms, and checked his eyesight and hearing. He was then herded stark naked into a cold room where a team of doctors fondled his testicles and made him cough, squeezed his penis to see if he had clap, and looked up his anus to see if he had hemorrhoids. They then verified his personal history and sought to ascertain that he wasn't a homosexual. "What they were really doing," one soldier recounted, "was stealing bits of our souls needle by needle."[11]

Next Jimmy took an aptitude test to determine which job options would be available to him. But for most draftees scores didn't matter. Their military trajectory was preordained. When the probing was over, Jimmy was reduced to a number on a medal tag—US51569003—that hung around his neck to identify his body if he was killed. The rest of his past, which barely amounted to a quarter pound of paper, sat in a filing cabinet in the records office at Fort Dix.

Shortly thereafter he was assigned to a unit—Company S of the Third Basic Combat Training Brigade—loaded on a bus, and transported to an isolated section of the fort where rows of two-story wooden barracks lined the streets. Built in 1940 to house the first mass mobilization of troops headed to Europe, the structures were in ill repair. In the late 1950s most of these old quarters had been demolished and replaced with three-story brick buildings complete with modern heating, gyms, and supply offices. But the entry into the Vietnam War increased enlistments by the tens of thousands and forced commanders to induct new soldiers twenty-four hours a day. Though the U.S. Army operated close to a dozen training facilities across the country, Fort Dix housed as much of a cross-section of the army population as any.[12] As a major training center for Vietnam-bound infantrymen, it was stretched for space to accommodate the large influx of conscripts. Camp personnel were left with no choice but to preserve what structures they could with more nails and thick coats of white lead paint. Even though the outdated barracks had indoor plumbing, most of the latrines and showers didn't work, and their obsolete heating systems—which consisted solely of coal-burning stoves—made them potential tinderboxes. Each night recruits were assigned two-hour shifts on fire watch. It proved to be the perfect time to write letters to his family, or to friends, including Gerry Shields, who had enlisted in the Navy:

Dear Gerry,
How are you, fine I hope. Training is getting harder each day, but the only thing I don't like is fire watch, that is to much. Every day someone is telling you what to do, I don't like that, but there isn't to much I can do about it. . . . I'm tired at the end of the day, but it isn't from marching, it is from getting up early every morning, right now I am getting ready to go back on detail so, I must close for now, so be good, write soon.
Your Friend, Jim
PS: Do you still watch Underdog?

It didn't take long for Jimmy and the rest of S Company, led by its young commander, Captain Arthur McAllway, Jr., to be fully inducted into the hellish environment of basic training. Everything was about time management and accountability, and every day began the same way: he woke at 0500 hours, quickly made his bed, hurried to the sinks with his toiletries, and—if time allowed—defecated. Early on some men who had trouble adjusting suffered from constipation. He then hustled into formation for roll call and marched off to complete his morning calisthenics. When Jimmy returned to the barracks he changed into the uniform of the day, and headed to the mess hall where a man with an automatic counter clicked off numbers as each man received his chow.[13]

The first weeks were the most difficult. They were designed to deprive recruits of all privacy and subject them to intense insults and strenuous exercises that were

Old barracks at Fort Dix.

physically demanding and mentally exhausting. This process was intended to erode each recruit's sense of individualism and replace it with a warrior identity centered on group survival and killing. The sole purpose of the ever-present drill sergeants, like James Cumberland, a combat veteran of the Korean War, was to transform the "low-life," "shitheads," "pussies," and "faggots" of S Company into a cohesive unit of "soldiers." In other words: "real men."

The intimidating demeanor of Sergeant Cumberland enabled him to maintain discipline and unquestioning obedience. Vicious taunts and harassment were critical to instilling a rigid set of regulations and procedures for the army's eight-week basic training program. His routine use of gendered and sexualized language was in line with army policy that was based on the assumption that it would foster manliness.

Indiscriminate taunts were intended to defuse class and racial tensions within the ranks, but very often they only served to promote bigotry and legitimize stereotypes. This was especially true of military instructors who referred to the Vietnamese as "dinks," "slants," and "gooks" during classroom exercises designed to introduce trainees to Southeast Asian "culture" and guerrilla tactics. But the series of lectures and anti-communist films that Jimmy sat through merely inculcated misconceptions and hatred. The Vietnamese were portrayed as unclean, deceitful, undisciplined, and timid. Because successful counterinsurgency depended on control over the civilian population, recruits were often warned that *all* Vietnamese—including women and children—were potentially hostile.

Although soldiers were informed of the articles of war, army training lacked instruction about moral responsibility. Despite having built a mock Vietnamese village at Fort Dix to acclimate soldiers to the physical and social environment of Vietnamese society, few infantrymen were taught how to communicate effectively with noncombatants and how to obtain accurate information from prisoners. The camp was filled with posters that further dehumanized the Vietnamese as the enemy. A prominently placed sign outside the barracks read: VIET CONG—BREAKFAST OF CHAMPIONS. Similar indoctrination methods were deployed at training facilities across the country. At Fort Polk's Tigerland, located in Louisiana's dense rainforest, the army prepared troops for combat by desensitizing them to violence. Billboards were strategically positioned outside the entryways to the barracks that affirmed: AGGRESSIVENESS AND FIRE POWER WILL WIN. Another with the caption, BONG THE CONG, showed a US soldier swinging the stock of his rifle to kill a Vietnamese peasant wearing black "pajamas."[14]

Soldiers also had to sit through numerous sermons in which army chaplains used lessons from scripture to lead discussions on "character guidance" to ensure that recruits saluted officers correctly and obeyed their NCOs.[15] The payback for defying drill sergeants ranged from profane insults, having to run several miles in full gear, or pull extra hours on the infamous Kitchen Patrol (KP): peeling potatoes, cleaning dishes, and dumping trash. Those who refused to conform were threatened with court martial or sent straight to the stockade; slackers were sent to the fort's "Special Processing Detachment," and risked having to repeat boot camp. Jimmy's misbehavior never amounted to more than "smart aleck" responses for which he was ridiculed in front of the company. Once he fell asleep on guard duty, thus potentially putting his unit at risk. He was ordered to do pushups until he collapsed. Random inspections for cleanliness were viewed as especially peevish. If just one soldier failed, the whole platoon could lose its precious weekend passes.

Jimmy's barracks smelled of gun oil and wax polish. Two rows of stacked metal beds lined the walls on each floor. He was assigned a top bunk with a footlocker placed exactly in the center of the end rails of the bed. Next to it was a wall locker that held his combat equipment and Class A dress uniform. Both had to be locked at all times (to save a few precious seconds in the morning, some men carefully situated the shackle bolt into the mechanism without having it clasp to give the impression it was secure). Army rules detailed the precise placement of every soldier's belongings within the footlocker. Toothpaste had to be positioned in the rear of the trunk and arranged so the words of the brand name appeared upside-down when the lid was opened. A trainee's shaving cream must be placed in the right corner, while his razor was required to be facing down on a white towel in the middle of the chest. The toothbrush had to be pointing in the same direction as the razor, with the bristles on the right side, also facing outward.

If a man used cologne, the same directions applied to it as for the toothpaste. A recruit's comb, handkerchiefs, and dish soap were required to be neatly lined on the same white towel. A soldier's boots had to face toe out with the heel even with the frame of the bed and ought to be completely dry and free of dust and dirt. If a soldier was religious, a Bible was allowed. It was positioned right side up in between the handkerchiefs and shoe polish. This was the only permitted deviation from the footlocker guidelines. A trainee's bedding was also regulated by the *Soldier's Handbook*.

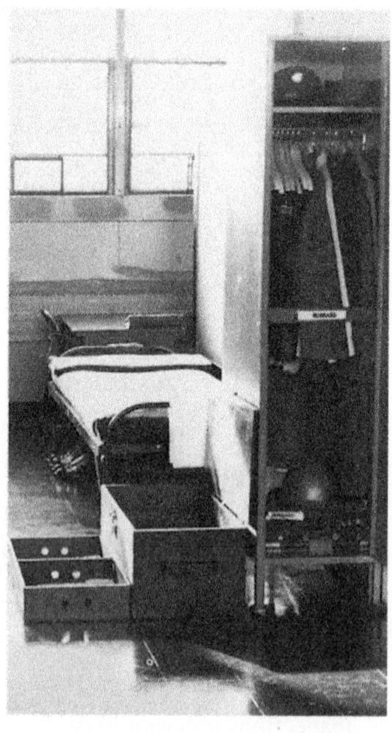

(Left) A solder at Fort Dix adjusts his footlocker to meet army regulations.
(Right) A typical bunk with foot and wall lockers.

Clean sheets had to be fitted on the mattress so tight that if a coin were tossed on the bed it would bounce off without the sheets ever being ruffled. Notorious for his messy bedroom at home, Jimmy found keeping his footlocker organized and living space spotless the most annoying aspect of regimentation. By the third week, trainees were out of the classroom and into the field.

Drill had drained Jimmy of his vigor; training came as a shock. As he lay awake at night, he wondered what he had gotten into. In a letter to Gerry, who had also registered similar complaints about his basic training, Jimmy expressed a lack of enthusiasm for military life that he would take with him to Vietnam. Trying to hold on to what was left of his civilian identity, he focused on life back home:

Dear Gerry,
How are you, I got your letter today, and I'm glad your getting out [of the Navy] if you can because it [the military] is no place to be when you don't have to be, if you do get out I can get you a job down the hosiery mill for $2 an hour. . . or with my father who is selling trees and flowers this year. . . it doesn't seem like many know what we are fighting for, Pres. Johnson doesn't know either. . . about that girl you met, take her out you ass, the most that can happen is her husband will find out and kill you, well, I got to go to bed. . . When you come home, Wildwood here we come. Take it easy, and I will say a prayer for you about getting out.

In the second half of boot camp, recruits began to master the basic weapons of the infantry. The most important of these was the 7.62 magazine-fed, gas-operated, air-cooled, semiautomatic M14 rifle, which was soon to be replaced by the smaller caliber M16A1. Fully loaded, the M14 weighed over eleven pounds. In addition to understanding the functioning parts of their gun and how to clean it, each soldier was tested for accuracy and rate of fire on the range. If he demonstrated high proficiency in "zapping" targets, he was awarded a ribbon and moved on to learn how to detonate claymore mines and set ambushes as well as fire an M-60 machine gun, a .45 pistol, and the M72 Light Anti-Armor Weapon. Marksmanship training was followed by vigorous instruction on how to live in the field or, according to military jargon, "the bush." As trainees began to build camaraderie during shooting contests and physical competitions against other units, the role of the drill sergeants was minimized. Instead, squad leaders were picked from the ranks of the trainees to manage organizational tasks and discipline. But despite the drill sergeants' reduced role, many trainees had internalized their animosity toward the "Cong" and "draft dodgers."

As verbal abuse waned, most of the trainees in S Company had become accustomed to the physical exertion. But some could not adjust to army routines. The most proactive of these men often gathered in small groups to discuss the possibility of desertion, and some headed north to Canada or south to Mexico. By the end of the war nearly 500,000 men had deserted from bases across the United States. Those who felt they had exhausted all other options sought to have "accidents" on the shooting range. Every week at Fort Dix there was an average of four attempted suicides, and by the end of the Vietnam War a record two hundred men killed themselves at the New Jersey base alone. But Jimmy figured there was no way for him to back out. What would people think of him? He was stuck, again. Basic training was getting harder, and his nerves were wearing thin. Numerous studies conducted among trainees in the 1960s found that by the middle of the eight weeks of training, recruits had become so intensely anxious and angry that their stress levels surpassed those of frontline soldiers.[16]

Unfocused rage, however, was not the intended outcome of military training. In weeks six and seven, the main goal was to channel the recruit's anger through violent exercises designed to replicate anticipated combat situations. Brutality and fatigue were meant to produce "mental callouses." Trainees learned how to handle bayonet assaults by fighting each other with pugil sticks, three-foot long PVC pipes with padded foam on each end. They were also instructed in the "ten to twelve different ways to kill" a Viet Cong guerrilla. Jimmy related the experience to his brother:

> *. . . I learned more about hand-to-hand combat today and boy can you really hurt a guy if you want too, but what the army is teaching is nothing to play around with, it doesn't take much to hurt a person no matter what their size or weight, if you have good foot speed and fast moves it is hard to be beat, but the enemy is not just standing there singing. If you are slow when you come in contact with him [you're dead], but once you get him down you smash his head into the ground 7 or 8 times, and give him the heel of your boot, then you decide how to finish dispose of him, and that's where I'm told the fun starts. . . .*

Soldiers also learned other crude killing and maiming techniques. These included eye gouging, kneeing men in the crotch, and biting off ears. Fortunately, Jimmy didn't have to sit through slide shows where pictures of mutilated Vietnamese corpses were shown to psychologically numb young army "derelicts" to the atrocities of war. He was also spared what Marines called the "rabbit lesson," in which an NCO placed a rabbit on a table while he lectured recruits about to leave for Vietnam on the necessity of elusiveness, vulnerability, and survival. At first the rabbit distracts the men, and some display affection for it. But then the instructor slams it on the table, breaks its neck, skins it, disembowels it, and throws the creature's entrails at the stunned soldiers. Though the mutilation of the rabbit was left out at Fort Dix, the lesson Jimmy and his fellow trainees were meant to learn was: If you want to stay alive, you have to kill the gooks, especially since the little "bastards were responsible for you being there."[17]

To further build their survival skills, troops practiced how to properly throw grenades, treat gunshot wounds, and care for minor burns and head injuries, which entailed wrapping medical gauze around plastic heads that didn't bleed. War games that emphasized tactical training went on both day and night, and stressed the art of concealment on Fort Dix's eleven square miles of nutrient-poor, barren soil that

At Fort Dix, soldiers are trained how to fight in close combat using a mixture of martial arts.

bore no resemblance whatsoever to the jungles of Vietnam. To further simulate the war zone experience, soldiers carried a full pack through the pine forest. A thick belt supported by suspenders held a pair of universal ammunition pouches, a first-aid bag, a compass, a folding entrenching tool or "little shovel", a bayonet, and a plastic canteen that fit into a mess kit. A small combat pack fastened to the back of the strap held a pair of dry socks, gun cleaning tools, and wire-cutters. Two twenty-round M14 rifle magazines filled each ammo pouch, and several fragmentation grenades were fastened to its side. Additional grenades (smoke and white phosphorus) and a flashlight were clipped to the suspenders. An infantryman also carried a light, aluminum frame rucksack. It held a minimum three days' C-rations, extra water and magazines, a rubber mattress, a poncho, a poncho liner, a mosquito net, toiletries (razor, soap, toothbrush and toothpaste), letter writing materials, C-4 explosive, trip flares, and claymore mines. Though most of the extraneous items were left at base

Recruits at Fort Dix prepare for a field inspection during an overnight training exercise.

camp—specifically the thirteen-pound sleeping bag, a small tent, and bulky gas mask—the whole load weighed over sixty-five pounds.[18]

Trainees were also introduced to chemical, biological, and radiological warfare. They memorized the procedures needed to survive, and then waited anxiously in long lines to enter the bunker where they would be exposed to chlorobenzylidene malononitrile (tear gas). Jimmy's squad walked into the chamber with their gas masks on. But once the doors were shut and sealed, the soldiers had to spend from three to five minutes with their masks off. Many began coughing and dry heaving as they felt the effects of the chemical. When Jimmy stumbled out of the door, gagging and drooling, his skin burning, he was told to lift his arms and keep walking.

Near the end of the training cycle, Jimmy's family visited him at Fort Dix. His mother brought a picnic lunch to eat on the parade grounds before they took Jimmy

James Gilch with his mother Kate and father George during a family visit at Fort Dix.

home for the weekend. Kate and George expressed increasing concern about their son's future. But Jimmy sought to calm his mother by letting her know that he had recently put in a request for a desk job as a colonel's aide. He was confident he would have a decision sometime soon. The position would keep him out of combat, and he assured her that if he were sent overseas, he would be pushing paper in an air-conditioned trailer.

In a letter to his parents shortly after he returned to base, Jimmy made little of his failure to get the desk job. He also left out the fact that his Military Occupational Specialty, infantryman 11B, meant that he would undergo two more months of learning how to kill. Although Jimmy would later describe his Advanced Infantry Training (AIT) as a lot like basic training, it wasn't. He would no longer be a trainee; he would be a "grunt," a ground pounder. His training would emphasize "instant reactions" and "quick kills," which meant that he would discharge his weapon at any sound or movement without consciously aiming. He would also learn how to search thatched houses for booby traps, and use friendly villages for cover when in "killing zones."

His ultimate fate would soon be determined by a computer technician feeding two separate decks of cards, one white, one green, into an IBM card sorter. Jimmy's aptitude test scores, educational level, language proficiencies, and physical skills were all deciding factors. The white card identified locations around the world where the army had an opening for a rifleman. The green card listed the names of trainees who were waiting to be assigned. When fed into the sorting machine, each card exited paired with the opposite color, and the odds were high of going to Vietnam. As one personnel officer explained, "a lot of guys, by the toss of the dice, went to Europe," and the "unlucky ones" went to Vietnam.[19] Recruits who did not want to take a chance with the system, as Jimmy remarked, "never came back."

In a letter written near of the end of his Advanced Infantry Training, Jimmy reflected on lost opportunities that landed him in the army and, eventually, Vietnam:

> *Dear Mom,*
> *. . . Too bad I did not know what I know now when I was home because I would have had more respect for both you and dad and the kid's. I wish you made me study in school, and I wish you were a lot harder on me. Tell Georgie to leave the girls alone, he doesn't know what it is like to be away. I've learned a lot that I would not otherwise have if I stayed in [Runnemede] all my life. . . thank god I found this out now while it is not too late. I would like to go back to school when I come out and make the family proud of me like I'm proud of dad and you and Georgie. I don't see how dad kept the family like he does, I don't blame him for being mad sometimes because he has a lot on his mind. . . and everything he tried to teach me I thought I knew, but I didn't know anything. When I get out, I will really try my best to be a help instead of a pain. . . .*

Major General Charles Beauchamp sat in his office at Fort Dix writing a letter for the camp's 1965 yearbook that would be given to the graduates. To promote the Defense Department's new "Action Army" philosophy, which focused on the use of sophisticated weaponry, electronics, and guided missiles, Beauchamp assured recruits that they were as well prepared for combat as possible. He tried to convince all who read the letter that the army produced "better citizens" who would be able to defend America by being thoroughly disciplined and "technically qualified, and physically, morally, and mentally conditioned to survive on the modern battlefield."[20] But despite Beauchamp's rhetoric, which was reflected in the camp's motto, "Home of the

Ultimate Weapon [the soldier]," the training provided at Fort Dix had not adequately prepared the men in his charge for the type of combat they would face in Vietnam.

Renewing the War for Independence

As the French arrived to restore their control over the Saigon region in 1945, nine-year-old Le Van Tra joined several of his schoolmates in pilfering ammunition, grenades, and other supplies from soldiers passing through his local marketplace in the town of Binh Duong. In his teenage years, he became a part-time messenger for Viet Minh units fighting in the southern districts. An ardent patriot, Tra shared the deep disappointment of the majority of the Vietnamese people with the 1954 Geneva Accords. Despite a decade of devastating revolutionary warfare, the agreement did not ratify their most nonnegotiable demand: a unified, fully independent Vietnamese nation. In the months that followed, Tra yearned to join his older brother and other family members, who had fought against the French, and now were ordered by the Viet Minh leadership to regroup in the Democratic Republic of Vietnam (DRV) in the north, where they were to receive additional training. But Tra's parents insisted that he stay in Binh Duong to finish his schooling and, because he was the only child still at home, his brother urged him to remain behind and care for them. Although saddened by his brother's departure, Tra was somewhat consoled by the opportunity to march with hundreds of other young people alongside the oxcarts that stretched for miles on the dusty roads carrying the fighters to Xuyen Moc, the coastal town from which they would board ships bound for the North.

In roughly the same time span, a young but seasoned Viet Minh veteran, Houng Van Ba, who had fought for years in the famed guerrilla Battalion 307, made his way to Vung Tao south of Saigon, where he was assigned a Soviet ship for a similar journey to the North. Though he had often been away from home during the years of combat against the French, Ba recalled the intense homesickness that he and his compatriots felt long after they arrived in the liberated northern half of Vietnam. But he immediately added the same refrain that resounds in interviews and captured diaries of the great majority of fighters mobilized to overthrow the American-backed regime in Saigon: the willingness to accept sacrifices in order to reunify the Vietnamese people.[21]

In the months after the Geneva settlement arbitrarily cleaved Vietnam in two at the 17th parallel, American politicians and journalists made a great deal of the mass migration that occurred in the opposite direction from that traveled by Tra and Ba. An estimated 800,000 Vietnamese—many of whom were Catholics—fled from the newly established Democratic Republic of Vietnam in the north to the faction-ridden regions in the south, where US operatives scrambled to bolster an anti-communist regime, soon to led headed by Ngo Dinh Diem. It is unclear whether intimidation of and physical assaults against Catholics preceded or were sparked by their decision to abandon en masse their homes in the North. But their flight was depicted, often in sensationalist terms, in the

American media as yet another example of communist brutality and the threat it posed for all citizens of the "free world." Little notice was given to the tens of thousands of southerners who simultaneously moved north, including an estimated 100,000 Viet Minh officials, soldiers, and party supporters. But the decision on the part of the communist leadership to transfer guerrilla fighters and support personnel to North Vietnam for further training and indoctrination, left little doubt that they were convinced that the struggle for Vietnamese independence was far from over. They also ordered operatives remaining in the South to store weapons in concealed locations and to continue expanding party membership. The Americans' refusal to sign the Geneva Accords, and their efforts after 1954 to find alternative leaders to Ho Chi Minh, made it clear that the internationally supervised elections mandated by the 1954 agreement would never be held.

Deprived of the opportunity to form a government for all of Vietnam in an election that virtually all knowledgeable American and international observers were convinced Ho Chi Minh would win by a landslide, the communists and their allies paused in the mid-1950s to consolidate their control in the North and clandestinely expand their political networks in the South. Even before they were officially in control of Hanoi in May 1954, the Lao Dong (Vietnamese Workers' Party) launched an overly ambitious, and at times brutally executed, campaign focused on the redistribution of agrarian landholdings and the repression of individuals and social groups viewed by the party collective (at times erroneously) as hostile to the communist-led regime. The excesses committed in the dispossession of the landlord classes and purges of noncommunist individuals and groups that had been allied with the Viet Minh resulted in major social disturbances, disrupted party and government operations, and led in some areas to violent clashes. Although Ho Chi Minh, Vo Nguyen Giap, and other communist leaders sought to moderate the pace and intensity of the sociopolitical transformations propagated by the doctrinaire revolutionaries, measures to check indiscriminate vilification and repression did not restore a semblance of social equilibrium until well into 1958. Preoccupied with these internal disorders and the need to establish a competent structure of governance from the capital in Hanoi to the far-flung villages across the DRV, the communist regime in the North vacillated in its defense of the increasingly hard-pressed revolutionary forces that had gone underground in the South after 1954.[22]

Soon after his American backers made it clear they would provide ample support for what was soon to be the Republic of [South] Vietnam (RVN), Ngo Dinh Diem set about eliminating potential (and often imagined) political rivals. Diem put his brother Nhu in charge of South Vietnam's rapidly expanding, US-bankrolled army (ARVN) and police forces, which were ordered to crush the religious sects and a crime syndicate that had carved out semiautonomous enclaves in the fiercely contested southern provinces. After the sham election that was staged to give some legitimacy to Diem and his cronies, Nhu's paramilitary units and secret police focused on the Western-influenced political parties that varied from those on the right advocating the restoration of Vietnam's imperial dynasty to the ultra-Marxist splinter parties on the far left. Under the legal system the regime implemented, anyone accused of belonging to or collaborating with the communist or other leftist parties had no rights of appeal whatsoever. Even those suspected of cooperating with the communists, were arrested, imprisoned, tortured, and murdered with impunity. Although the southern Viet Minh activists who had not migrated North after 1954 had retreated to clandestine operations and sought to blend into the civilian population, the draconian repression of the Diem regime forced them to renew the guerrilla insurgency that had vanquished the French. They armed themselves with weapons they had hidden as the French withdrew, and then retreated to the forest and underground sanctuaries they had established to survive the government onslaught.

As the repression of the Saigon regime intensified in the late 1950s, particularly in the districts surrounding the capital, rebels in the South called upon the North Vietnamese leadership to intervene in their support. Ending the division of Vietnam remained the ultimate objective of communist leaders on both sides of the 17th parallel. But disagreements among the top leaders delayed Hanoi's responses to the threat that Diem's push for dictatorial control posed for the very survival of the communist party in the South. Having concluded that there were no viable constitutional options for achieving power, in December 1960 the southern communists and other political factions who shared their opposition to Diem formed the National Liberation Front (NLF). In January of the previous year, the Politburo of the DRV in the North had voted to provide assistance to the rebels in the South.

As American military and financial support for the Saigon regime increased alarmingly in the years that followed, newly ascendant communist leaders in the North, most notably Le Duan and Le Duc To (who had both fought in the war against the French in the Mekong Delta region) accelerated Hanoi's efforts to reinforce NLF units with weapons, critical supplies, and training for combat and propaganda operations. The Lao Dang Political Bureau in the North also tightened its control over the NLF through the Central Office for South Vietnam (COSVN), headquartered just over the border with Cambodia northwest of Saigon. Ongoing connections between communist forces in North and South were established by both land and sea, with the most critical and enduring linkages forged by the establishment and steady expansion of the multiple routes traversed by the Ho Chi Minh trail. The porous northern borders along the 17th parallel and increasingly the sanctuaries in Cambodia made possible an acceleration of the infiltration of regular North Vietnamese Army (NVA) units into Diem's contested fiefdom. NVA soldiers would soon become a major factor in combat operations in the war for control of the South and an essential counterforce against the massive US military buildup than began in early 1965.[23]

Both the top-down, hierarchical command structure of communist guerrilla forces and the pivotal impact of the conventional North Vietnamese forces engaged in the South complicate the prevailing—but misleading—impressions of the conflict as an insurgency fought by small units with a good deal of autonomy and improvisation. As the Vietnamese people had through two millennia of history, the Viet Minh and NLF-NVA fighters relied on both guerrilla and

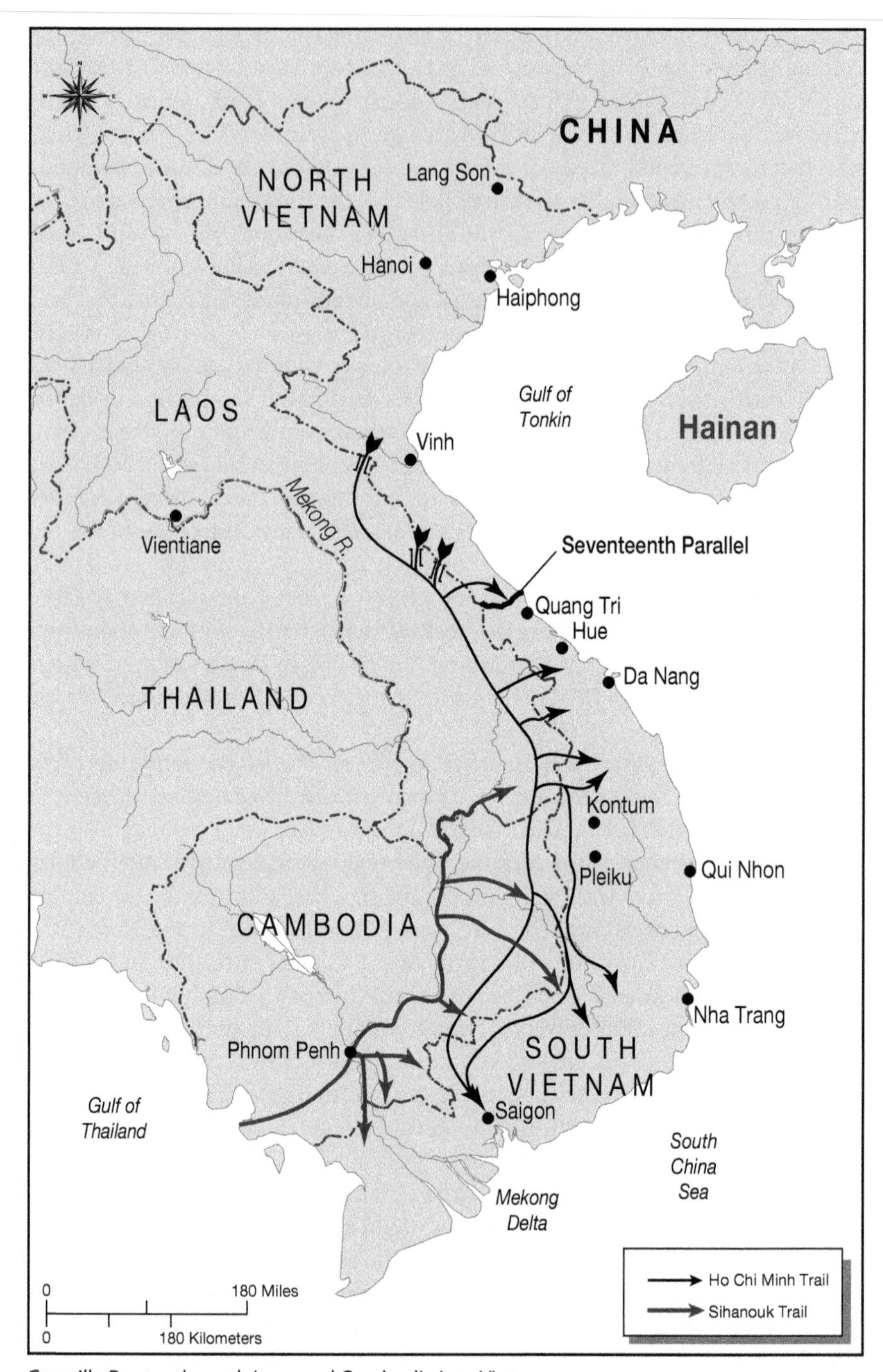

Guerrilla Routes through Laos and Cambodia into Vietnam

conventional warfare to defeat their internal rivals and drive off powerful foreign invaders. Viet Minh forces fighting the French after World War II as well as NLF insurgents battling the Diem regime in the 1950s and 1960s relied heavily on traditional tactics long associated with guerrilla warfare. They used the widespread support of the local populace and their superior knowledge of the terrain in their base areas to carry out sabotage operations, mount ambushes, devise elaborate ruses to draw enemy units into minefields, and evade contact in situations where their adversaries had amassed superior firepower. By contrast, regular NVA soldiers deployed in the South often engaged in conventional combat operations against pursuing or entrenched American or ARVN units. Both approaches contributed to ultimate victory; in fact, during the French phase of the wars of liberation massed assaults on the fortifications at Dien Bien Phu had been tactically and strategically decisive. But guerrilla operations proved critical by making it possible for the communists to sustain what soon became a prolonged war of attrition against escalating US military interventions.

The training that Ho, Giap, and other key Vietnamese leaders had received from Maoist revolutionaries in China before and during the Second World War reconfigured traditional Vietnamese approaches to both conventional and guerrilla warfare in significant ways. Modifications in organizational structure, methods of maintaining discipline, training of recruits, and the nature of the weapons deployed by the Viet Minh were sustained by the National Liberation Front during the war in the South. These changes greatly enhanced the insurgents' potential to counter the high-tech reconnaissance, communications, and weapons systems wielded by all branches of the American military and (to a lesser extent) allied ARVN forces.

Similar to their Chinese communist and Soviet prototypes, the organization of the Vietnamese military—both the regular forces of the NVA and in NLF guerrilla units in the South—was centered on officers called cadres, who combined both military and political authority and responsibilities. Cadres were the highest-ranking officers in units at every level of NVA and NLF forces, and thus their approval was required for all military operations. Those chosen as cadres were almost always party members. Literacy, loyalty to the communist party, integrity, and courage in battle were deemed essential candidate attributes. Both in the NVA and the NLF, cadres were responsible for the maintenance of discipline and high morale within the units to which they were assigned. They relied on ongoing indoctrination sessions that stressed the reasons why the Vietnamese were at war in order to ensure their subordinates' willingness to endure personal losses for the greater national causes of liberation and unification. Cadres attached to guerrilla forces in the South were in charge of intelligence gathering in the areas in which their units were operating, and were responsible for critical liaisons with the civilian population. In order to maintain widespread support among the general populace, they also organized propaganda offensives, oversaw the recruitment of guerrilla fighters, and ordered reprisals against informers and headmen collaborating with the Saigon regime.

Most of those who fought in guerrilla forces in the South were young to middle-aged males, including many who joined as teenagers. In a revealing comparison with NVA soldiers from the North, almost all of whom were literate (many actually had some secondary education), less than half of the trainees in the South were literate—evidence of the ineptitude of the Diem regime. Among the best prepared for guerrilla operations were those—including Le Van Tra and Houng Van Ba—who went north in 1954, where they were given further schooling, and more rigorous training and intensive political indoctrination, than most of those recruited in the South. The Hanoi government gave the so-called "Autumn" soldiers or "regroupees" who volunteered to return to the South to support the insurgency against the Saigon regime extra pay and rations, and their parents were provided with stipends by the Hanoi government.

The level of training of guerrilla fighters in the South varied considerably. Cadres and "main force" or fulltime, regional fighters were the best trained, while part-time, "local force" recruits usually received more rudimentary weapons and tactical instruction. Almost all guerrilla recruits were from settled agrarian or urban areas, and thus struggled to survive in the rainforest environment where many units operated for weeks or months at a time. Clashes with American or ARVN forces were frequent and casualty-ridden.

Women played critical roles as intelligence gatherers and couriers, saboteurs, doctors, and nurses. They maintained the Ho Chi Minh trail, and in many instances were combatants, some of whom became high-ranking officers and decorated war heroes. Both NLF-affiliated and non-communist women's groups were deeply involved in organizing mass protests in Saigon and other urban areas. In 1963 they joined in the demonstrations that contributed to the collapse of the Diem regime and destabilized the military governments that followed. Older men and children also supported rebel operations as messengers, spies, and guides. Village communities in NLF-controlled areas collectively hid and stored food and weapons for guerrilla units.

As the escalation of US military interventions accelerated rapidly in the mid-1960s, the communist government in Hanoi sought to bolster NLF forces by sending increasing numbers of regular NVA troops into battle in the South. Throughout Vietnamese history, conventional armies and set-piece battles had long been as or more important than guerrilla warfare in power struggles between rival dynasties, resisting enemy invaders, and expanding kingdoms. From this perspective, the formation of the Army of the Democratic Republic of Vietnam marked the reemergence of an ancient Vietnamese military tradition that had proved a match for powerful Chinese and Mongol adversaries and had impressed numerous European observers in the centuries dominated by Vietnamese dynasties before the French conquests.

Similar to those of its predecessors, NVA units were made up mainly of peasant conscripts, but they also included urban workers, and at least in the initial stages of the American buildup, substantial numbers of volunteers. A small percentage of combat forces came from elite and middle-class backgrounds. But very few were the sons or daughters of party officials, many of whom found

Women fighters of a local force prepare for an air raid in Hanoi, North Vietnam, April 1967.

government positions in the North or were sent abroad to Eastern Europe or the Soviet Union for advanced education. Once inducted into units assigned to the southern front, leaves were rare, and both regulars and guerrillas were in service for the duration of the conflict. In the mid-1960s, only a small percentage of guerrilla fighters in the South were soldiers drawn from the ranks of the NVA. By 1968, however, especially after the massive losses inflicted on NLF forces engaged in conventional combat during the Tet Offensive, one third were reinforcements sent from the North.

The basic training for those inducted into the NVA was similar to that found in most twentieth-century armies. It included routinized drill, marching in step, presenting arms, etc., designed to instill discipline and group coordination through rigorous physical exercise, and intensive instruction in the weapons and combat tactics deployed by the regular armed forces of the North Vietnamese regime. Additional training was provided for inductees selected for specialized assignments, such as logistics, engineering, and emergency medical care.

A young Vietnamese soldier is measured for his uniform and medically evaluated by a team of doctors as other recruits await their turn in line.

Substantial doses of political indoctrination were also provided for all military personnel, and these sessions almost certainly had considerable impact on the very low desertion rates among soldiers sent to fight in the South. NVA units were given extra instruction in how to counteract, destroy, and recycle the types of military hardware that US and ARVN forces would use against them. They also received better pay and rations than those who remained in the North. They learned how to survive and fight in the rainforest, and cope with napalm and B-52 carpet-bombing as they made their way down the Ho Chi Minh trail.

There was an obvious and daunting asymmetry between the high-tech weapons and communications systems the US unleashed against both NLF guerrilla fighters and NVA soldiers and the means the Vietnamese had to counter American forces. But the commonly held notion that the communists fought back with little more than obsolescent firearms and ingenious yet rather rudimentary booby traps vastly underestimates the sophistication of the military hardware the Vietnamese were able to import or manufacture themselves. It

Training for NLF recruits encompassed both simulations of stealth maneuvers and training in highly lethal and up-to-date weaponry.

is true that at the start of the French phase of their wars of liberation the Vietnamese were short on firearms and ammunition, so much so that some of their fighters used World War I vintage rifles. But Viet Minh operatives were adept at appropriating the weapons of the departing Japanese in 1945, and they repeatedly ambushed French convoys in the following decade. In the first years of

NLF mobilization against the Diem regime at the end of the 1950s, and even after America forces began to arrive in 1965, some local guerrilla units were still poorly armed. But after the Communist Party came to power in China in 1949, the Chinese funneled a steady supply of pistols and low-caliber ordnance—much of which had been captured in the Korean War—to their fellow revolutionaries in French Indochina. Chinese support waned considerably due in part to disagreements over the Geneva Accords, and by the late 1950s the Soviet Union and its Warsaw Pact satellites had eclipsed the Maoists' arms deliveries to North Vietnam.

By the time of the American military buildup in 1965, NVA, NLF main force units, and local fighters were well supplied with machinery, transport vehicles, and advanced weapons—from the famed and ubiquitous AK-47 automatic rifles to machine guns, mortars, grenade launchers, and surface-to-surface rockets. As we shall see, the Vietnamese guerrilla fighters also made very good use of captured or discarded American equipment, which they recycled into deadly weapons or sandals, blankets, bandages, and other essential items in short supply. By the last stages of the war, NVA forces, which had become the main adversaries of the US–ARVN alliance, deployed armor-piercing recoilless rifles, grenades, tanks, and large field guns.

Estimates of the food and clothing provided Vietnamese soldiers vary somewhat, but differences between regular NVA and guerrilla units were generally slight. In his *Viet Cong Memoir*, Truong Nhu Tang recalls that NLF guerrillas kept the things that they carried in their backpacks "to a minimum."[24] Clothing was limited to two pairs each of black pajamas and underpants and a small sheet of nylon (or plastic in other accounts) that served as a raincoat or cover when sleeping. Weapons and ammunition made up the bulk of their load, which also included their provisions that consisted of a cotton tube stuffed with rice, a chunk of salt, a bit of monosodium glutamate, and dried fish or a little meat. Other NLF or NVA narratives mention sandals (made from enemy truck tires), canteens (often made in China), little oil lamps (made from perfume bottles), green tea, *nuoc mam* (a Vietnamese sauce made from fish), and tobacco. Southern fighters returning from the North in the late 1950s and 1960s recount discarding NVA pith helmets in favor of the soft, floppy hats of NLF guerrillas, and being equipped with flashlights and hammocks. When lapses in US surveillance and pauses in bombing permitted, both regular and guerrilla forces supplemented their meager diets with vegetables raised in concealed plots or provided by villagers in "liberated" zones as well as "bushmeat" from monkeys and birds that were trapped or shot in the forests.

Whether they were draftees or volunteers, both NVA and NLF combatants had a mixture of motives for risking their lives in the last—and most lethal—phase of the Vietnamese wars of liberation. Particularly as the conflict escalated in the late 1960s, the majority of NVA soldiers from the North were conscripted, and were often subjected to intense pressure from their families, friends, and village communities to serve. Government propaganda was also a major factor motivating those compelled and those more willing to fight. Legendary heroes,

The surfeit of equipment provided for American soldiers and what was available to NLF fighters underscores the great discrepancy in wealth and material abundance between the two adversaries.

including the Trung sisters who led a rebellion against the Chinese nearly two millennia earlier, and centuries of struggle against invaders and colonizers were used to frame calls to defend the Vietnamese nation and avenge the deaths and destruction American military interventions were inflicting on Vietnam, North and South. Testimony or diary entries by NVA soldiers captured during the war or providing oral interviews afterward stress the importance of reunifying the Vietnamese people and alleviating the suffering of their "Southern blood brothers."[25] Reunification is also a recurring motivation emphasized in interrogations of NLF prisoners. In some cases, traumatic personal losses—a fiancée killed in a US bombing raid in the North, a farmer driven off his land—drove aggrieved students or peasants to enlist as soldiers or insurgents. The potential to raise one's social status by advancing in the hierarchy of the communist party or the ranks of the NVA or NLF was also very likely a significant factor in decisions to join the resistance. Similar to Jimmy Gilch and many other young Americans, young Vietnamese sought to find a larger purpose or some excitement in their lives, and perhaps even imagined returning from the war as heroes. As Le Thi Dau, a Viet Cong nurse, remarked, "The war was horrible. [But] it gave me something to do that was out of the ordinary."[26]

Off to War
January 1966

When Jimmy's final orders came, he used what little time remained to say his farewells. After his brother's wedding celebration, he kissed his girlfriend Louise goodbye and paid her bus fare home. Walking back from the station, his new uniform gave him a sense of purpose, but it did not rid him of his newfound feelings of cynicism. At home he joked about the things he learned in basic training, and conducted cleaning inspections of the den and bedrooms. His mother was happy he had kept his sense of humor, and she was pleased by how meticulous he had become about the placement of his belongings. He wouldn't allow his sisters to iron his fatigues; they had to be pressed a certain way and only he knew how to place the pins on his uniform in accordance with army code.

On his last day in town, Jimmy went to visit Mrs. Shields. He knocked on the door, and then greeted her with a smile and hug. He shared stories about his experiences at Fort Dix. When he got up to leave, she broke down in tears. He offered his handkerchief. Walking to the door, she told him that she couldn't wait to see him when he returned. He paused. "I'm afraid, Mrs. Shields, when you see me again, I'll be in a pine box."

By 1959 guerrilla fighters from the South who had gone North after Geneva were returning to their home bases to join the resistance to the Diem regime. Leaving their villages and families in 1954 to continue their training in the liberated North was the most memorable part of the journey. Half a decade later—and all throughout the American phase of the war—the trip south was physically taxing, dangerous, and often lethal for many of the guerrilla fighters making their way back home as well as for the regular NVA soldiers from the North who soon followed. In late May 1964, Huong Van Ba rode in a truck convoy to a concealed rest area on the North Vietnam-Laos border where he shed his NVA uniform, identification card, and any other personal belongings that would mark him as a soldier from the Democratic Republic. Ba had been appointed the deputy commander of an artillery unit of forty-five returning guerrilla fighters. He and his unit made the journey down the Ho Chi Minh trail on foot, walking on average over eight hours a day. They carried seventy-pound packs along crude trails that snaked through rainforests and across mountains and rivers to the NLF stronghold in the vicinity of Tay Ninh northwest of Saigon.

Ba appreciated the auxiliary support unit that was assigned to transport his company's disassembled heavy weaponry and ammunition, an arduous task that most NVA soldiers and guerrillas would soon have to handle themselves in addition to their own backpacks in similar terrain. The travails of the journey south were amplified by the enervating humidity and sudden bursts of torrential rainfall in the midst of the predictable monsoon showers. There were rest areas, but no permanent shelters. Infiltrating NVA or NLF forces had to sleep in their hammocks or on the ground out in the rain with some protection from plastic or nylon sheets. Having soon used up the rations they were given at the start of the trek, Ba and his companions were dependent on the irregular and often meager foods supplied by local supporters along the way. But much of the journey was through sparsely inhabited areas, and hunger and disease soon began to thin their ranks. Despite the quinine pills that had been provided, malaria wore down and then ravaged those who were able to plod on. The commander of the force, who was Ba's good friend, struggled to continue. He died shortly after laying down to rest at one of the way stations on the trail. Ba did not contract malaria, but was badly infected after stepping on a punji stake and spent time recovering at a makeshift clinic.

After the remaining soldiers of the artillery force moved deep into the southern provinces, they succeeded in evading ARVN patrols that sought to intercept and kill or capture them. Unlike communist forces entering the South after the Americans arrived in force in the summer 1965, Ba and his comrades did not have to contend with high-tech American surveillance systems or weapons fire. On August 1, 1964, over two months after Ba and his unit set out they finally reached their assigned destination. Of the forty-five who had begun the journey south, fewer than ten made it to Tay Ninh. After two days of rest, the weary survivors were ordered into combat in the tunnels of Cu Chi where US forces were launching a search and destroy operation.[27]

NLF solders making their way up the Truong Son mountains on the Ho Chi Minh trail and U.S. soldiers arriving in Saigon courtesy of Pan American Airlines.

CHAPTER 4

Into the Quagmire

> "The ability of the Vietcong continuously to rebuild their units and to make good their losses is one of the mysteries of this guerrilla war. We still find no plausible explanation for the continued strength of the Vietcong. . . . Not only do the Vietcong units have the recuperative powers of the phoenix, but they have an amazing ability to maintain morale."
>
> —US GENERAL MAXWELL TAYLOR, then ambassador to South Vietnam, November 1964; as quoted in *The Pentagon Papers*, Gravel edition, 3:668.

> "Their [the Vietnamese] economy is agrarian and simple, their population unfamiliar with the modern comforts and conveniences that most of us in the western world take for granted. . . their morale has not been broken, since they are accustomed to discipline and are no stranger to deprivation and death."
>
> —ROBERT MCNAMARA, as quoted in Tom Mangold and John Penycate, *The Tunnels of Cu Chi.*

> "Well, I'm afraid that bad days are coming. There is no way to make this Vietnamese war decent. There is no way of justifying sending troops to another man's country. And there is no way to do anything but praise the man who defends his own land."
>
> —JOHN STEINBECK, Letter to Jack Valenti, *Life in Letters,* 1965.

In the weeks after the arrival of the Marines in Da Nang in March 1965, President Johnson expanded the air war against North Vietnam to include bridges, ammunition dumps, rail lines, and other channels of transportation. But the effort to destroy Hanoi's will and bring its people "to their knees" was unsuccessful. Over 600,000 Vietnamese volunteered to repair the damage to the North's infrastructure, and in the interim relied on wheelbarrows, oxcarts, and bicycles to transport supplies across otherwise impassable roadways and water systems.

Many were motivated by the slogan: "Each kilogram of goods . . . is a bullet shot into the head of the American pirates."[1] The aerial bombardment was meant to destabilize the Democratic Republic of Vietnam and force the communist regime to surrender before "the game had grown too costly."[2] But LBJ and his inner circle of advisors soon considered the assault to be "a colossal misjudgment." Neither the president nor McNamara could have imagined that the Soviets, Chinese, and other allies of North Vietnam would contribute a total of $600 million in economic aid and another billion in weaponry and supplies, which equaled more than four times what the North Vietnamese had lost in the bombings. During the monsoon season of 1965 NLF guerrilla operations were driving ARVN forces out of formerly contested areas throughout South Vietnam. The number of soldiers and the amount of equipment Hanoi sent down the Ho Chi Minh trail astonished General William Westmoreland, the commander of American forces in Vietnam. His intelligence staff estimated that the influx of North Vietnamese troops reduced the ratio of American to NLF/NVA battalions from 3 to 1 (which at the time was considered the disparity necessary to defeat guerrilla warfare) to approximately 2 to 1. If additional US forces were not introduced, the military warned, the number of American casualties (already at 4,877) would rise significantly. NVA and NLF units had already decimated several ARVN battalions and overrun compounds housing US advisors. The reverses suffered by the South Vietnamese military forced key White House policymakers and army planners to admit that just "holding the line" in the South and bombing the North was not going to deter the communists or bring an end to the war anytime soon.

Angst and Escalation

The unanticipated buildup of Vietnamese guerrilla forces beginning in early 1965 precipitated a series of clashes that the Americans and their southern allies were quite unprepared to fight. Increased casualties and desertions from ARVN ranks had created what Westmoreland claimed in early June was a "near-catastrophic state." Unable to repel decisively NLF advances, he cabled Washington to inform Johnson and the Joint Chiefs that the situation had deteriorated to a point of perilous desperation. "In pressing their campaign," Westmoreland wrote, "the Viet Cong are capable of mounting regimental-size operations" in strategic areas around Saigon. To prevent a collapse of the South Vietnamese regime, he insisted that an additional 175,000 ground troops were necessary to clear hostile areas. At the same time, the general recommended expanding bombing runs to include Haiphong harbor, where most of the arms and supplies from the Soviet bloc flowed into North Vietnam. But neither of these measures, Westmoreland predicted, would raise the chances of a military victory much above 30 percent. He insisted that what was needed was a steady flow of troops to locate enemy forces. The Commandant of the Marine Corps, General Wallace Greene, also agreed that the military needed to raise the tempo of war. "The Marines were not in Vietnam to sit on their dittyboxes," Greene declared at a press conference, "they were there to kill Viet Cong."[3]

Although an increase of 38,500 American soldiers in South Vietnam had been recommended by an American mission, led by Robert McNamara, that met with its South Vietnamese counterparts in Honolulu in late April, President Johnson remained hesitant to commit additional forces. He was determined to succeed in Vietnam, but wanted more time, more options. In order to free himself from the pressure of the decision, he instructed his most outspoken staff members—George Ball and Robert McNamara—to prepare reports fully developing their opposing positions on how to proceed. Ball's dissent from the views of hawkish cabinet members allowed Johnson to use the undersecretary's arguments against escalation to delay a decision on troop increases while he pushed for passage of the Voting Rights Act. In order to forestall an impending ground war at least through the summer, Ball offered additional alternatives. He proposed that the military use the monsoon season as a "test period" to weigh the odds and price of eventual success. Depending upon the results, the undersecretary concluded, the military could either draft plans to withdraw or mount an offensive if the army had made significant strides in "throwing back the Viet Cong without unacceptable US losses. . . ."[4]

Ball's memorandum did not reach LBJ's desk until mid-June. But even before the undersecretary's recommendations were available, Johnson's key advisors were convinced that McNamara's lengthy, methodical report calling for extended counterinsurgency operations was the more sensible option. Although the defense secretary seemed personally at odds with his own advice, he nonetheless recommended on June 10th that Westmoreland's request be granted. But Johnson continued to vacillate, arguing that: "Not a damn human thinks that 50,000 or 100,000 or 150,000 are gonna end that war. We're not getting out, but we're trying to hold what we got, and we're losing at the rate we're going."[5] That night LBJ took Westmoreland and McNamara's proposals home to his ranch to study over the weekend. He made no decision. In the meantime, the Pentagon had endorsed the army's troop request, and the Joint Chiefs had asked McNamara for a "substantial further build-up of US forces in Vietnam, at the most rapid rate feasible on an orderly basis."[6] With slight modifications, McNamara approved the deployment schedule, which Johnson after many meetings with his advisors announced in a press conference on July 28th.[7]

Because combat operations by American troops had been approved in April, even before Johnson's announcement, Westmorland had begun testing key elements of his "search and destroy" strategy. In early July, he had ordered attacks in War Zone D northeast of Saigon to "shake the confidence of the Viet Cong." Though these probes had reportedly turned up "lots of rice," they yielded few contacts with guerrillas. After action reports on a 2,500-man sweep of the same area on July 8th included the claim that over one hundred NLF casualties had been inflicted. But there was little evidence that a direct engagement with the Vietnamese ever took place. NLF forces continued to plague US "pacification efforts." On June 30th, guerrilla sappers infiltrated the Da Nang air base, killed an American, and destroyed six planes. Two days later, a mortar attack on the US airfield in Soc Trang allowed NLF forces to seize control of neighboring towns and delay flights in and out of the base. By the end of the month, forty Americans were dead.

CIA reports showed that the army's multiple attempts to regain ground since the start of the monsoon season had not only failed, but had actually given a boost to NLF recruitment. Intelligence director William Raborn doubted that commanders of NLF or NVA units would concentrate their forces in large fixed battles. Instead, he concluded, "the enemy would continue harassments intended to bleed and humiliate US forces, trapping and destroying isolated units where possible."[8] Despite these reverses, Westmoreland continued to believe that the Democratic Republic of North Vietnam was too deeply committed to be influenced by anything other than the application of overwhelming force. He soon requested further troop increases, but a reluctant LBJ continued to express doubts about the likelihood of victory. Before he met with select advisors to discuss more deployments, the president sought the opinion of a senior politician and highly respected former military commander.

His phone call to Dwight Eisenhower's Gettysburg farm came early on July 2. Wasting no time, LBJ asked Ike his thoughts about another major troop deployment. "When you once appeal to force in an international situation involving military help for a nation," Ike told Johnson, "you have to go all in!" Johnson expressed skepticism about the escalation's effectiveness, and asked, "Do you really think we can beat the Viet Cong?" Eisenhower replied, "We are not going to be run out of a free country that we helped to establish."[9] Assured of Eisenhower's backing, Johnson was still concerned that his domestic programs were imperiled. LBJ lamented, "every time we have gotten near the culmination of our dreams, the war bells have rung. If we have to fight, I'll do that. But I don't want . . . to be known as a War President." Johnson mused that he had begun to feel the same "gloom that belonged to that unhappy wretched Abraham Lincoln" when he realized he had crossed the threshold—escalation was inevitable.[10]

Once LBJ had resigned himself to additional deployments, he sent his defense secretary to confer with the military in South Vietnam in order to determine the precise number of infantryman needed. Shortly after landing at Tan Son Nhut airport, McNamara met with Westmoreland. The general estimated an additional 100,000 men were needed by the start of 1966 in order to maintain a tactical advantage. The following afternoon, McNamara met with South Vietnam's Prime Minister Nguyen Cao Ky and President Nguyen Van Thieu to discuss the security of Saigon. McNamara questioned Ky and Thieu about how many US troops they felt were needed. Thieu replied: "thirty-four battalions, plus another infantry division . . ." As McNamara waited for Thieu to finish talking, he scribbled notes on a yellow legal pad and then, according to one observer, "fired questions about numbers, organization, management, and logistics as if he were bent on assembling all the factors and components for the solution of some grand mathematical equation."[11]

When McNamara returned to Washington early on July 21st, he found LBJ reviewing unsettling CIA reports. That morning the president had met with his National Security team, which included the Joint Chiefs, to debrief McNamara.

When LBJ entered the room, it was clear to McNamara that the president's mood had changed. He had just learned that his Medicare bill had the votes needed be approved by the Senate later that day, and his antipoverty bill was expected to pass in the following days. Prompted by Johnson, McNamara began by summarizing the Pentagon's recommendation to send 200,000 more troops to Vietnam by early 1966, and then call-up approximately 600,000 conscripts, volunteers, and reservists over the remainder of the year. Despite George Ball's repeated interjections, General Wheeler tried to reassure the group that "greater bodies of men [would] allow [the U.S. Army] to cream the Viet Cong."[12] After several hours of debate, Johnson was still skeptical. In addition to the prospects of high casualties, which Clark Clifford had estimated to be over 50,000 in five years, Johnson was worried that the projected twelve-billion-dollar price tag for 1966 alone would kill all of his Great Society plans. He was also concerned that his approval rating would plummet due to opposition to raising the draft call.[13]

To ease Johnson's anxiety about voter disaffection, McNamara outlined a social scheme he had been developing. His plan would expand the manpower pool, placing the burden of the war on the less privileged without having to resort to unpopular measures, such as mobilizing the reserves or ending college deferments. When McNamara's "Project 100,000" was unveiled in October 1966, he tied it to the president's Great Society initiatives because it would apply military training and discipline to rehabilitate America's "subterranean poor." "These youths," McNamara asserted, "have not had the opportunity to earn their fair share of this nation's abundance, but they can be given an opportunity to return to civilian life with skills and aptitudes which for them and their families will reverse the downward spiral of decay." He concluded that by the end of the war the Department of Defense would become the "world's largest educator of skilled men."[14] But limited funding meant that the inductees slated for Project 100,000 went through the same training process as other recruits. Despite McNamara's original intention, no special curriculum was ever developed to improve the education levels and or vocational skills of the over 320,000 soldiers who enlisted under the auspices of the program.

Still confronted with a fateful decision, Johnson invited Robert McNamara and Clark Clifford, Chairman of the President's Intelligence Advisory Board, to Camp David on July 25 to ponder yet again the extent of America's commitment to Vietnam. The debate was at times heated. Clifford at one point slammed his fists on the table and adamantly exclaimed, "If we don't win after a big buildup, it will be a huge catastrophe . . . .It will ruin us . . . ." To counter Clifford's pessimism, LBJ brandished a letter from John Kenneth Galbraith and began reading aloud:

> Vietnam is not of intrinsic value—if there is no high principle involved. . . .[The] basic issue is not to get thrown out under fire. . . .Political questions are what we make them. . . .Stop saying we are going to pacify the country. [Use] patience—pressure—quietly marking areas we can hold. Hold these for years if need be. Make a safe haven. Viet Cong cannot attack these areas formally. . . . Gradually stop bombings. . . . Keep offer of negotiations open.[15]

When he finished, Johnson turned to McNamara and asked for his response to the letter. Without more US troops, he told the president, South Vietnam would fall to the communists and pose an intolerable risk to American security and credibility.

Finally, after much deliberation at Aspen Lodge, Johnson reached a decision. Additional troops would be sent, and he would go public with his decision in a brief midday television address to the nation. Deflecting responsibility for his approval of Westmoreland's mounting requests for more troops, on July 28 Johnson announced in a nationally televised address: "I asked the general what more he needs to meet this mounting aggression. He has told me. We will meet his needs."[16]

Johnson later described his predicament with the off-color sort of analogy he favored: "If I left the woman I really loved—the Great Society—in order to get involved with that bitch of a war on the other side of the world, then I would lose everything at home. All my programs; all my hopes to feed the hungry and shelter the homeless; all my dreams to provide education and medical care to the browns and the blacks and the lame and the poor. But if I left that war and let the Communists take over South Vietnam. . . there would follow in this country an endless national debate—a mean and destructive debate—that would shatter my Presidency, kill my administration, and damage our democracy."[17] By early 1966, the military statisticians disclosed that the combat force ratio in Vietnam was still only two American soldiers to one Vietnamese guerrilla. That was not good enough to guarantee success, especially if the army was going to be able to expand its operations and build base camps, such as the one planned for the Cu Chi region, an area that had long been one of the most fortified and formidable NLF strongholds in the South.

Contested Ground

The half-decade of war from 1965 to 1972, which devastated the villages, croplands and forested areas in the vicinity of the little market town of Cu Chi, encapsulated both arrogant miscalculations on the part of the invading Americans and the remarkable capacity on the part of the Vietnamese guerrillas for perseverance and improvisation. These qualities contributed in major ways to the defeat of the global superpower by a divided, war-ravaged, postcolonial nation.

In the abstract, the US planners' choice of the of Cu Chi region as a focus for offensive operations against the NLF guerrillas seemed to make good strategic sense. In early December 1965, an advance party of army officers visited the region and soon after recommended building one the largest military bases in Vietnam just to the east of the town. In the years that followed the camp became the epicenter of a succession of counterinsurgent offensives against NLF guerrilla forces operating northwest of Saigon. The report submitted to William Westmoreland stressed that Cu Chi straddled Highway One and was proximate to the Saigon River. Both were major thoroughfares linking Saigon to the villages and plantations to the north and west as well as the coastal areas to the

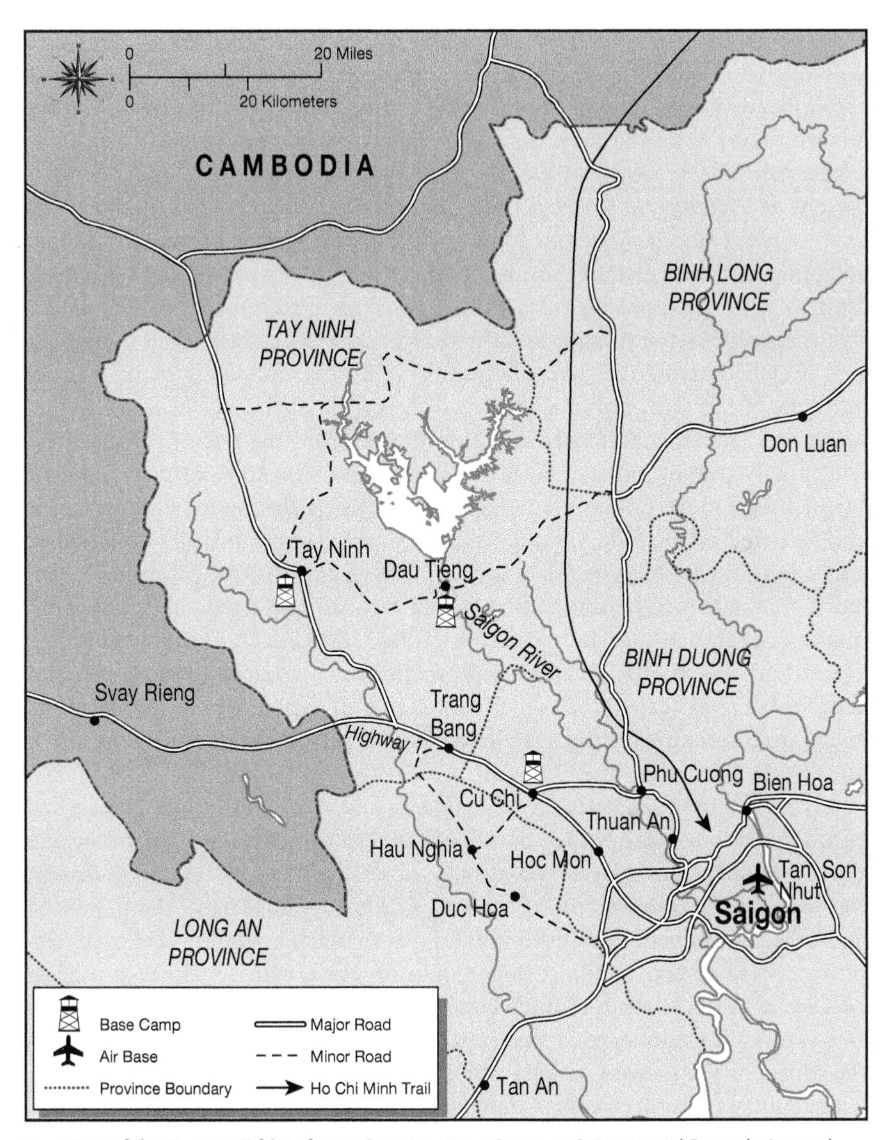

Location of the Twenty-Fifth Infantry Division Base Camp with Provincial Boundaries and Lines of Communication

east. The highway also connected the capital to the borderlands of Cambodia to the north, which had become both the southern terminus of several strands of the Ho Chi Minh trail and a sanctuary for several communist command centers. The authors of the report noted that the flatlands to the east of Cu Chi could readily accommodate the concentration of forces that Westmoreland envisioned. Once established, the camp would be within firing range of several zones that had been guerrilla strongholds for decades. The authors of the report also assumed that the base could be readily defended from enemy assaults because it would be located away from heavily populated areas.

As was the case in many of the decisions that determined the course—and very often the outcome—of American interventions in Vietnam, Cu Chi was recommended as the site of the main base camp north of Saigon by a team of advisors who knew little about the region's history or the nature of the surrounding terrain. Their report to Westmoreland was written soon after most of them arrived in Vietnam for the first time, and their findings ignored the warnings of Americans who had been in country a good deal longer. Perhaps even more troubling was their dismissal of the concerns of ARVN officers who were quite familiar with the problems the area had posed for government-friendly forces. By the mid-1960s, the villages, French-owned rubber plantations, and rainforests that stretched across the flatlands from Cu Chi to Cambodia had for decades been one of the most formidable areas for guerrilla operations of first the Viet Minh and later the National Liberation Front. From the late 1940s the overwhelmingly peasant population of the region had been mobilized in the fight for an independent, united Vietnamese nation. Guerrillas were well provisioned and sheltered by the local villagers, and were increasingly armed with weapons and reinforced by NVA regulars funneled down the Ho Chi Minh trail from North Vietnam. American soldiers would face similar resistance throughout much of South Vietnam. But by the early 1960s, the Cu Chi region had become a zone that Saigon officials and ARVN soldiers were anxious to avoid. The liberation struggles against the French and the Diem regime had transformed the entire area into arguably the most imposing and resilient communist bastion in all of South Vietnam.

During most of the century of conquests and colonial rule, the French had encountered only localized resistance in southern provinces of Vietnam, which they governed as the separate colony of Cochin China. In most instances dissent was forcibly repressed and short-lived. But enduring movements that espoused antiforeign sentiments emerged in the form of religious sects. The most significant were several Buddhist millenarianism cults, which merged in the last decades of the nineteenth century into the Hoa Hao, and the more eclectic Cao Dai, whose adherents were concentrated in the vicinity of Saigon. The impact of the spread of Vietnamese nationalist resistance in the first decades of the twentieth century was enfeebled in Cochin China by deep political divisions among the Buddhist sects, bourgeois loyalists, an array of patriotic splinter parties, and various communist and socialist factions. However, as the First Indochina War intensified and spread among the peasantry after the end of the Second World War, the Cu Chi region and the provinces in the Mekong Delta became highly contested regions of refuge and resistance for Viet Minh forces, and major targets of French counterinsurgency campaigns.

Beginning in the late 1800s on the plains north of Saigon and in the vast swamp and rainforest zone formed by the Mekong River to the south, the French had devoted substantial resources to promote agricultural production. French engineers and managers supervised Vietnamese workers in clearing and draining the land, dredging existing waterways and cutting canals, and recruited peasants and indentured laborers from the more densely populated areas of north and central Vietnam as well as China. Within decades both regions were extensively cultivated and became economic mainstays of the French colony. They were also strategically vital due to the road, rail, and river connections they provided between Saigon, the southern provinces, and access to port outlets for overseas commerce. Of the two areas, the Mekong Delta's environment was clearly the better suited for guerrilla warfare. By contrast, French and American military planners assumed that the flat and open terrain centered on Cu Chi north of Saigon favored the heavy weaponry, air power, and rapid movement of their regular military forces.

To offset the daunting asymmetry in killing power that their adversaries possessed in combat operations in provinces in the vicinity of Cu Chi, communist guerrillas literally went underground. Taking advantage of the depth of the region's water table and its clay and laterite soil, which peoples of the tropics have cut into bricks for housing and monumental construction for millennia, they carved out a massive tunnel network that crisscrossed Cu Chu and neighboring provinces and at its peak extended over an estimated 120 miles. At the southern end the network's trap door exits formed what Westmoreland called "a dagger" pointed at Saigon. The tunnels also connected NLF units with most of the villages and towns in the districts into which the networks extended.

The tunnels of Cu Chi provided shelter that greatly enhanced the odds of survival for NLF fighters and staging areas for attacks against French, ARVN, and American forces. They gave the Viet Cong[18] control of the night and

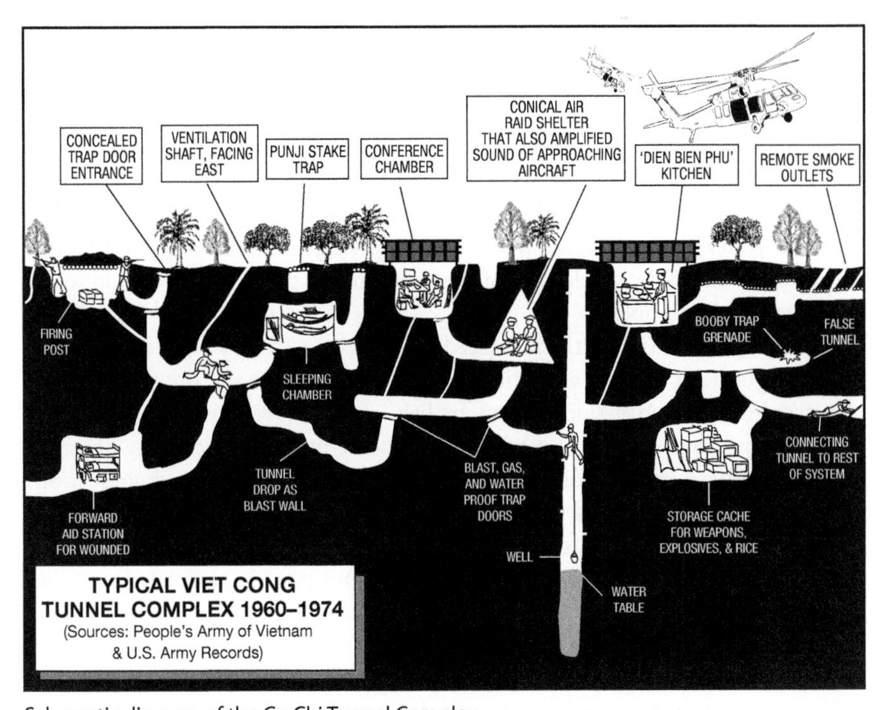

Schematic diagram of the Cu Chi Tunnel Complex

everything underground, while conceding surface areas from dawn till dusk and the skies above to better armed American and ARVN forces. Rooms close to the surface served as sniper's nests and gathering places for raiding parties. Tunnel entrances were cleverly disguised with forest cuttings or planted patches of undergrowth, and they were purposely made as small as possible to allow the shorter, slighter Vietnamese access and make entry difficult for their taller, heavier American pursuers.

Over time the tunnel networks developed into increasingly complex systems that included sleeping quarters, conference rooms, intricately ventilated kitchens, aid stations, rudimentary hospitals, and sizable chambers for printing presses and manufacturing firearms—including even small-gauge artillery pieces. Pedal-pumped generators, as well as batteries discarded by Americans and spent shell casings that were made into nut oil lamps, provided power for machines and lighting. "Safe" zones were reinforced with tree trunks to serve as air raid shelters, particularly after the Americans began to use B-52s to carpet bomb the region. Water "traps" were used to absorb a variety of gasses and other chemical weapons US forces used to kill or drive enemy forces out of their refuges. In some segments of the tunnel system there were two or even three levels, and they were equipped with booby-trapped doors and dead-end passages to frustrate tunnel rats who dared to pursue NLF guerrillas underground.

In addition to shelter, sustenance, and bases for assaults on occupying forces that the tunnels provided guerrilla cadres, they became major channels for the NLF to connect with and control the peasants of Cu Chi and surrounding districts. Tunnel links were built to most of the main villages in the region and NLF cadres assisted local populations in digging shelters for individual dwellings. Rice and other supplies were stored in small household shelters as well as common village caches. Peasant families were held responsible for the upkeep of their household shelters, and periodically recruited by guerrilla operatives and village notables as laborers for building and repairing neighboring portions of the tunnel network. During major offensives mounted by occupying forces, the peasants' water buffalos, which were vital to plowing and fertilizing the rice paddies that produced the staple food of the Vietnamese, were sometimes hidden in the main tunnel complexes.

Although essential for the sustained resistance—and very often survival—of both the guerrilla fighters and villagers who supported them, the tunnels were claustrophobic, vermin-ridden, and hellish places of refuge. Blackouts were common and the complex as a whole was poorly lit. Despite cleverly designed ventilation ducts, the air was stagnant. During enemy offensives whole sections of the tunnels were flooded with gases that burned the eyes and skin, and were often lethal. Rats, poisonous snakes, scorpions, and outsized centipedes throve in the underground networks. Insects from mosquitos to chiggers burrowed into the occupants' skin, spreading disease and intense discomfort. Waste disposal was a constant problem, and especially because fresh air was chronically in short supply, the smell of areas where latrines were located could be nauseating. The difficulties of day-to-day existence were compounded by the structural damage inflicted on the tunnel networks during aerial bombardments or assaults by enemy armored vehicles across the terrain overhead.

During these operations, which became more and more frequent in the American phase of the Vietnam wars, guerrilla fighters and support personnel huddled in darkness contemplating the very real possibility that they could be buried alive. As a NLF captain who lived underground for most of five years recounted, the cries of wounded fighters intensified the terror experienced by all who lived through enemy offensives from above:

> They used to beg us to kill them, said Linh. They used to scream for one look at light and one breath of air, not fresh air, but air. The wounded, their discipline diminished, their minds and bodies hurt, preferred death to lying underground. It was unpleasant to hear them. We offered them nothing: neither death, nor light, nor more air.[19]

The fact that many guerrilla fighters lived in the tunnels for years with only sporadic forays above ground underscores their capacity for enduring hardships and dedication to the struggle for national liberation.

The Americans' disregard for the warnings about the perils Cu Chi and the surrounding districts posed, which had been so inexplicable given their selection of the site for a major military base, carried over into the construction of the sprawling encampment that began in early 1966. From the outset, substantial portions of the base were located directly over sections of the tunnels, which meant that guerrilla fighters could emerge from entrances to launch nighttime raids on construction workers and equipment as well as newly arrived US soldiers and their armored vehicles. Because these assaults continued for well over a year after a presumably impenetrable defensive perimeter of fences and dugouts had been completed, they were a major source of concern and enduring tension for base commanders and ordinary soldiers. Even after the tunnels under the camp had been located and destroyed,[20] guerrilla fighters intermittently emerged from tunnel openings just outside the camp's perimeter to direct mortar fire into the compound.

Well before the tunnel threat was solved, an area directly west of the town of Cu Chi, the size of 115 football fields, had begun to be transformed by US construction crews into an enormous building site. After the 173rd Airborne Brigade secured the zone around the camp with artillery barrages and B-52 bombing runs, huge Rome Plow bulldozers demolished what remained of the homes of local peasants, who had been forced to move to a strategic hamlet nearby. Bulldozers were also used to scrape away all of the vegetation in areas surveyed for the base, including fields cultivated by local villagers and along the roadsides of supply routes from Saigon and Long Binh. Even before the arrival of the Twenty-Fifth Infantry Division that was to carry out most of the American offensives against the guerrilla forces north of Saigon for the next four years, truck convoys and cargo planes—on average four a day totaling 268 vehicles—delivered massive amounts of construction materials. These included cyclone fencing and barbed wire, office and hospital equipment, tents and beds, kitchen and mess

Cu Chi Base Camp

appliances, and a dazzling array of advanced weaponry. Soon a steady flow of food, drink, and consumer goods followed that were deemed essential for the sustenance of the four to five thousand US military personnel who would occupy the base through more than six years of operation. Within months a sizeable town that exuded American affluence was fabricated in the midst of the impoverished, war-ravaged countryside of South Vietnam.

Any notion that the fortified encampment at Cu Chi was secure was fleeting. The heat, humidity, and pervasive stench of burning feces served as constant reminders of the alien terrain in which the base was located and the constricted and beleaguered lives of its American occupants. Vietnamese laborers dug ditches, cleaned barracks, laundered clothes, and washed dishes in the clubs and general mess hall. Some were barbers, messengers, waitresses, and even office clerks. Many were spies for the NLF. Though executed if caught, informers working inside the base supplied guerrilla operatives with intelligence about preparations for search and destroy missions, the location of landing zones or ammunition dumps, and even guided raiding parties through vulnerable sections of the defensive perimeter.

Because of their close contact with officers and enlisted men, barbers and women working as waitresses, cashiers in the PX, and "bar girls" often proved to be the best informants. Prostitutes in nearby towns, or those who regularly solicited clients just outside the entrance to the base, also provided information for communist units. Espionage from within was combined with intermittent harassment from what became known as "the belt" of Viet Cong tunnels and firing positions beyond the barbed wire and bunkers. On some occasions, nighttime raiding parties were able to make their way through the camp's defenses and launch brief firefights, which, even if they inflicted few casualties, called into question assumptions that the base was a safe zone. On several occasions, guerrilla infiltrators acting on information provided by Vietnamese working inside the base were able to damage helicopters and armored personnel carriers that were among the most menacing war machines the Americans deployed.

Arrival in Nam
February 1966

Jimmy was in the pipeline—the army's labyrinth of processing stages between training and combat. It was always the same story: you waited. He listened inattentively to announcements and absently watched safety demonstrations; then things were finally set in motion and the plane took off. He leaned against the window and watched the Oakland Military Terminal fade from view. The Bay Area had become a stockyard for soldiers heading to Vietnam. He was a little hung over, and slept much of the twenty-two hour flight. At each stop a buzzing loudspeaker woke him giving the local time, and he set back his watch. When he landed in Bien Hoa airbase, much of what he learned in training about the war conflicted with his first impressions. He envisioned a scorched countryside pocked with craters and devastated towns. But from the air, it was just a mass of men and machines kicking up dust in a dirt field surrounded by jungle. There was no gunfire, only a constant coming and going of helicopters. There was oppressive heat and an unforgettable stench "and poor little kids running after you while you are marching and saying GI do you have candy, you give me candy, and if you give him a peace you the greatest, but if you don't, he will call you every name in the book."

Waiting again, he took out paper from his duffel bag. He addressed a letter to his father. Despite just finishing a crash course in Vietnamese geography, he crossed out "Fort Dix, New Jersey," and on his stationary wrote, "I don't know. . ." He was sweating. It wasn't a rolling, beaded sweat. It was thick, muggy sweat that seemingly pushed—all at once—from his insides out to this skin. It was heaviest on his neck and buttocks. He itched and felt unclean. He had orders to report to the First Air Cavalry Division. Robert McNamara had increased the number of airmobile squadrons in country after the success of helicopter warfare was demonstrated in the November 1965 offensive in the central highlands of the Ia Drang Valley. But on Jimmy's arrival, he was reassigned to the First Battalion (Mechanized), Fifth Infantry Regiment that was attached to the Twenty-Fifth Division. As the third oldest regiment in the American army—descended from a unit formed in 1808—the Fifth Infantry had participated in every major US engagement since the War of 1812. Over a century later, the Fifth Infantry was sent to Vietnam as a mechanized unit that used Armored Personnel Carriers (APCs or "tracks" as the GIs commonly called them). Initially deployed for ARVN troops, thousands of APCs were already in country when the First Battalion arrived. A track required only two crewmen, a driver and a commander, and carried eleven passengers. The boxy structures looked similar to tanks, but lacked a large caliber gun turret. All APCs were similar in design, but the soldiers who operated them made their own modifications to increase protection, boost firepower, and add comfort. Though all were equipped with a swiveling .50-caliber machine gun, some were altered to include mortars and rocket launchers, flamethrowers, and several .30-caliber Browning Automatic Rifles. Appropriately nicknamed the "battle taxi," the APC was originally designed to transport troops to the killing zone near the front lines of theoretical battles fought on the plains of Europe. Engineers compared it to the landing crafts used in WWII to carry GIs safely across waterways when they then stormed enemy beachheads. Similar to landing crafts, APCs were not designed for inflicting heavy damage on enemy forces and, compared to modern day artillery ordnance and fighter planes, the tracks were not formidable fighting machines.

During the early 1960s the combat record of the South Vietnamese mechanized forces was dismal. Multiple reports—including those written by one of the more perceptive and seasoned American military advisors in Vietnam, Colonel John Paul Vann—were commissioned to explain their failures. Vann stressed the hesitancy of ARVN track commanders to maneuver their APCs properly to suppress attacking guerrillas, while minimizing exposure and maximizing what U.S. Army doctrine called "superior firepower." Although APCs were considered virtually invincible

The M113 Armored Personnel Carrier deployed in Vietnam

by the army—and mechanized infantrymen were effective as shock troops and capable of handling small arms fire—in a counterinsurgency role the vehicle itself was flawed. It was highly vulnerable to a variety of mines and grenades, hidden tank traps, and 57-mm and 75-mm recoilless rifles. On grassy and lightly wooded terrain, its top speed of thirty-five miles per hour made it an optimum war machine for reinforcing infantry units and temporarily holding strategic positions. But in Vietnam its speed was compromised by thick jungles and the lowland flood plains of the Delta. The vehicle's intimidating presence was offset by its noise, which alerted the enemy to an impending attack. Not only were APCs useless on night patrols, their thirteen-ton metal bodies, powered by their heavy 209 horsepower Chrysler V8 gasoline engines, often sank deep into the mud of rice paddies and other flooded areas.

Indications of the APC's weaknesses had been made clear by the defeat of ARVN forces at the Battle of Ap Bac in 1963. Colonel John Paul Vann, circling the battlefield in a spotter plane, was enraged at ARVN troops, whom he thought were blatantly disobeying his orders to assault entrenched guerrilla units. But Vann was not an armored specialist. He was ignorant of how time consuming it was for APCs to cross irrigation ditches, morasses, and high-walled canals. If troops were not careful, water would rush into air-intake vales and flood the engines—or if the depth was misjudged, breach the sides. Without portable bridging equipment, ARVN soldiers had to cut brush for traction and set up a towline around trees to pull each vehicle across the rice paddies. When the tracks finally arrived, commanders were forced to assault head-on guerrillas who had strategically positioned themselves between marshland and patches of heavy forest. Three years after the rout of ARVN forces at Ap Bac, an army inquiry into the organization, equipment, and support needs of the South Vietnamese armored units stressed that the need for more mechanized divisions was so urgent that deployment of US troops would be necessary to combat advancing Viet Cong forces. In January 1966, soldiers of the Fifth Infantry landed at the port of Vung Tau, and moved toward their final staging area at Cu Chi base camp. Jimmy was among the additional reinforcements that arrived in the following months.

As Jimmy waited at the airbase to receive his equipment, he cashed in what little money he had in his pocket for South Vietnamese dongs. The night before he left California he had spent most of his pay on drinks and lap dancers in San Francisco strip clubs. He felt somewhat embarrassed about that. He told his mother "not to get mad, remember I am almost 21 now. . . " Everybody he knew was assigned to different regiments and companies. "I don't know anyone here," he wrote, "but that is just the way things go." His early letters were written in a stream of consciousness format, and his thoughts were strung together by commas. His spelling and grammar were terrible. At the top of the page of the letter written after his arrival in Cu Chi, he warned, "BEFORE READING IT I ALL READY KNOW WORDS ARE SPELLED WRONG"—and he underlined "wrong" three times.

Jimmy Gilch's transfer to the Twenty-Fifth Infantry Division meant that his tour of duty would be spent in one of the most contested and lethal centers of NLF guerrilla resistance in South Vietnam. His combat unit had been formed at the Schofield Barracks in O'ahu, Hawai'i just before the Japanese attack on Pearl Harbor in December 1941, and it served with distinction in both the Pacific theatre of World War II and the later Korean conflict. In 1956, the division established a Jungle and Guerrilla Warfare Center in the foothills of the Ko'olau Mountains. The center taught survival skills and how to fight in the jungle against guerrillas. Instruction at Kara, one of the twelve mock "Southeast Asian" villages, set up by the Twenty-Fifth Infantry, was intended to provide all recruits in the U.S. Army's Civil Affairs Program with techniques for training the local population in self-defense. The soldiers were also instructed to establish positive relationships with the peasants, and help them find ways to improve their standard of living. Because they were assumed to be somewhat acclimated to tropical environments, the odds were overwhelming that they would play a major role in the American counterinsurgency campaign in South Vietnam. But once in combat in Vietnam, GIs trained at Schofield made little use of what they had learned. Falling in line with the plan of battle set out by Westmoreland and the Joint Chiefs of Staff, the soldiers of the Twenty-Fifth "Tropic Lightning" division waged a conventional, high-tech war against an elusive and resilient enemy that was able to make optimum use of the maze of tunnels at Cu Chi.

In retrospect it was supremely ironic—but quite consistent with the American conduct of the war as a whole—that Jimmy and the men of the Fifth Infantry Regiment were attached to the one division in the US armed forces that had been extensively trained in counterinsurgency and jungle warfare. Jimmy and most of the grunts in his company were hardly, if at all, drilled in counterinsurgency techniques or properly educated in mechanized combat. The NCOs of B Company, to which Jimmy was assigned, were only slightly better trained than the men they commanded. Many of the young lieutenants were ordnance officers or paratroopers trained to identify bombing targets and organize airdrops. Several replacements were from military intelligence and other noncombat branches in which their previous duties focused solely on supply management and medical evaluation. Jimmy's platoon commander was a 101st Airborne paratrooper, whose ten-week Organizational Maintenance schooling on how to recover and repair tracked or wheeled armored vehicles made him one of the few "qualified" field officers in the unit.

At the camp's orientation session Jimmy watched a movie about Vietnamese culture, signed mimeograph papers, and was issued a helmet and an M-14 rifle. He sat through slide shows where medical officers warned about cholera, dysentery, and how prostitutes were vectors of disease. He was warned about malaria, gonorrhea, rabies, tapeworm, and the plague. Sergeants cautioned about booby traps, spider holes, and punji pits, and how the shit-covered bamboo sticks were so sharp they could poke a man's dick off. The NCOs stressed that just about every animal and insect that looked innocent was poisonous—and that went for the civilian population too. He was informed about how boredom and curiosity were killers in motor pools and along the barbed wire perimeter.

The morning following orientation, Jimmy traveled in a convoy from Bien Hoa to Saigon and then on to Cu Chi. He initially found what he was seeing "funie" but much of what he witnessed on the forty-mile trip through the countryside along Highway One was sobering. He saw ox carts and men on bicycles piled with enough boxes and food to press down the back shocks of his Chevy back home. Children rode atop water buffalo; others, mostly naked, ran alongside pointing sticks like swords at the convoy while older villagers just stared. Jimmy remarked, "Its hard to believe the way they [the Vietnamese] live, and even dress, every family has 9 or 10 kid's and you can't tell one from the other, it just like the war story you see on TV, they sell silk clothes ceap here, every thing is a lot ceaper here than the states, when I get paid I will send some clothes home for the kid's and I'll give you 5 cents in Viet Nam money. . . " Drawing comparisons with the poor, urban areas of Philadelphia and Camden, he wrote his sisters: "if you could see how the people over here live, you would think a lot different, if a girl 7 or 8 has a dress, she must come from a rich family. . . " On one of the stops near the hamlet of Cu Chi, several Vietnamese were squatting along the road and peeing. Those not laboring in the distant rice paddies were selling everything from silk shirts to shoes and jackets. There was a flea market for soldiers. Jimmy bought a cowboy hat.

Consumerism was spreading in South Vietnam. Locals who were connected with the black market understood what goods American troops wanted. Most of the buildings in Cu Chi were little more than huts made from local bamboo and thatch harvested in the rainforest; others were makeshift shacks tied together with rope and pieces of scrap metal. The villagers wore wide conical hats and black cotton pajama-like shirts and pants. Some women blackened their front teeth, which Jimmy later learned they thought attractive. "If the little green and yellow barn which is in the back of the house was over here," he remarked, "you would think a King lived in it."

He bounced up and down as the bus hit potholes. "These people" he wrote, "are so far behind us in everything that in ten years we will pass them again like going around the world (I don't know whether you know what I mean)." His contempt for the "lazy" Vietnamese people and the poverty and backwardness of the country confirmed his notion that the United States was there to assist and uplift them. "The girls, that is all you see here, they all work for the government of the US in the PX and as taylor's, etc, they have the men working here to, laying pipe, for water, but they sleep most of the time, the people here are living way better now than ever before, because they all work now." As for the Viet Cong, he concluded, "they are not afraid to die, I guess not, they have nothing to live for, all of them live like pigs, the men are only about 5'6" at the most, about 135 or 140 pounds, they all wear black pajamas and GI clothing," and he was surprised to learn that some even wore boots. These

A typical Vietnamese family dwelling in the vicinity of Cu Chi, 1966.

impressions gave him a cause to fight for, especially for the children. He concluded his letter with a few Vietnamese phrases he had been studying from an appendix of a manual he was given at orientation:

Đúa tay Lèn (Put up your hands)
Đúng Lai (Halt)
Tŏi Khám ông (I will search you)

The base camp at Cu Chi was a flat wasteland. A red talcum-like dust swept through the air, and the treeless patches of earth had a top layer of soft soil that looked greyish brown. Behind the camp, parallel to the French-built Highway One, the Vam Co Dong River flowed, feeding marshes and swamps that frequently flooded the base, leaving soldiers to flounder in an ocean of mud. To the west of the base was the Nui Ba Ben Mountain, and to the east rubber plantations could be seen. The more cynical GIs told new arrivals that the real reason they were in Vietnam was to protect the interest of the Michelin Rubber Company. Jimmy and the First Battalion,

Fifth Infantry (1/5 Mech) were positioned on the camp's northeast perimeter and assigned to guard a bridge over the shallow Soui Ben Muong River. The outpost was later named Ann-Margret in honor of the concert the seductive performer gave there in March 1966. Across the marshland there was an entrance into the heavily fortified Viet Cong strongholds in the Ho Bo Woods and Filhol rubber plantation. During the First Indochina War the French referred to the area as the "Iron Triangle" due to the refusal of the outgunned and often-outnumbered guerrilla units entrenched there to yield to opposing forces. The Viet Minh leaders, however, glorified it as the "Land of Fire." In the post-Geneva decades, the very name, Cu Chi, evoked heroic resistance, similar to the significance the Battle of Saratoga assumed for American revolutionaries who won a turning point victory there using guerrilla tactics.

By the beginning of February 1966, the base camp was about a half mile across, and it expanded each day. In order to attack it, raiders or sappers would have to cross several hundred yards of defoliated ground, exposing themselves to mortar and machine gun fire. If they survived that gauntlet, claymore mines awaited them, backed up by barbed wire and opposing American forces in crude bunkers. Nonetheless, the "no man's land" surrounding the camp's circular boundary actually favored the guerrillas in a number of ways. The open terrain proved ideal for snipers, and small reconnaissance units pinpointed US positions and coordinated mortar and rocket attacks from the cover of the distant tree line. Yet, despite the bold attacks of Viet Cong fighters, within a two-month period Cu Chi base camp was a mile in diameter. In the early months of construction, the living conditions for GIs in Cu Chi were well below the poverty line in the United States. Before pup tents were distributed, soldiers slept in holes. On guard duty they shared dugouts with rats and other nocturnal vermin, and they relieved themselves in primitive latrines that spread typhoid and hepatitis. The low level of the land and the high water table made it nearly impossible to build proper sewage facilities. To get rid of human excrement, soldiers mixed it with flaming kerosene in empty gasoline drums. Burning feces was regarded as the worst of all duties, and was often assigned as punishment for insubordinate or negligent GIs. It was also one of many menial, but essential, tasks provided by the local Vietnamese population.

To dispose of urine, army engineers constructed a system of iron tubes that poked out of the ground. These "piss pipes" were filled with used motor oil to reduce the *odor*, but the urine seeped into the dirt and often contaminated nearby wells. Vietnamese women were hired to wash clothes and clean the barracks and offices. An army surgeon surmised that employing "local undereducated natives" was a fine way to create a middle class in Vietnam. Similar to Jimmy, the surgeon believed in America's civilizing mission, and assumed that "the exposure these women had to middle-class Americans by working for them was very enlightening. Just as the presence of our [US] troops inexorably changed the way of life for Filipinos, the Japanese, and the Koreans."[21]

Terms of Engagement

In January 1966, a month before James Gilch arrived at Cu Chi, the province had been a verdant region of rice paddies, orchards, and nut trees. Villagers raised pigs and chickens, and water buffalo to plow their fields. But by February when Jimmy arrived, and traveled through it for the first time, the land was ruined. Even before the bulldozers had finished clearing the forest cover and peasants' homes to make way for what would become a mammoth base camp, a combined American-Australian force mounted the largest offensive yet attempted in South Vietnam. Aptly named "Operation Crimp," the central aim of the mission was to destroy what was believed to be the headquarters for NLF forces operating in the districts around Saigon. Its broader objectives were to kill or capture as many of the guerrilla fighters as possible, and deprive them of staging areas for raids on the bases occupied by the ARVN or US forces. The overall offensive strategy and the tactics deployed by specific units were in many respects the same as those that would be adopted in major operations during the half decade of American military interventions in Vietnam's civil war.

After weeks of aerial surveillance, which yielded little information about enemy positions, the Ho Bo Woods was bombed by B-52s, napalmed by fighter jets, and shelled from artillery positions on its perimeter. The resulting craterization and defoliation initiated a process that over time turned once lush forest and paddy lands into a "white zone" of burnt-out forest and grasslands, and pock-marked, desiccated fields. As the aerial assault wound down, American and Australian infantry brigades were transported by helicopter to positions to the north and west of the forest to begin search and destroy operations towards the Saigon River. Other units established a defensive line south of the woods in order to trap guerrilla forces that military planners assumed would flee the infantry advances from the north. Compared to offensives that followed in both the Cu Chi region and elsewhere in Vietnam, armored vehicles were conspicuously marginal in Operation Crimp. But tanks and especially APCs would soon become requisite components of the search and destroy emphasis that characterized most American military operations against NLF guerrilla forces. The asymmetry of killing power between the two sides was evident. Eight thousand soldiers were deployed in the American-Australian offensive against an estimated one thousand NLF guerrillas defending the tunnel stronghold. In the seven days of the operation, allied forces pummeled the Ho Bo Woods with tens of thousands of artillery shells and hundreds of thousands of rounds of mortar, grenade, and small arms fire.[22]

Although American and Australian infantrymen had been briefed about the tunnels, none of the newly arrived units had sufficient intelligence or training to deal with them. To make things worse, neither their commanders nor their line officers had any idea how extensive and sophisticated the guerrillas' underground networks were or where they were located. Enemy fighters, on the other hand, had received detailed intelligence on the buildup to the offensive, and even the timetable for the assault, from spies both inside the base camp under construction and stationed in neighboring towns and villages. As the allied forces

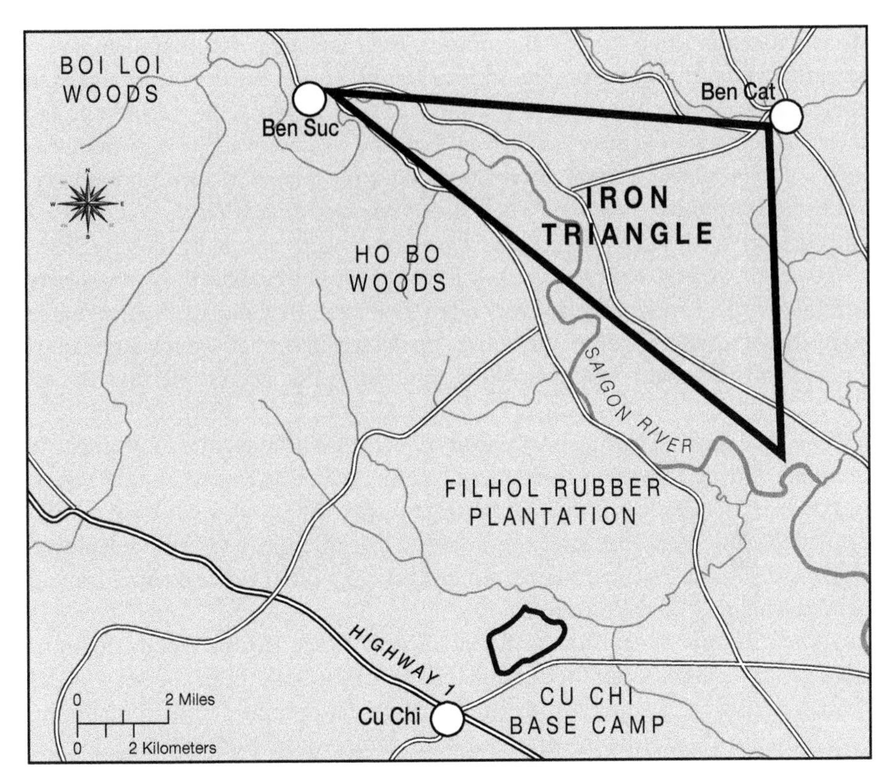

Areas of Operations of the Twenty-Fifth Infantry Division

advanced into the rainforest or sought to set up defensive positions along tree lines or the dikes of paddy fields, NLF snipers—often popping out of spider holes at tunnel entrances—were able to inflict numerous casualties, then disappear with impunity. Small guerrilla units also harassed the advancing infantrymen who, oblivious to the nature of enemy defenses, proved easy targets in the early going. After inflicting casualties on advancing allied forces in brief firefights, guerrilla fighters disappeared into the tunnels. The frustrations of chasing an enemy that refused to stand and fight were compounded by the intense discomfort caused by the heat, humidity, and ever-present insects, reptiles, and leeches in the forest zone. But far greater perils were posed by the booby traps that ranged from improvised explosives to pits with *punjis* or sharpened bamboo stakes that had been cleverly camouflaged and positioned near tunnel entrances and approaches to areas where the networks were concentrated.

When tunnel entrances were discovered, US units mainly used explosives and noxious gases to kill or flush out enemy fighters. But as the operation continued, individuals or small groups of soldiers, who would become known as "tunnel rats," were sent into the dark unknown to engage adversaries that had very often moved to other parts of the network. Though smaller American infantrymen were usually selected for these operations, they still struggled to move about in the claustrophobic maze under the Hobo Woods. By contrast, their equally hefty Australian counterparts (whom the Aussies called "tunnel ferrets") fared better in their efforts to explore and map the networks. At the outset of their advance, the Australians had included volunteer engineers in their probes, and had managed to capture documents that provided detailed information about the guerrillas' underground networks and defensive measures. They also discovered that what they considered garbage—from tin cans to expended shells—were eagerly sought by the guerrillas.

Realizing that their trash was being recycled into weapons, the Aussies were careful to collect and cart away every bit of their rubbish. Guerrilla fighters made good use of almost all of it, very often turning it into booby-traps and explosives to kill and maim enemy soldiers. Soon after the Crimp offensive ended, the Australian units were assigned to other areas in South Vietnam, and these lessons were ignored by most American officers and infantrymen. The growing numbers of American troops, including Jimmy Gilch, who moved into the region in the years that followed did not manage to put the tunnels out of operation until 1970, and then only after the Twenty-Fifth Infantry had been redeployed elsewhere. Unlike the Australians, Americans were often careless about leaving behind what they considered trash.

The outcome of the first battle for control of the Ho Bo Woods ought to have given American military commanders reason to rethink the search and destroy approach to counterinsurgency that would become standard operating procedure for US ground forces in Vietnam. But because Westmoreland and his subordinates assumed that their vastly superior resources, far more advanced weaponry, and better trained soldiers would ultimately prevail, they played down the troubling level of casualties inflicted on US and Australian forces in proportion to the number of guerrillas killed, wounded, or captured. American planners also sought to obfuscate the obvious conclusion that the offensive had not achieved any of its main objectives. The enemy's headquarters had not even been located, much less destroyed, the tunnel system remained intact, and NLF still controlled the Ho Bo Woods. The tunnels and forest would remain a major NLF stronghold and refuge area for nearly the whole of the US phase of the Vietnam wars. In the years that followed, American combat forces and the Vietnamese people would pay a very high price for the failure of US military planners to evaluate critically and thoroughly the outcomes of a conventional military operation against guerrilla insurgents that had clearly failed.

In Pursuit of an Elusive Enemy
Late February 1966

It was Monday, and it started off like most other days. It was hot. Jimmy collected a dollar from everyone in his squad and bought a case of beer. It was a bonding agent, and a stress reliever, and sometimes it was cold. By the afternoon—still waiting for a reply from his first letter—Jimmy made his way to his foxhole and again wrote home. He had just cleaned his rifle and was finishing a warm beer with lunch. He heard muffled machine gun fire in the distance. His squad was placed on stand-by, while

"Company A [and a platoon from C Company] was out in the bush" clearing more land "and burning the small town's . . . There are no front lines here, everywhere there are VC's around, even underground," Jimmy told his father. But he tried to ease George's apprehensions by adding, "the VC's are only poor farmer's, who really does not know to much about fighting, it is up North where all the action is, around Cam Ranh Bay, once in a while a sniper fires a shot or two into camp, but it really is nothing. . . ."

He spoke of guard duty and how "day's sure do go fast around here," but the nights drag on forever, "2 hours on, and 2 hours off until 5 in the morning . . . " He hated the anxiety of watch, and expressed doubts about the quality and resoluteness of his leaders. During a recent ambush, "the VC have fired a few shot's into our camp, you should see these Sgts they all our afraid, most of them stayed up all night awake scared . . . and had no idea what was going on." Jimmy was dismayed by the fact that the NCOs who gave the orders didn't seem to know what they were doing, and he "wanted to take charge." To add to his frustration, the army "messed up with his records," and he was unable to wire his pay home. He promised his family to write as much and as often as he could and, concerned with his ability to express himself, he asked his mother to "for get about sending my sun glasses, just send me a spelling book or something so I can spell some word's right . . . ."

Although he had reassured George that "everything was fine," Jimmy failed to write that the fourteenth of February had been a busy day for camp doctors and air medical support. At 06:30, Company A set out from Cu Chi, moved across the Ben Muong stream, dismounted from their APCs, and carried out a reconnaissance patrol. Jimmy's squad stayed behind to secure the crossing site. At 07:30 the patrol came under small arms fire, and by 09:00 it requested immediate dust-off transport. Four men had been wounded—one shot in the head. In the meantime Company A was making slow progress on its mission to destroy houses, tunnels, and food caches. By 11:00 thirteen men were wounded, and eight had been killed. Two were forward observers from an artillery battery; the others were noncombatant photographers. Gripped by fear and succumbing to enemy fire, Company A withdrew towards Cu Chi. Jimmy watched the company retreat. He would soon be ordered to "attack [that same] small town about three miles from camp . . . find the VC burn their homes and kill them."

On Wednesday, the sixteenth of February, back from his first patrol—something that would soon become a daily occurrence—Jimmy took out a pen from his fatigue jacket. He smoothed out a piece of stationary and wrote "Viet Nam" under the header: *The United States Army Training Center, Infantry*. Still not having heard from his family since his arrival, he was unsure if the mail was getting home. Experiencing war for the first time opened Jimmy's eyes to the realities of death and chaos, and those revelations gave mail a new importance. Letters became lifelines linking troops to their families, helping keep many sane. In addition to fighting for their squad mates, letters gave GIs a purpose to continue. For Jimmy they became his defense against fear, and they formed a bridge between Vietnam and Runnemede, New Jersey. For the first time he wrote about combat:

> *Dear Dad and Mom: How are you, well its about 7:30 in the morning here, the sun is just starting to come up, it feels like it is really going to be a hot one today, well yesterday I thought I would see JC* [Jesus Christ] *for sure, there were 11 of us in the tank* [APC], *our mission was to burn up a small town, on our way there we were being shot at, but that is the everyday thing here, any way, the APC hit a anti-tank mine* [and] *the VC's were just ahead, we had to get out and find cover, last night they were all around us again, but you never see them . . . the sergeants are fighting with each other a lot and nobody seems to know what is going on, one say's one thing, another say's something different, I'll guess I will take over and show them how to do it, we have a lot of old timer's here from World War II, during the day there is never anything to do, just stay in your bunker, and look out for the VC, most of the men getting hurt here, is done by their own men, they keep telling us to be careful but how do you really do that, when you don't know what to be careful of, there is so much to watch for . . . last night I fired my rifle for the first time, it was about 11:30 at night and they started to fire on us, you would have thought hell broke lose, during all the shooting, guy's were running around looking for their beer, that is most important thing here . . . I will write you again later, so good by for now, and every body take care of them self's, P.S. by the time I get out of here I will know how to write letters, love Jimmy.*

Vietnam was one giant trap. As Cu Chi's American military population rose, so did unexpected casualties and injuries. Men were crushed by APC engines in the motor pool, greenhorns mistakenly shot other GIs while on guard duty, and boredom seemed to become death's co-conspirator. Soldiers accidently shot themselves in foxholes, fell on barbed wire, and one man from Jimmy's company was shot on patrol when he turned on his flashlight to find a suitable place to relieve himself. Nobody used a flashlight after that. The next night, third squad was again ordered to head out on an ambush operation. Patrols typically consisted of a squad sergeant, medic, forward observer, a machine gun crew, radio operator, and five grunts. The team used a compass and a map to navigate, and usually a GI capable of keeping a good pace counted out the meters traveled. Mechanized units used a similar method to maintain an accurate sense of their location, especially when mortar teams pre-plotted firing zones around the ambush site. Once the squad reached their objective, it broke into three groups of four men and planted claymore mines around their perimeter.

Jimmy saw no action on the patrol, and wrote home trying to capture the darkness in the rainforest. Again he hadn't seen any Viet Cong, but commented on feeling being watched. The night was so dark he couldn't see his hands in front of his face. Above the black "nothingness" of the jungle, he could see an impressive display of stars that were as bright as those he'd seen on the clearest nights in the Pine Barrens in South Jersey. "Every little noise made [him] jump . . . ", and he readied his finger tightly against the trigger guard. To keep his mind off the eeriness, Jimmy occupied himself with stray thoughts: "This place gives you time to think," he wrote. He usually thought about home and his girlfriend, Louise, and his future plans after the war—which were what he increasingly counted on to get him out alive. Frightened and homesick, he sat in the rain dwelling on his past. The next time he got a chance to write home, he asked his sister Maureen how she was doing in school. Thinking about how he ended up in the army, he told her that she "better not give up, because if she does, I will kick her ass when I come home. . . . " He questioned all the things he had done wrong, and wondered, ". . . boy who was I fooling. . . ." Although he claimed, "if I had to do it all over again, I would do the same thing," his letter suggested otherwise:

> *I miss home a lot, far more than I can put into word's, you always's think the grass is a lot greener on the other side, but when you find it is not, well you know what I mean, this is all doing me good, don't get me wrong you must see how other people live before you know how good you have it, I don't want you to feel sorry for me or any thing like that, but I am going to tell you how I live each day so the girl's will know how lucky that have it, first thing is I never get more than 2 ½ hours sleep at one time at night, and its to hot during the day to sleep, this is the good part, washing yourself, there is a well here on this old farm, but the house and every thing else has been burned down a while ago, you hook a rope on the [5 gallon] can and let it go until you hit water, bring it back up . . . soap yourself up, than pour the water over yourself, now for eating, the food is good, you eat out of your mess kit, of course you sit on the ground, in the sun, when I do sleep, it is on the ground, in a foxhole or under a tree, so see there girl's, I hope you learn from me . . . I have to accept the fact that I'm here, but I will make the best of it, this place will bring the man out of a boy, an it sure did in my case, I hope every body is feeling fine, and thing's are going good, for Daddy . . . (and of course mom, who always's tried to tell me stuff for my own good, but I knew it all) . . . and Georgie too, because he has a lot to worry about now, I was thinking of the fights we had, remember the one during the summer out in the field, looking back on that makes me feel bad, and so does all the times I talked back to Mommy and Pop and putting my hand on the girl's but that is just part of growing up I guess. . . .*

As patrols led to more tension and worry, he convinced himself that if he wrote enough about the future, it would come true. He made his father a proposition: "Let me send the money [I make] home each month, use it as you see fit, I would like it to go toward the station's rent, when I come out [of the army] it [the bank loan] should be down a lot and I can help pay it off, then WE can cut it [the gas station], down the middle when we sell it, or rent it, or [use it.] I have to start thinking of the future, when I get as old as twenty-two I must think ahead. . . . " He soon found out that the army did not offer the sort of career he thought it might. Instead, if he was going to "make it in the world," he needed a secure job and a good education.

When Jimmy returned the next morning at first light, he and B Company were ordered back out into the bush on their first extended search and destroy mission: Operation Clean Sweep. Similar to Crimp, Clean Sweep was designed to "uproot" and "neutralize" Viet Cong emplacements by searching out enemy tunnels, villages, and bunkers. Once found, they were to be destroyed along with everything inside. Tactics in Vietnam had a very different purpose than in prior wars. If an American unit was sent to a place like the Ho Bo or Filhol Woods, it was not to hold and exploit a valuable objective. If contact was made, the ensuing firefight was often fierce, quick, and lethal. Jimmy discovered that it was almost impossible to locate enemy forces. Combat units from the Twenty-Fifth Infantry Division were constantly in motion. For the men of the Fifth Mechanized, this meant that endless numbers of small operations took place, day and night, over terrain visited again and again. Beyond trying to locate the Viet Cong, the GIs rarely understood the purpose behind search and destroy missions, and there was something absurd about the way the war was fought. Jimmy was beginning to realize that futility. Yet, he continued to believe in America's mission: He was there to "free the farmers of Vietnam from communism" and help them improve their lives.

The Fifth Mechanized with B Company on the right crossed the LD (Line of Departure) at the prescribed time of 08:30. The ARVN troops attached to the Fifth Mechanized were late leaving the area, and held up the operation. They also never dismounted to search and destroy their first object. The frequent occurrence of this sort of negligence led many Americans to believe the South Vietnamese forces didn't care about winning about the war. Within a matter of hours, as if they had been followed, B Company came under sniper and light arms fire. They tried to flank the enemy, but failed to find them. In the process of trying to engage them, the company found an opening to a tunnel complex and the "rats" were called in. Tunnel rats like Gerald Rolf, a friend of Jimmy's from Second Platoon, found weapons in a tunnel that was over two hundred meters long, and an APC collapsed a large "underground classroom" filled with eight hundred pounds of rice and twenty U.S. Air Force bombs reassembled as booby traps. As night fell, Jimmy curled up under his poncho, which he used as a sleeping bag, and hoped to be asleep before the rain came. Throughout the night he was awakened several times for guard duty, and he had scratched his face and neck so many times from insect bites that his skin was raw.

In the next few days, American forces destroyed twenty-five bunkers and a total of seventy-nine tunnel complexes. Though it was estimated that the enemy lost a total of twenty-four fighters, only eleven bodies were "tagged." A number of the casualties taken by the Fifth Mechanized were a result of foolish errors. Men who stuck their heads out of the APC during heavy fire were killed, and one man was injured when the mounted .50-caliber machine gun fired accidentally and knocked him unconscious from its hard recoil. Another was shot in his left buttocks. The unit lost one APC to enemy fire, and an additional two malfunctioned and needed to be towed. The after action report mentioned that heavy civilian traffic on Highway One delayed the operation and allowed the Viet Cong time to set up ambushes and mines. They also noted that "the woods were much thicker than anticipated . . . and it was extremely difficult to coordinate and control the movement of the APCs through heavily wooded areas." An air observation helicopter was needed to help navigate APC drivers in the forest and "control the rate of movement." Moreover, the tracks consumed too much gasoline to sustain a long operation.

Many of the infantrymen, including their platoon leaders, felt that forward observers were needed to estimate the timing of the mission and identify difficult terrain that could slow the operation. Other GIs questioned why air observation was not used to aid ground troops with surveillance as well as supporting fire and bombing. Though the mobility and swiftness of helicopter squadrons enabled them to "waste" large enemy units, their real value was in resupply, medical evacuation, and troop transport. But helicopters were noisy and prone to being downed by light weapons fire and RPGs (rocket propelled grenades).

Following his return to base, Jimmy took a shower by the well. He lathered the soap in his hands and pulled up the bucket, and let the water trickle over his head:

> *Then the funiest thing happened . . . a little old sniper started shooting at me, at first it was funie, but then I thought they were real rounds he is shooting, I hit the ground fast, I did not know what to do, get dressed or what, so I just finished washing, anyway, a sniper only shot's once or twice and then leaves (I hope), besides that nothing new. . .*

He was becoming numb to fear. The next day he was ordered to start cutting down trees on the edge of camp, burn them, and hide claymore mines in the cleansed areas. A claymore is about twelve inches wide and seven inches high, and has "little legs" of wire. Inside its plastic casing is over a pound of plastic explosive that discharges 700 steel ball bearings that blow out in a fan shape. Soldiers who remotely fired this device had to be at least forty meters away or they were burned by its back blast. Many times out in the bush, GIs made their own mines with a steel ammo box and C-4 explosive, and packed it with anything they found in the motor pool: pistons, sparkplugs, wheel bearings, nuts and bolts, screws, and chain links. They then punched a hole in the back and inserted the charge. It tore through anything it hit within its "optimum distribution range" of fifty-five yards.

When he got back to his post, Jimmy drank a few beers with his squad mates. He was exhausted. His company was finally issued tents, but they didn't keep the rain out. Every so often someone broke the silence and talked about home or recent patrols. For those who hadn't seen it, Jimmy told them about his showering experience—how he was scrambling in the mud, naked, with soap in his eyes, praying he wouldn't get shot—and just when it got quiet again, he started to laugh, "and before you know it, every body [was] laughing, but know body knew what was funie, neither [did] I. . . ."

A Huey Helicopter delivers Army Air Cavalrymen to the Battle of Ia Drang.

North Vietnamese troops advance under cover to attack enemy positions.

CHAPTER 5

In Dubious Battle

> "The courage and skill of our men in battle will be matched by their magnanimity when the battle ends. And all American military action in Vietnam will stop as soon as aggression by others is stopped."
>
> — PRESIDENT LYNDON BAINES JOHNSON, August 21, 1965. From "The Enemy in Your Hands," an instructional card given to all troops upon their arrival in Vietnam detailing how to treat a prisoner of war humanely.

> "To his modern armament, one opposes a boundless heroism to vanquish by either harassing or combining military operations with political and economic action; there is no fixed line of demarcation, the front being wherever the enemy is found... each inhabitant a soldier, each village a fortress, each party cell and each village administrative committee a staff."
>
> — VO NGUYEN GIAP, *People's War, People's Army*.

> "The losses we had today hit home, as my best friend in this shit hole was killed. He was only 22 years old and was going on R&R on the first of June to meet his wife in Hawaii. I feel that if I was only a half second sooner in pulling the trigger, he would still be alive . . . If there is a place called Hell this surely must be it, and we must be the Devil's disciples doing all his dirty work. I keep asking myself if there is a God, then how the hell come young men with so much to live for have to die."
>
> — STANLEY HOMISKI, B Troop, 3/4 Cavalry, Twenty-Fifth Infantry Division, May 25, 1968.

Several weeks into the basic training that was intended to prepare Jimmy Gilch and his cohort of inductees for combat, the major adversaries in what would become the American phase of the Vietnamese wars of liberation were locked in the first, and one of the very few, conventional battles in that decade-long conflict. American planners and commanders in the field were unanimous in their contention that US forces had decisively won the battle of Ia Drang, which raged from November 14–18, 1965 and was named after the river valley where it was fought. More significantly in view of the conduct of the war to come, the officers in country and the Joint Chiefs in Washington concluded that the margin of victory demonstrated the effectiveness of ratcheting up the high-tech approach to America's military intervention in Vietnam's civil war. But their communist counterparts, from Senior General Giap in Hanoi to generals Chu Huy Man and Hoang Phuong, who directed NVA units in the field, had drawn very different conclusions from the first major engagement with US forces. North Vietnamese leaders found that their soldiers would fight bravely despite the seemingly overwhelming firepower the American military could deploy against them. Communist combatants at all levels also began to devise ways to offset the Americans' potentially demoralizing technological advantages and counter the tactics and overall strategy that US leaders believed that Ia Drang had validated. Thus, though the battle was relatively small in scale compared to most conventional engagements in the industrial era—or even compared to wars of early modern or ancient times—it was atypical for the Vietnam conflict on the whole. Nonetheless, it profoundly shaped the nature of the combat operations that Jimmy and his company would be ordered to carry out. It also foreshadowed the casualty-ridden war of attrition that would engulf all armies involved as well as the devastation that would be inflicted on the country and the civilian population of Vietnam, North and South.

The Lessons of Ia Drang

By mid-1965 there seemed to be very good reasons for communist leaders in Hanoi and NLF commanders in Cambodia and South Vietnam to transition to the third and final phase of the Maoist formulation of revolutionary guerrilla warfare: a full-scale general insurrection or "counteroffensive" against the imploding Saigon regime. In the preceding decade guerrilla forces had moved back and forth between the first or "strategic defensive" and the pivotal "tactical offensive" phases. The ebb and flow of guerrilla operations underscored the NLF's recognition that it was crucial to regard the transitions between phases of the insurgency as fluid, reversible, and calibrated to counter the repressive measures taken by successive governments in Saigon. Well-trained propaganda teams provided the entering wedge into the villages and market towns that ARVN soldiers occupied sporadically in the daytime and very often abandoned after dark. Through radio broadcasts, theatrical performances, and impassioned diatribes against the "US puppet-regime" in Saigon, agitprop operatives sought to win the peasantry's support for the insurgency. They appealed to Vietnamese patriotism, and stressed the indifference and ineptitude of government functionaries and their allied landlords and village chiefs.

NLF recruiters skillfully dramatized both the corruption of Saigon politicians and bureaucrats and the atrocities government police and ARVN forces had committed against the civilian population in rebel-held areas. The former was exemplified by a huge, float-style tableau featuring two enormous dummies that was erected at a heavily trafficked highway junction just outside of Saigon.

An NLF rally in the Cu Chi district in 1965

One of the figures resembled the American ambassador Frederick Nolting who was attempting to seduce the other, Madame Nhu, the callous and notoriously outspoken wife of Diem's brother Ngo Dinh Nhu. Both were sprawled across a bed of super-sized dollar bills. A sign attached to the display warned officials who would be ordered to dismantle the mock monument that it was wired with explosives. But perhaps the most poignant of the efforts to publicize the regime's brutalities against the civilian population arose when ARVN soldiers raiding a village suspected of sheltering guerrilla fighters shot a young mother and her five-month- old baby. The bodies of mother and child were placed in a small boat and left to float downriver to a busy market town where they were on view for several hours before government forces arrived to remove them.

As was the case in the revolutionary China, respect and support for the peasantry were instilled in recruits to NLF forces and regular NVA units. Communist soldiers were harshly punished for maltreating all but hostile or suspect villagers in the areas in which they operated. Although the resources available were often meager, NLF teams sought to build schools and clinics in communities that supported their resistance to the Saigon government. Very often their assistance provided the only opportunities for healthcare and education that rural Vietnamese had ever known. More critically, communist operatives forcibly introduced land reform in areas that came under communist control. They lowered rents, and turned over confiscated rice paddy plots to poor villagers. Oppressive landlords and local notables who resisted were driven into the towns, compelled to cooperate, or in some cases publicly executed. In contrast to the Diem regime and its allied US aid agencies, which sought to uproot peasant communities and relocate them in sterile, vulnerable "strategic hamlets," NLF infiltrators fortified villages and dug escape tunnels and underground shelters to store food, weapons, and animals if they came under attack.

In areas where there was substantial resistance to rebel incursions—particularly in major towns and cities where dictatorial government control was somewhat more secure—terrorist tactics were regularly deployed. From car bombs and raids on the haunts of the fashion-conscious urban elites to the assassination of government officials or American advisors, guerrilla operatives systematically and *selectively* for the most part targeted the leaders and local supporters of the Saigon regime. Successful terrorist operations proved effective ways to demonstrate the ineptitude of the South Vietnamese government and its military forces. Creating an atmosphere of destabilization and disorientation that permeated Vietnamese society gave rise to a widespread longing for order and support for a strong state. Guerrilla raids also provoked often indiscriminate and counterproductive police and military reprisals that bolstered NLF recruitment efforts and garnered increased support on the part of the broader civilian population.

From the early 1960s, ever-larger guerrilla offensives marked the transition to an emphasis on the second ("tactical offensive") phase of revolutionary warfare. The NLF and infiltrating NVA forces took advantage of the steady disintegration of the Diem regime amid widespread protests in Saigon and other urban centers to expand the territory they controlled outright. To the chagrin of American military advisors in country, many ARVN commanders were mainly engaged in intramural plots and coups, and readily obeyed orders to avoid combat with communist forces. Guerrilla fighters regularly mauled poorly led and demoralized ARVN forces in firefights and larger engagements. By mid-1964 it was clear to the new American ambassador, Maxwell Taylor, that the Saigon regime the United States had propped up for barely a decade was on the verge of collapse. General Westmoreland, who had taken command of American forces in Vietnam only weeks before Taylor arrived, warned that the steady communist advance increasingly put American advisors and military bases in peril and demanded significant reinforcements to defend them.

As the direct involvement of US combat units in the civil war in the South and aerial assaults against North Vietnam intensified in the early months of 1965, the communist leadership on both fronts launched major offensives designed to spark widespread insurrections that would finish off the Saigon regime before the Americans could fully commit their vastly superior military power. In October, a force of over four thousand regular NVA soldiers converged on the Ia Drang valley in the interior highlands of South Vietnam. They were massed to launch an assault against a Special Forces camp located in a decrepit former French fortress at Plei Me. By mid-1965 the camp had been manned by a dozen American advisors and nearly four-hundred *Montagnard* (non-ethnic Vietnamese peoples living in the mountainous regions in Vietnam's interior) irregulars loosely allied with the Diem regime.

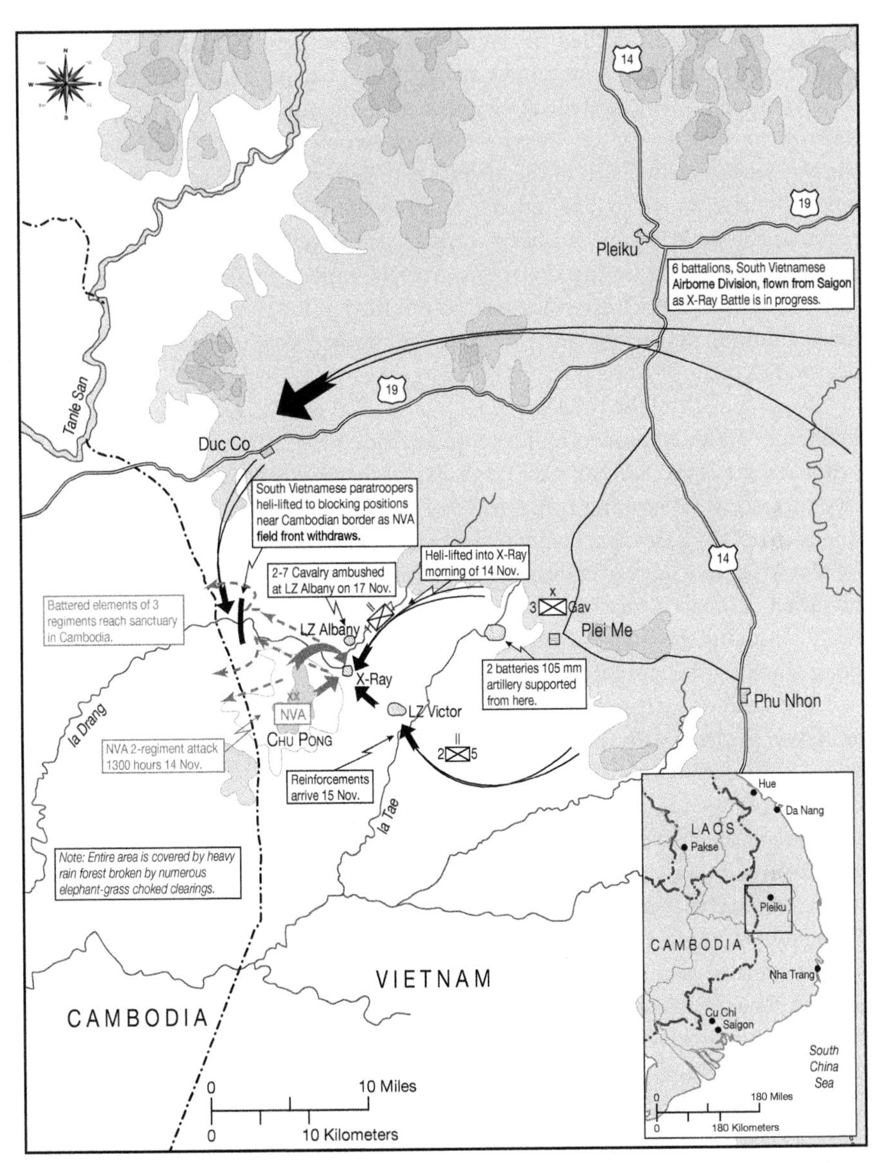

The Key Contested Locations and Troop Movements in the Seige of Plei Me and the Battle of Ia Drang

Operating on the long-standing assumption that whoever controlled the highlands could dominate South Vietnam, communist commanders viewed the siege of Plei Me as the prelude to a major offensive focused initially on the capture of ARVN headquarters and the airbase at Pleiku to the northwest. Once control of the central highlands was secured, NVA forces would descend to the plains to the east, capture the city of Qui Nhon, and gain control of a portion of Highway One, the main north-south artery in the heavily populated coastal region. If successful, the operation would cut Saigon off from the northern half of South Vietnam.

The assault on Plei Me was mainly a feint intended to compel ARVN commanders to launch a counterattack from Pleiku, where the bulk of their forces were stationed. NVA strategists planned an elaborate ambush to intercept and destroy the anticipated ARVN relief column, which they calculated would clear the way for the completion of the operation to gain a foothold in the coastal lowlands. But they failed to take into account the fact that what had been an ARVN regional camp at Pleiku had been transformed over the course of 1965 into a major air base for incoming US troops. An NLF raid on Pleiku in early February, in which nine American service men were killed and 128 wounded, accelerated the US buildup at the base, and proved to be a major factor in President Johnson's decision to commit combat forces to bolster the Saigon regime.

From the outset the NVA offensive against Plei Me bogged down. Reinforced by a force of ARVN Rangers and resupplied from the air, the garrison managed to beat back the NVA's human wave assaults. Decisive in this regard were the artillery support and bombing runs provided by newly arrived American units stationed in nearby bases that decimated attacking and retreating North Vietnamese forces. After five days of mounting casualties and the failure of the elaborately prepared ambush to prevent the advance of the ARVN armored relief column, NVA commanders ordered the two regiments engaged to retreat towards the Chu Pong massif and Cambodian sanctuaries to the west.

Encouraged by the successful defense of Plei Me and determined to destroy as many of the enemy as possible before they crossed the border, American and ARVN commanders mounted a counteroffensive to locate and destroy the retreating NVA regiments. Westmoreland in particular pushed for an aggressive pursuit of elusive enemy forces because he believed that a major engagement would provide an excellent test of the Air Mobile approach to counterinsurgency warfare that he advocated. Developed initially in response to President Kennedy's demand that American forces come up with effective ways to deal with the spread of guerrilla warfare in the peasant-based societies of Latin America and Asia, Westmoreland fixed on its capacity to respond rapidly to assaults by these elusive adversaries and destroy them with massive firepower. Prodded by his loyal and highly opinionated deputy William DePuy, Westmoreland was convinced that a high-tech response would prove the best way to inflict intolerable casualties on communist insurgent forces, and thereby salvage the South Vietnamese regime.

Drawing on reinforcements from Da Nang and Saigon, and deploying massed artillery as well as an impressive range of attack aircraft and helicopters to move combat forces into position, Westmoreland and his staff launched the first major American offensive of what was to become a long war. On November 14th, troops from the Seventh Calvary Division were air lifted to a recently cleared landing zone, dubbed X-Ray, on the southern bank of the Ia Drang River, just northwest of the Chu Pong massif. Chosen initially because it would place US troops within striking distance of enemy forces, X-Ray was also—purely coincidentally—in the vicinity of the headquarters of NVA units operating in the valley. Though taken by surprise, North Vietnamese commanders ably reoriented their retreating forces, and a newly arrived support regiment, to renew the offensive, now targeting Americans in pursuit. After being delivered by the first helicopter lift, fewer than two hundred US infantrymen soon found themselves confronting nearly 1,600 well-trained NVA soldiers in and around the landing zone. In the four days that followed American and Vietnamese forces clashed in a series of firefights that, taken together, proved to be one of the largest and most fiercely fought engagements of the war.

Although initially dauntingly outnumbered, American advanced forces managed to form a defensive perimeter at X-Ray. As additional units arrived by helicopter, their firepower increased and they were able to advance against NVA forces approaching through the rainforest. In the opening days of the battle, the North Vietnamese mounted human wave assaults against X-Ray and the cluster of landing zones that were established nearby. Hand-to-hand fighting at close quarters dominated the early clashes, and X-Ray and its satellite landing zones were often in danger of being overrun. But as Westmoreland and DePuy anticipated, the outcome of the battle would be determined by the potent and, they presumed, precise air and artillery support that beleaguered American units could summon. The Vietnamese, on the other hand, lacked sophisticated antiaircraft weaponry at this stage of the war. Thus there was little they could do to shield their massed infantry forces from being strafed by jets and helicopter gunships, incinerated by napalm, and blown apart by B-52 carpet bombings.

Those NVA fighters who were able to close in on American positions were more often than not cut down by artillery strikes delivered from distant firing bases. Inevitably, however, assaults that succeeded in engaging US soldiers in combat at close quarters also resulted in GI deaths by friendly fire. Nonetheless, the demoralizing and disorienting impact of American firepower on NVA fighters was graphically captured by Sergeant Ernie Savage. Fighting in a platoon cut off from the main force, he found it unsettling that, "It seemed like they [NVA assault troops] didn't care how many of them were killed. Some of them were stumbling, walking right into us. Some had their guns slung and were charging barehanded . . . An hour before dark three men walked up on the perimeter. I killed all three of them 15 feet away."[1]

After three days of assaults and counterattacks, North Vietnamese forces had begun to retreat. Westmoreland and his staff had little doubt that, despite the fact that American units had taken unexpectedly heavy casualties—305 killed and 524 wounded in the Ia Drang campaign as a whole—they had won a significant victory. Though frustrated by the refusal of LBJ and the Joint Chiefs to allow them to pursue enemy forces into their Cambodian sanctuaries, Westmoreland and his field commanders were confident that they had found a formula for defeating both the NVA regulars and NLF guerrillas. The success of the Air Mobile campaign they had mounted in the Ia Drang valley set in place the core components of the war the US military would wage until the end of Westmoreland's command in June of 1968. In a process repeated over and over again, aircraft surveillance would first locate enemy positions, then a diverse constellation of helicopters would be deployed to transport rapidly and provide cover for the insertion of infantry units to carry out "search and destroy" missions. Finally, once battle was joined, American aircraft and artillery batteries would unleash wave after wave of massive firepower that was intended to overwhelm adversary troops caught up in the operation.

Most military leaders in country and back in Washington saw in the battle of Ia Drang confirmation of their assumption that they had developed a combination of military operations that would defeat North Vietnam's aggression and prevent communist totalitarianism from spreading to the South. There were, nonetheless, different estimates of how long it would take, and how high the cost would be to secure a stable regime in Saigon. Some of the officers involved in the battle were concerned that most of the American forces deployed were withdrawn from Ia Drang immediately afterward, leaving the valley open for NVA and NLF units to reoccupy. Most sensed that Air Mobile combat meant that capturing and holding territory would no longer be the measure of victory; some realized that body counts would soon become the gauge of success and failure in battle. Field officers and ordinary grunts, who had actually grappled with the enemy firsthand, were given pause by the courage and determination shown by their Vietnamese adversaries throughout the weeks of combat. As Charles Beckwith, one of the American advisors working with the hard-pressed forces defending Plei Me, admitted when asked for his assessment of the North Vietnamese soldiers in a nationally televised CBS documentary on the siege that began the battle: "I would give anything to have two hundred of them under my command. They're the finest soldiers I've ever seen . . . that's right. They are dedicated and they're good soldiers. They're the best soldiers I've ever seen." Wrestling with a pointed follow-up question about how the Americans and Vietnamese fighters defending Plei Me compared to their communist adversaries, Beckwith sought to qualify his praise for the enemy by lauding the "outstanding job" done by the US advisors, whom upon further reflection he considered "a hell of a lot better than the Viet Cong."[2]

The Good Soldier
March 1966

From a tactical standpoint, the war seemed to be going well. Whenever the NVA chose to stand and fight, they were defeated by conventional American formulas. In the counterinsurgency operations in southern Vietnam, however, the military situation was deteriorating. The U.S. Army sought to reverse the erosion of civilian confidence in America's ability to contain the brutality of guerrilla warfare with solutions similar to those used in the Ia Drang Valley. The military buildup in the Cu Chi region was fully assembled by the end of March 1966. The increase in the strength of the Twenty-Fifth Infantry's ground combat forces was matched by the addition of more mechanized units and armored cavalry squadrons at the insistence of the division commander, General Fred C. Weyand. He argued that armored units were far more effective than foot soldiers in clearing trails, destroying mines, and disrupting enemy defenses.[3] When Weyand arrived at the Cu Chi base camp, the situation was so grim that he quipped: "Before I came out there a year ago, I thought we were at zero. I was wrong. We were at minus fifty."[4] His frustration with the failure to contain the Viet Cong militarily was intense and widely shared. He seconded Major General Arthur S. Collins's conclusion that the objective in limited war is not destruction of the enemy's military machine, but rather neutralization of their political and military influence among the people.[5]

Weyand's frustration was compounded by the fact that American commanders had difficulty in determining the effectiveness of search and destroy operations. The U.S. Army's field manual on counterinsurgency operations offered limited advice on how to measure success in an unconventional war. Thus, officers used evaluations of their unit's proficiency in battle as evidence of progress. Within regular military parameters this amounted to recording body counts, seizing war materiel and foodstuffs, and capturing prisoners.[6] In striving to compensate for the destruction involved in accomplishing these objectives, genuine acts of charity and compassion that American soldiers participated in, such as building bridges, churches, schools, orphanages, and roads, were often undermined when the civilian population—unarmed and exposed—became targets of military operations. In a perverse twist of logic that characterized so many American efforts in Vietnam, the good intentions of civic initiatives generally produced adverse effects. An estimated $800,000 worth of materials—including clothing, hand tools, children's toys, canned goods, soap, and medical supplies—that Weyand had secured and donated to villagers through his "Operation Helping Hand," a program designed to help American soldiers counter the terror and harassment of the Viet Cong, instead sparked calculated communist raids on villagers in which guerrillas confiscated the consumer goods and sanitary equipment for their own war effort.

The American response to the growing strength of the communist forces and the continuing weakness of the South Vietnamese regime magnified the hostile environment into which Jimmy Gilch and other young soldiers were thrust. The uncertainties posed by these opposing trajectories were central to the difficulties combatants had in understanding, much less committing to the American mission. The guerrillas' hit-and-run tactics, which killed and wounded some of Jimmy's friends, quickly erased any sympathy he may have had toward the Vietnamese. He depersonalized the enemy, making it possible to kill without remorse. Jimmy's hardened attitude became apparent during Operation Waikiki.

As part of the larger operation, the Fifth Mechanized Regiment was working on a seven-day-a-week schedule to eliminate a recently discovered tunnel network in the Cu Chi region. In the preceding patrols, the Second Brigade had reported 163 Viet Cong killed and a further 356 possible dead. Field officers had been notified beforehand that "howitzers had been pummeling the area on a 24-hour a day basis to soften Viet Cong strongholds before ground probing action . . . and heavy support [would be] supplied from raiding Air Force jets and armed army helicopters." Since its deployment to Cu Chi on January 19th, the Eighth Artillery Regiment alone had fired over 25,000 shells into the nearby provinces. By the end of April the unit would double that total.[7]

When Jimmy and the men of B Company arrived at their primary objective, they found that the village of Xom Moi, an "island" positioned in the middle of a rice paddy, had been partly destroyed by the bombing. What was still standing they torched, and any tunnels were blown up. Once the food and weapons were confiscated and destroyed, the company remounted their APCs and left the burnt-out village. Jimmy, who had recently been made point man of his squad, sat atop the APC providing suppressing fire with a .50 caliber machine gun, a weapon noted for its ability to chop down trees. Jimmy had been given the nickname "Cowboy Jim" for his confidence and rebelliousness. He had been letting his hair grow out for weeks, and when it was long enough he was going to shave it all off, except for a strip running down the middle of his head. He figured a "mohawk brought out the animal in you." Jimmy admitted that the most important life lesson his father had taught him was "never take shit from anyone, [and though I was] no Cassius Clay, I learned to take care of [myself] in Vietnam." He had begun to enjoy the adrenaline rush of war, and of the two celebrities he revered as a kid, he began to phase out the less heroic of the two: "I've given up on Elvis for now, until I get out of the army." His attachment to his new persona reflected a combativeness that was evident in his letters: "I am starting to like it, sometimes I feel like John Wayne, it is very exciting, don't worry I am not going to be a hero, but I hope to get me a VC pretty soon, just for something different . . . I've [also] been getting a pretty good tan each day, I hope nobody say's when I come home, 'boy you look good, I bet you had a nice time,' I'll kill them . . . "

The nature of the war itself had come to shape Jimmy's responses, and made it possible for him find purpose in the midst of its hellishness. He fought to protect his buddies by killing the enemy before they killed them. As Army Specialist George Olsen wrote, "You're scared, really scared, and there's no thinking about it. You kill because that little SOB is doing his best to kill you and you desperately want to live, to go home, to get drunk or walk down the street on a date again."[8] The feelings Jimmy expressed to his family about heroism were similar to Marine Lieutenant Brian Sullivan's remarks to his wife: "I guess I should be honest. I've been nominated, I hear, for the Silver Star . . . . Please don't get upset. I didn't try to win it—I was just trying to keep my people alive and doing the best I could."[9] Like most GIs, Jimmy's feelings were also affected by a general distrust of the villagers in the areas he was ordered to defend. A recent occurrence had been circulated in the division's newspaper about an engineering battalion that was working to remove dirt from a quarry not far from the base camp. A group of children had gathered throughout the day to watch the men at work. Suddenly two villagers walked up behind the crowd and tossed a grenade in the direction of the Americans. The explosion seriously injured two of the children. The attackers escaped.

Later in the afternoon Jimmy and B Company conducted additional searches of nearby villages. As they were returning to base camp, they surprised several Vietnamese men gathered in a small clearing off the trail. Because it was virtually impossible to tell the difference between a guerrilla soldier and a civilian, Jimmy's squad sped forward to check out the group. He described the incident that followed: "We were really trying to run them over, but they ran so fast." Seeing the suspected guerrillas stumble as they zigzagged around trees and low-lying brush, Jimmy laughed. It reminded him of a scene from an "old time silent film." He wrote that he "had never seen a funnier sight than" four or five men fleeing for their lives. He added in a letter: "our mission was to make friend's with the people living in the small towns . . . but I would rather shoot them because then we don't have to worry about them later, and besides, I learned it takes a long time to make friend's, and I don't want to spend to much time out there in the field . . . "

Shortly after he returned from Operation Waikiki, Jimmy was assigned to a security detail responsible for cutting down and burning trees along the Ben Muong River in order to lengthen the base's northeast perimeter. While working, he noticed a wild boar rooting around the edge of the woods. The area had once been a farm, possibly one that had water buffalo and pigs. But now it was just scorched earth. He returned to his foxhole in the afternoons covered in soot and red clay. His hands remained stained for days. When he wrote home, his palms would sweat, loosening the grime on his skin and stamping his fingerprints on the margins of the paper. Since he was a little boy, Jimmy had been obsessed with personal hygiene. But in Vietnam staying clean was futile. His laundry always came back looking dirty, and the recent monsoons had collapsed the well that serviced the showers.

One morning soon afterward, Jimmy spotted the boar running wildly. He kept an eye on it while continuing to hack away at the scrub growth. A platoon coming down the road had also seen the creature. It had become a trendy amusement to shoot at animals that wandered around the countryside—none of which posed a threat to the soldiers. An eight-foot monitor lizard had recently been killed, and the "hunters" dragged it back to camp and nailed the carnivorous beast to a wooden cross like a trophy for all to see.[10] With each gunshot, Jimmy heard laughter, then shrieks, from the wounded boar. Finally, as if seized by decency, one soldier killed the boar. Turning away disapprovingly, Jimmy continued to shovel the earth and ashes. He later wrote: "They shot the wild pig that lived here, to bad, I was just starting to like it." Jimmy commented no further, but it was that type of war, one that made for random slaughter.

Private Reginald Edwards of the Ninth Marine Regiment described a similar rampage: "I don't know how many chickens I shot. But it was a little pig that freaked me out more than the chickens. You think you gonna be shootin' a little pig, it's just gonna fall over and die. Well, no. His little guts be hangin' out. He just be squiggling around and freakin' you out. See, you got to shoot animals in the head. If we shoot you in your stomach, you may just fall over and die. But an animal, you got to shoot them in the head. They don't understand that they supposed to fall over and die."[11] Troops went for days out in the bush, seeing their friends die, yet never encountering the enemy. Lacking human adversaries they resorted to killing innocent livestock and wild animals.[12]

Some soldiers found killing animals or civilians similar to hunting. Jimmy alluded to this when he told his uncle that "he should see some of the guns over, and maybe since E & E [a hunting and fishing shop] is kind of dead right now in Runnemede, he could move over here and start up a sporting goods store." One soldier, First Lieutenant James Simmen from the Sixtieth Mechanized of the First Division, made the resemblance more explicit: "You'd be surprised how similar killing is to hunting. I know I'm after souls, but I get all excited when I see a VC, just like when I see a deer. I go ape on firing at him. It isn't that I'm so crazy. I think a man who freezes killing a man would freeze killing a deer. I'm not perverted, crazy or anything else. Civilians think such thinking is crazy, but it's no big deal. He runs, you fire."[13] Jimmy expressed similar feelings to his father:

> *Daddy, how's thing's, I hope good, are you making plan's for hunting this year (or did mom make them for you?)... I just got back off a 2 day field problem, we killed 26 VC, guess what I was shooting, the new M-16 auto-rifle, everybody said, I had done real good. I would make John Wayne look sick. I was on top* [of the APC], *when we were going through the jungle burning houses, and trying to get the VC. Rounds were going over my head, I figure that was it, so I cut lose, 20 rounds in about 4 sec., and that went on for about 1 hour, I was tired, we were only suppose to go for one 1 day, but we had them trapped, we ran out of water, don't think that was not hell, it got so hot, and my hair is still long... I have some better story's... but I'll have to save them until I get home because I don't want Mommy to get a hold of the letter... my CO* [commanding officer] *said this place will make a man out of you, and boy was he right. . . . I had a run in with a SGT* [sergeant] *out there again, he started giving me a hard time, but I told him where to get off, he said, 'son, you are looking for an ass kicking.' I said maybe your are right, but it wont be by you, he got so mad that he just walked away... well, tell everybody I said hello, and send my love. (Everybody in my squad lives in the south, like TENN, KY, SC, NC, FL, places like that, so I am the only yank here, the way they talk they think they won the civil war, but I keep telling them that the North did).*

Some American soldiers found killing invigorating. They recall never feeling as alive as when they were in a situation in which they felt the adrenaline rush that comes with confronting death. Facing mortality bonded men together, and the communion between them could be profound and affectionate. When the time came to go home, many opted for another tour. In *Dispatches*, Michael Herr relates an episode in which a soldier who had engaged in the fiercely fought siege of Khe Sanh had to be placed forcibly on the plane that would take him home. In *Rumor of War* Phil Caputo comments on the physical and emotional appeal of combat and the bonding it engendered. Having watched a fellow soldier parting with his dying friend, Caputo writes, "It was a conversation of two lovers who were about to be separated."[14]

Despite Jimmy's cowboy image, passages in his letters home hint that his attitude towards combat was beginning to change. In mid-March he expressed excitement about an upcoming patrol. He told his parents he was going on what was officially designated "as a Good-Will Tour, [which meant that his unit would be] visiting the small town's in the region and helping the poor farmers . . . About Time!" Toward the end of his letter, he asked his mother, "Can you send me some books to read and a radio, I have a lot of time, and please tell everybody that I cant write them, but that James Xavier Gilch will not fail." In spite of the seeming abandon he displayed in combat situations, he was increasingly eager to learn and grow. He continued to write home every day, and his ability to articulate his ideas began to improve. He still wrote in a stream of consciousness mode and mistook plurals for possessives, but his spelling got slightly better once the dictionary his family mailed to him arrived. "When I get the hell home," he wrote, "I'll be able to write a letter pretty good (I hope) and write better too." He was also anxious to show—and not just through his more polished writing—that he was maturing in ways his father would appreciate, thus proving that he would be able to run the family business when he returned home.

Rethinking the Path to Liberation

The heavy losses NVA forces suffered in the mass assaults that they repeatedly mounted against American positions in the Ia Drang valley forced NLF commanders in the South and the Politburo in Hanoi to reassess their assumption that the time was ripe to move to the final stage of revolutionary guerrilla warfare. It was evident to the communist leadership that not enough of the peasantry and urban dissidents in South Vietnam were ready to rise up in revolution. The sheer numbers of combat personnel the United States deployed in the month-long series of engagements also left no doubt that the Johnson administration had opted to escalate significantly American support for the Saigon regime. Accounts of the battle provided by the People's Army Publishing House decades after the end of the war make it clear that the North Vietnamese commanders were both surprised and, at least initially, stunned by the size and firepower of the US forces arrayed against them.[15] Ferocious American air assaults and infantry incursions smashed NVA communications systems, cut officers off from their subordinates, and broke down the cohesiveness of units advancing to assault US infantry forces landing in the valley. Especially sobering for commanders and ordinary soldiers alike was the realization that the asymmetry between the firepower regular North Vietnamese fighters could muster and that unleashed by American infantry, artillery, and air assaults made conventional NVA offensive operations nearly suicidal.

North Vietnamese regulars (NVA) advance in a wave assault

Although enemy body counts tended to be exaggerated by both sides, and American casualties exceeded expectations, whole Vietnamese regiments were decimated and total NVA losses numbered in the thousands. There was no doubt on the part of the communist leadership that they were up against an enemy far more mobile and technologically advanced than their former French colonizers. Setpiece battles, such as the one at Dien Bien Phu, would be far more lethal—perhaps prohibitively so. Unlike their American counterparts, Giap and the NVA commanders did not claim victory after the battle of Ia Drang. They were willing to settle for a draw, which they viewed as a significant achievement in view of the fact that they were up against a global superpower. Nonetheless, the lessons they took away from the first major clash with American forces were very different from those of Westmoreland and his staff.

The battle convinced communist leaders that NVA forces had the leaderhip, training, and courage to engage frontline US units in conventional warfare. But the full-scale American commitment made it strategically necessary to curtail offensive operations that had become more frequent and bold against ARVN forces in the months before the major US military interventions. Communist leaders also found it telling that the Americans had withdrawn from the valley soon after they had driven NVA regiments into Cambodia. They correctly surmised that Westmoreland's superiors in Washington had denied his field officers permission to pursue the North Vietnamese into that neutral country.

Communist military strategists concluded that the Americans had sought in the Ia Drang campaign to overwhelm NVA forces by deploying all of the advanced weaponry and fully implementing the tactical innovations that would henceforth characterize Air Mobile operations. But rather than demoralizing North Vietnamese and NLF fighters and prodding Hanoi to negotiate, the battle had exposed some of the vulnerabilities and underlying strategic flaws of the war that Westmoreland had decided American forces would wage. Most crucially, in reviving their reliance on guerrilla tactics and avoiding setpiece battles, communist operatives were able reduce the effectiveness of US air power and mobile artillery. When pitched battles or firefights did occur, communist soldiers were instructed to get as close to the enemy as possible. Nguyen Hu An, an NVA commander who led the attacks on the X-Ray landing zone at Ia Drang, later revealed that his troops were told to "hug them by the belt buckle" so that napalm, strafing, and artillery barrages were prohibitive.[16] Though American helicopters were the key to locating and attacking elusive guerrilla and regular NVA units, they were noisy and vulnerable to ground fire, and slow especially when they were delivering GIs to landing zones.

Communist leaders in Hanoi and in the South were also emboldened by the realization that Westmoreland and his subordinate officers had adopted body counts instead of territory captured as the metric for determining which side had won the battle and who was winning the war. NVA and NLF commanders were resigned to a war of attrition, but not because, as McNamara and other American policymakers suggested,[17] they were indifferent to ever-higher levels of casualties and the widespread suffering that a long conflict would inevitably entail. Rather they were confident that the resolve to expel the invaders and the stoical patience of the majority of the Vietnamese people would inevitably bring victory. Whether fighting for reasons that ranged from personal revenge for the deaths of family and friends in bombing raids or infantry assaults, or the desire to liberate and unite their country, communist leaders were convinced that NVA and NLF volunteers and draftees were far more motivated, and thus better able to endure the hardships of combat than American GIs. They also foresaw that mounting casualties in a prolonged conflict would provide further impetus for the antiwar protests that had already begun on college campuses from California to New York City. Above all, the leaders in Hanoi and COSVN (Central Office for South Vietnam) headquarters in eastern Cambodia realized that the overall US strategy, which concentrated on defeating NLF and NVA forces rather than gaining the support of the peasant population, was ultimately destined to fail.

Ambivalence and Disillusionment
March 1966

Jimmy lifted the poncho that was covering his face, and sat up on the mats that were spread out under him and his squad. A dense fog had set in. Resupply helicopters had been unable to reach the company during the night due to "enemy fire and darkness," forcing the men to share what remained of their provisions. They chewed their salt tablets and to conserve water they took small sips from their canteen and swished the warm liquid that tasted of chlorine and plastic around in their mouths. They had been told that such an exercise tricked the body into believing it was hydrated. It was kind of crazy, Jimmy thought, that the whole country was full of water, but so little of it was safe to drink. From their first day in country, the men were told not to drink the water from the many small steams and canals because they were cesspools. Every now and then there was an outbreak of dysentery when soldiers filled their canteens from flooded bomb craters because they thought the water was potable. Jimmy never took that chance.

The men were without their company commander, Captain Ellison Vickery. He had been wounded on the first day of their current mission, Operation Honolulu. They themselves had narrowly escaped an ambush a few days earlier. On March 14, the platoon had to dismount their APCs due to the wet conditions and, according to Jimmy's estimate, "walked about 12 miles through water and rice fields, burning up all the houses along the way, and crossing river's, and lake's, and swimming in water that was over [their] heads." He wrote that, "It was about 2 or 3 in the evening when the VC set up an ambush on us just as we were crossing a river." The guerrillas had presumably been following the company all day, and chose to dig in on the opposite side of a canal that was heavily protected by a thicket. When the Viet Cong opened fire, all hell broke loose. Men from different platoons were running around, exposed and looking lost, while Jimmy and several others "quick hit the ground." As the Americans returned fire, an argument broke out among the platoon sergeants about how to escape. One of the sergeants, fed up with the bickering, jumped up from his cover behind a dirt mound and sprinted toward a nearby open field. Jimmy followed suit and the rest rallied behind him. "We all got up," he wrote, "and I started to run across the rice field's, which were full of water, if it was not for Sgt. [Robert] Bennett I guess we would have been in a lot of trouble, it was his idea that we run across the field to get away from the heavy VC attack . . . so much happened that I could write a book about it."

After they were resupplied on the morning of the 16th, the men tore down their improvised shelters, and tied their ponchos and mats to the top of the armored personnel carrier. They also stacked sandbags along the top edges of the track to provide additional protection. They then opened the hatch and ducked into the machine. The first thing they always saw when they entered was a big bold-lettered

Although the M-16 was prone to jamming, it was relatively light, easy to grip, and capable of rapid firing—thus well suited to firefights in densely wooded terrain.

sign posted over the engine cover: DANGER: MONOXIDE GAS, which reminded them to make sure the engine compartment was closed. The space inside the APC was about the size of a sleeping compartment on a train with a four-and-a-half-foot-high ceiling. Jimmy bumped against his squad mates as the track made its way over the uneven terrain. David Berry, Richard Gill, Larry Van Clief, Samuel Harris, John McGough, Leo Hinterlong, Nat McLean, and Sergeant Wilberto Sanchez sat around him. They had all recently been issued the army's new M-16 automatic rifle. Though it "looked good," Jimmy noted, an early design flaw made it unreliable in combat. Cartridges would jam in the chamber, and a rod had to be inserted down the barrel to remove the bullets. When confronted with the malfunction, army officials responded by informing the soldiers they were not keeping the weapon properly cleaned. It was not until 1967 that a Congressional hearing on the problem forced the army to redesign the weapon.

As the track lurched through the woods, it tore off low-lying tree branches that then dropped into the open hatch. Medical kits and ammunition boxes stowed in the overhead compartments fell to the floor and startled those who had nodded off. Occasionally the driver would abruptly shift gears, jerking the men out of their seats and slowing the track to a crawl. He was being cautious in an attempt to avoid hidden explosives. The Viet Cong had littered the area with booby traps and mines, which several APCs from C Company had hit earlier in the operation. One of the APCs exploded an antitank device that wounded several of the men inside. But they all escaped with their lives. It was common for those who survived such a blast to wander out of the machine in a daze. Many vomited from having inhaled the thick smoke of burning rubber and the engine parts. Others, their ears ringing and their faces stained black with oil and grease, just stood beside the smoldering heap of steel, mumbling and sobbing in deep shock.

The tension in the APC was high. Sergeant Sanchez felt that he had been humiliated, especially because Jimmy had disregarded his orders during the ambush on the previous day and followed Sergeant Bennett's lead. Jimmy described the situation to his father:

> *The Sgt. . . . said I think everything is a big joke, and I am trying to turn the whole team against him . . . he got mad again and wanted to fight me, he kept on me for the longest time, I know if I was to stay on him he would blow his head, he took me to the squad leader, and boy did I make an ass out of him, when he started telling the sq. leader what happened, that I didn't follow him and made a joke out of the war, before you knew it, the squad leader was laughing right along with me . . .* [That evening] *it rained all night, 'this is the weather VC come out in' my Sgt. said, but I told him this is the kind of weather you can get a cold in too, he didn't say too much after that . . .*

Jimmy used humor to diffuse tense situations and ward off the hostility of some officers. His parents were comforted by their son's humorous stories, which they felt showed that he'd kept his self-confidence and hadn't lost his ability to push back. But jokes had become a means of coping that masked fear. Jimmy's letter to his mother describing the run-in with the sergeant was even more humorous and lighter in tone than the one addressed to his father: "Mom, help, write our congressman, I'm being picked on by my sergeant . . . give my love to everyone, even President Johnson, wait, I'll take that one back." For Jimmy, the Vietnam War was becoming a cruel joke, and he was far from the only one who believed this.

For most of the ride the nine of them sat on hard folding benches and stared at each other. They were en route to the Hiep Hoa village, located in the Duc Hoa district of the Hau Nghia province. Not one of the Americans in the APC knew about Hiep Hoa's thirty-year history of foreign military occupation, and thus had no sense that most of the villagers had experienced violence, treachery, and deep human sorrow. During World War II many of the villagers had joined the resistance in retaliation for heavy Japanese taxes. They burned crops, assassinated Japanese officials, and raided enemy garrisons and munitions depots. When the French returned to reclaim control of Hiep Hoa, they were driven away by well-armed Viet Minh soldiers. The Viet Minh movement grew stronger even as the French tried to reestablish control over the countryside, working outward from the towns and cities where their control was more secure.

Villagers who had earlier remained neutral were forced to pick a side. In the 1950s a teenager named Hai Chua[18], whose father had recently been driven into hiding by the Viet Minh for having worked as a French civil servant, desperately tried to avoid commitment to either side of the conflict. For years, Chua managed to escape both armies' recruiters who regularly swept through the village cajoling or forcing young males into military service. But General Giap's victory at Dien Bien Phu convinced him to join the Vietnamese Nationalist Party. After the French were ousted, and before his local unit was disbanded, Hai Chua's last major task during the First Indochina war was to carry hundreds of weapons and various munitions to storage caches in Cambodia, which he would later retrieve to be used against the Americans. On March 17, 1966, when Jimmy and B Company neared Hiep Hoa, they were riding into a communist stronghold where they possibly confronted Chua and his fellow revolutionaries. Whatever the approaching Americans had in mind, the rice farmers of Hiep Hoa were willing to risk their lives to disrupt the intruders' plans.

By early evening, the men of B Company had detained fifty-six residents of Hiep Hoa. Thirty of them were children. During the search, Jimmy tried to recall how to pronounce several of the Vietnamese commands that he had studied from an appendix card given to him on his arrival in country. Nothing came to mind. Only one man, who was interrogated by the Republic of Vietnam National Police (RVNP), was thought to have links to a Viet Cong regiment. He was found hiding in a tunnel and driven out by tear gas. He had emerged from the smoking hole with his hands up, crying, "Finis, Viet Cong! Finis, Viet Cong!" Once calmed, he was asked where he had hidden his weapon. He replied: "I lost it." Realizing his slip, he quickly retorted: "I'm just a simple farmer." Jimmy was haunted by encounters with the villagers, especially since he was unable to communicate with them. He was deeply troubled by "what a feeling it was to hold a gun on a person, you are telling him what you want him to do and he is telling you too, but neither one of us can understand what one is saying to the other."

Jimmy was beginning to realize that he had become caught up in missions that were anything but what his company commander had characterized as "good-will tours." American casualties in the first few days of the operation were nearly equal to those of the enemy. In order to capture nearly a hundred seemingly ordinary Vietnamese peasants, the battalion had expended over 30,000 rounds of ammunition and close to one hundred pounds of explosives. Any village caught harboring supplies for the Viet Cong was evacuated, burned, and later bombed. Jimmy was assigned "to go into the houses and get the people out." Given short notice, some villagers buried what they could not carry, hoping to someday return to their homes and dig up their valuables. Suspected Viet Cong collaborators, such as the one Jimmy had detained at Hiep Hoa, were immediately interrogated and then sent to prisoner of war camps or civilian jails. Many of them never returned.

Though Jimmy and his company strove to treat their captives with a degree of respect, they often used brutal tactics to extract information from suspected Viet

Cong. Age or sex didn't matter. Douglas Anderson, a medic in the Third Battalion of the First Marines, was put in charge of guarding an old man who was arrested in a raid on a village not far from Da Nang. The old man sat still. He was missing a hand, and the wound had long been scarred over. The American medic pointed his M-16 at the man's head, trying to figure out just how the "old guerrilla could fire" —let alone accurately—an automatic rifle. Anderson recounted: "I remember [him] sitting there knowing he was going to die that day and just staring straight at me . . . .I was very close to crying. He was looking right into my eye . . . he knew who I was. He knew that I did not want to kill him, but he knew that I would." Soon thereafter, an American and a Vietnamese intelligence officer began to torture the prisoner. They forced his head deep into a bucket of water and made him confess between gags that he was a communist sympathizer. The Marines then tied his feet together, strung him to the back of a track, and dragged him until most of skin was torn off. "I'll never forget the man's face, and I will never forget his eyes, and I will never forget holding the rifle at his face," Anderson recalled, "There was something about the internal solidity of this human being that I will never forget. I feel that's the closest relationship I ever had with a Vietnamese . . . . [It was something] that changed my life."[19]

The following day, Jimmy had a similarly defining experience while guarding a female prisoner. What he was ordered to do went against every value he had been raised to believe in. He could justify burning houses: they harbored the enemy. Without thinking, he could kill those who fired at him. But holding an unarmed woman and her baby at gunpoint was morally reprehensible. He knew he didn't want to kill her, and if he had been ordered to do it, he might not have been able to pull the trigger. While Jimmy guarded the woman and child, several of the men in his squad questioned some of the children rounded up in the village. Children were favored for impromptu interrogation because US Intelligence officers thought they were less inclined to lie because they had yet to be indoctrinated by the Viet Cong. Sensing the children's hostility, it suddenly occurred to Jimmy that if the woman were able to get his weapon, she might kill him. So he tightened his grip and "held his gun a bit closer to her head because [he] was told she was a VC and she could shoot a rifle just like a man." It was the most disturbing situation he had encountered so far. He later described the event in several letters, each time remarking that his parents should have seen the young woman's expression as he held his gun to her head.

When the mother and her child were helicoptered out of the area, Jimmy knew what was going to happen to her village. As the encounter in the village demonstrated, the military's method of winning "hearts and minds" was counterproductive. Jimmy confessed to his father, "I think about the war and how it will come to an end over here, my CO told us things are no better now than 3 years ago, but people back in the states are getting mad so the newspapers put in what they think sounds good but never tell you the real things that happen, I don't think the war will end here, just because we might stop fighting, that doesn't mean [the Vietnamese] will . . . . Don't worry Dad, I am still just a beer drinker, and that's all I'll be, not a [politician or philosopher]."

Many soldiers who were becoming disillusioned with the brutalities and the indecisive combat turned against the military mission and focused on achieving personal aims. In a letter to the editor of the *Berkeley Daily Gazette*, Specialist Rod Baldra, angered by the actions of college protestors and feeling abandoned by his country, wrote: "Many of us [in Vietnam are] engaged in our own civic action programs on our own time. It might be giving undernourished children C-rations, teaching a teenage boy a little English or helping an old man tie a bag of rice to his bicycle."[20] Jimmy, like Baldra, began by helping the children. Many GIs were dismayed by the living conditions of Vietnamese children. Similar to Jimmy's own reactions when he arrived in Vietnam, one soldier commented on how they ran around naked and disorderly, while another was surprised they even survived to adulthood, "living like such animals."[21] Yet, many troops felt that the children ought to be helped. George Williams, who served with the First Infantry Division outside of Saigon just north of Jimmy's position, wrote, "There are a few kids who hang around, some with no parents. I feel sorry for them. I do things to make them laugh, and they call me 'dinky dow' (crazy). But it makes me feel good. I hope that's one reason why we're here, to secure a future for them. It seems to be the only justification I can think of for the things I have done."[22]

The relationships that developed between American GIs, who were concerned with the welfare of the many children orphaned by the war, were some of the most significant in a conflict in which Vietnamese civilians very often became targets of military assaults.

The lost parents, whose absence Williams regrets, were most likely victims of American aggression, and for many soldiers that alone was enough to push back against the ongoing depredations. As Private First Class Dan Bailey, assigned to the 101st Airborne Division, explained to his mother, "I went down to the orphanage the other day, and these little kids are pitiful. They sleep on plain floors and don't get hardly anything to eat. The reason I want you to tell everyone to help is because I feel I may have killed some of their parents and it makes me feel sick to know they [now have] nothing."[23] Another soldier, Bruce McInnes, a chief warrant officer with a helicopter company, wrote, "These children are victims of American terrorism [and their parents have died] defending their country." He continued, "I am ashamed because we [Americans] take our good fortune for granted, wasting so much that these people, especially the children in this orphanage, so desperately need."[24]

Jimmy expressed similar concerns soon after the episode involving the female prisoner. As if it were an act of penance, he described a rather different response he had in an encounter with a group of Vietnamese children: "When we were eating lunch along the road, while eating all the little kids would come out, I just could not eat in front of them, at first I could, but one of the little girls looked like our sister Barbara, then I thought this could be one of them, this could be us, so I gave them everything I had." In a later letter he mentioned the situation again, this time addressing his sister Barbara, "I have seen so many little cute girl's here, around your age just the other day, I thought I met you, down in one of those small town's, so I gave you all my lunch . . . " Jimmy could no longer think of the Vietnamese as "gooks, slants, or dinks." He had come to see that his world was not so different from theirs. He included his Batman pin in the letter for his little brother Joe. He felt he'd outgrown it.

McNamara's Predicament

General Westmoreland's upbeat assessment of the outcome of the first major engagement of American forces against regular NVA regiments in the Ia Drang valley bolstered the consensus of the inner circle of Lyndon Johnson's advisors that direct military intervention was the only way to salvage the Saigon regime. But reports of surprisingly heavy US casualties, the enemy's ability to withdraw its units in good order, and the continuing deterioration of the political situation in the South gave Lyndon Johnson cause for concern. Soon after the battle ended in mid-November 1965, he ordered Robert McNamara, who was conferring with allied leaders in Europe, to return to Washington via South Vietnam in order to evaluate the situation in country firsthand. Following a pattern that had worked for the military on earlier fact-finding missions by McNamara and other high-ranking administration officials, a well-choreographed tour was arranged for the Secretary of Defense. Westmoreland, DePuy, and other US staff officers brandished an array of statistics from estimates of NVA infiltration rates to kill-ratios to appeal to McNamara's fixation on quantification as the ultimate measure of effectiveness. Above all, they sought to demonstrate that Air Mobility, with an increasing emphasis on search and destroy missions, was the key to repelling regular forces from the North and defeating the guerillas in the South. But the American generals and the South Vietnamese leaders McNamara consulted were unanimous in stressing that substantially more troops and weapons were needed to meet the multiple challenges that communist operations posed, and win a decisive victory over the forces determined to destroy the Saigon regime.

Perhaps because McNamara had been through the rounds of well-coordinated presentations and highly selective consultations arranged for his earlier visits, he was more wary of the overly optimistic prognoses of the generals and officials in Vietnam than he had been in the past.[25] From the time of Diem's rule and Paul Harkin's tenure as the head of the American military mission, McNamara had rightly distrusted the statistical information sent from MACV (the Military Assistance Command Vietnam) to be fed into the Pentagon's computers. On his visit in November 1965, he found his conversations with several of the Marine commanders who were actually engaged in the Ia Drang clashes even more troubling. The field officers he consulted, particularly the lead commander Lt. Colonel Harold Moore, were clearly impressed with the courage and tenacity displayed by NVA fighters, despite the overwhelming superiority of the firepower US forces could unleash. The officers' openly voiced dissent arising from Washington's refusal to allow American forces to pursue retreating North Vietnamese regiments into Cambodia should also have alerted McNamara to a major constraint that communist forces would exploit with impunity.[26] On the broader situation in the South, his reports to the president made it clear that he was aware of the continuing political disarray in Saigon and the provincial capitals. He was also troubled by the repeated, demoralizing setbacks suffered by ARVN soldiers.

On his flight home McNamara began the draft of a memo for the president that summarized his intensifying misgivings about the military buildup that his long-standing advocacy in White House policy meetings had done so much to enable. McNamara's uncharacteristic indecisiveness regarding policy toward Vietnam was already evident in the Kennedy years. In agreement with JFK, McNamara did not initially see the fate of the Saigon regime as a concern that vitally affected America's national security. Consequently, he had urged the president on a number of occasions to reduce significantly the still relatively small number of American advisors in South Vietnam. As the most imposing and soon most famous member of Kennedy's cabinet, the views of the confident Secretary of Defense on the deteriorating situation in Indochina mattered. The young president and his brother Bobby had openly wooed the head of the Ford Motor Company to become a major player in the Kennedy administration. McNamara was widely touted in the press as the most brilliant member of Kennedy's "brain trust." His service as an Air Force planner during World War II, his achievements as a student and later faculty member at Harvard University, and his success as an innovative

A rather rare photo of a weary, and perhaps worried, Robert McNamara in the midst of a very taxing inspection tour on a hot, humid Vietnamese afternoon, November 1965.

corporate executive all served to enhance McNamara's reputation as the person to turn to when difficult decisions had to be made. His dismissal of prognoses based on personal experience, emotional appeals, or arguments that ran counter to his empirical data made him a formidable opponent in policy debates.

Even though the political and military situation in South Vietnam continued to deteriorate despite ever more massive infusions of American troops, weaponry, and dollars, McNamara usually kept his doubts to himself. He shared them privately with a few close associates, particularly his assistant secretary, John McNaughton. On the basis of the troubling combat and political trajectories that Pentagon statistics revealed, they concluded that incremental escalations could not win a war against an adversary willing to match each increase whatever the cost. Even then, McNamara balked at going public with frank assessments of these disheartening trends and the bloody stalemate that was building in Vietnam. But his post-Ia Drang briefings gradually forced him to set aside his sense of loyalty to the president, and even his own ambitions. He began to argue *within the administration* for a measured retreat from the quagmire.

In a memo to the president, which McNamara drafted as he crossed the Pacific and amplified on his return, he provided succinct policy recommendations that were based on a clear-minded calculus of the odds for eventual defeat and humiliation if the United States persisted in its quest for outright victory in Vietnam. He argued that the pacification campaign in the South was "thoroughly stalled," and there was no sign that an effective, or even stable regime would emerge in Saigon anytime soon. He admitted that the "willingness of the communist forces to stand and fight, even in large-scale engagements" with far more technologically advanced American forces was far stronger than anticipated. Equally ominously, McNamara estimated that the NLF-NVA coalition's staying power in a prolonged war of attrition was greater than that of the United States, and he predicted that their advantage would increase over time.

In considerable detail he compared estimates of existing and projected American, ARVN, and allied regiments and battalions with those mustered by the NVA and NLF, and concluded that even with major escalations, the US coalition could not achieve the 3:1 advantage that the military continued to insist was necessary to defeat a guerrilla insurgency. He estimated that due to the growing influx of troops from the North and rising levels of guerrilla recruitment, 400,000 US troops would be needed by the end of 1966, and an additional 200,000 in 1967 just "to hold our present geographical positions." He projected that the number of GIs killed in combat would rise to one thousand a month in 1966 and even higher in 1967—but still "not guarantee success." Having demonstrated that a military victory was highly unlikely, McNamara recommended that the president seek negotiations that would allow the United States to make "the quickest possible exit" from Vietnam and secure America's "withdrawal with honor."[27]

Despite McNaughton's urgings, McNamara refused to make the case for a phased withdrawal in either congressional hearings or in meetings of Johnson's inner circle of advisors. In fact, realizing that he would be confronted by a growing consensus of military and civilian leaders in favor of further troop increases, he sought to slow rather than halt the buildup. While continuing to go along with the expansion of the ground war and assuring the American people that he could see "light at the end of the tunnel," McNamara lobbied in closed policy sessions and private conversations for yet another pause in the bombing of North

Vietnam. Soon after the start of the Rolling Thunder bombing campaign in February, he had concluded that there were too few strategic targets north of the 17th parallel and too much aid flowing from the Soviet bloc and China for aerial assaults to compel the communist leadership in Hanoi to seek a compromise settlement. Troubled by rising levels of Vietnamese civilian casualties, and well aware that post–World War II studies found that bombing tended to strengthen the resistance of targeted populations, McNamara commissioned a study to explore the possibility of building a barrier along the 17th parallel to block the infiltration of NVA forces into South Vietnam. But it was soon clear that the cost of construction would be prohibitive, and that the "fence" would do little to deter enemy forces unless it was extended across neutral Laos and Cambodia to block the main pathways that made up the Ho Chi Minh Trail.

McNamara never submitted his pessimistic memo to Lyndon Johnson, but his role in persuading the president to temporally halt the bombing, which the North Vietnamese leadership subsequently dismissed as a ploy, eroded the defense secretary's standing in the administration's inner circle of advisors. As the influence of the Joint Chiefs and Westmoreland on the president's decisions increased, Johnson's private consultations with McNamara became less frequent. Gradually LBJ turned McGeorge Bundy and other civilian advisors who shared his conviction that he had put the nation on the right course to win the war in Vietnam, and thereby check communist expansion in Southeast Asia.[28]

Unfortunately for Johnson and the newly ascendant hardliners in the administration, especially the ever-upbeat Walt Rostow, McNamara's grim assessment of the mounting costs and likely outcomes of the US interventions in Vietnam were on the mark. The political situation in the South continued to unravel. Buddhist

In innumerable sessions before congress and with reporters, McNamara set out the Johnson administration's arguments for "staying the course" in Vietnam.

and anti-government protests, and the draconian repression they provoked, further shrank the base of the unstable military governments in Saigon. Equally ominously, NLF guerrillas and NVA fighters regularly routed ARVN forces, and steadily expanded communist control over the countryside. The escalating influx of American combat troops was met by significant alterations in the NLF-NVA approach to the war that yet again demonstrated the remarkable capacity of the Vietnamese to devise effective ways to counter the seemingly overwhelming advantages in weaponry and war-related assets wielded by foreign invaders.

Contrary to the then current American delusion that communist regimes formed a monolithic global phalanx controlled from Moscow, even within Vietnam there were major policy disagreements between the NLF in the South and among influential leaders in the fractious Politburo in Hanoi. The intertwined political and military strategies adopted by America's communist adversaries were decided only after months of deliberations that often devolved into heated debates among the various factions in both Hanoi and the South. Party leaders in the North ultimately reconciled the differences through a plan for protracted war that adroitly exploited the vulnerabilities of the US superpower. Drafted under the supervision of Le Duan, the top official in the Politburo who favored the Maoist option of military engagement over the Soviets' advocacy of peaceful reunification, their plan assured the NLF that it would not be abandoned by Hanoi. In terms of intra-party dynamics, this meant a decisive rejection of the insistence of the faction led by Troung Chinh that in order for the process of "social construction" to succeed in the North, the NLF and its allies had to fight the war for liberation on a "self-sufficient" basis. With the NLF clearly in mind, Le Duan proposed that channels for negotiations would be *officially* left open, but that no serious proposals would even be considered until all American combat troops were withdrawn from the South.

To retain the increasingly vocal support of neutral countries, and even some of America's allies, as well as to bolster the accelerating protest movements against the war in the United States itself, Hanoi did not explicitly rule out the possibility of a neutral transitional government in Saigon. But that option was clearly no longer acceptable to the communist leadership in either North or South. American military interventions would be met by increases in guerrilla forces and the continuing infiltration of regular NVA units at levels that would match or surpass each US escalation. Though acutely aware of the mounting costs in lives as well as resources that might have been devoted to national development, the majority of the Vietnamese communist leadership opted to continue the war of liberation and unification with a Churchillian fervor best captured by Nguyen Huu Tho. Formerly a Saigon lawyer and president of the NLF, Tho exhorted his comrades to:

> Point your rifles at the heads of the US aggressors. Strike night and day. Strike when it rains as well as when it is sunny. Strike at the enemy in the forests, on the mountains, in the delta, and in the cities. Strike at the enemy in large as well as small battles. All of you rush ahead and strike deadly blows at the heads of the US aggressors in order to exterminate them. [29]

Finding His Own Mission
March–April 1966

Operation Honolulu brought home to Jimmy that the war in which he was engaged was very different than the one he had expected to fight. He now realized that his mission had become an absurd paradox: he was burning villages to liberate the Vietnamese peasants. Although he couldn't escape the war's contradictions, Jimmy resolved to create his own mission. He took to calling patrols "field problems," and battalion operations would become genuine "good-will tours." In the process, his responses to the Vietnamese people became personal. An abiding patriotism was now tempered by the best of American ideals, most especially protecting women and children, and the Catholic obligation to uplift the underprivileged, which made him determined to seek ways to improve the lives of the "farmers." He was not alone in these pursuits.

On the last day of the weeklong mission, a telling exchange occurred: "I woke up early in the morning and had to go to this house and see if any young men lived there, there was just a little old lady there." She had gestured for him to come inside and offered him something to eat. "She wanted me to stay, so I did," he wrote. The meeting could not have lasted long. But in that brief encounter, the two sat looking at each other, "eating, and drinking cups of tea." Later that day while checking out dwellings in another village, Jimmy "mistakenly" forgot to pull the pin on the grenade he tossed into a thatched house. He later "got hell" for the lapse, and much to his embarrassment, he slipped and fell into the river on his way back to the APC. His thoughts were elsewhere.

Jimmy's interactions with the peasants during Operation Honolulu revealed contradictions in his attitudes toward the Vietnamese and how the war he was fighting was affecting them, and him. The day he returned to base he was immediately placed on guard duty. The incessant rain did little to improve his mood, and his sergeant's bravado aggravated him. He had trouble confronting his growing unease and how to resolve it. His thoughts turned to home:

> *The radio you sent work's real good, they play rock & roll between 4 and 6 every night, guess what was the first song I heard, Elvis singing wear my ring around your neck, it was just like sitting home, in the den, listening to the record-player . . . how is everyone doing in school? I hope nobody is failing, for once girl's, don't follow in my footstep's, at least not as school go's . . . I got my hair cut real short. . . mommy, I always think of you every night before going to bed, remember when I was young, and I went to sleep with my socks on all the of the time, well over here, you got to keep your boots on all night, well . . . don't laugh, but do you think I could still become a priest? For some reason lately I been think*[ing] *of it again, look kid's stop all the laughing before I get mad, I know you got to have gone get and education to high school but I'll bull shit my way in.*

By the end of the week the ground had become so saturated that his foxhole, which he shared with Sergeant Sanchez, "turned into a swimming pool." It didn't seem to matter how many sandbags they stacked around the hole, the water kept pouring in. He managed to save his radio and a handful of salt water taffy his aunt had sent from Atlantic City before the candy got washed away. He sucked on one of the candies as he stared across no man's land to the banks of Ben Muong River where the floodwaters were rising. That's where the VC always came from. By evening, the base's newly acquired 175mm cannons opened fire, hurling their 147-pound shells as far as twenty miles. At the push of a button and turn of a few knobs, the machine automatically loaded and rammed the shell into the breech. The detonation was so strong that it created its own breeze, and anyone standing a few yards from the blast could feel the earth tremble. Though the bombardments happened at least one hundred times a day, the noise was hard to get use to. The guns were supposed to make "any self respecting VC snuggle just a bit deeper in his tunnel at night."

After they had a few beers, the sergeant started to talk about his home life. Jimmy listened inattentively, and soon drifted off into thoughts of a future in which he returned to school and was happily married at "29 or 30 to someone who'd been lucky enough to meet [him]." Then he bought a house with the money he'd saved, and retired in his late fifties. These thoughts were most likely brought on after Jimmy read in the camp newspaper about the Veterans' Readjustment Benefits Act. When signing it, President Johnson praised, "[the] brave Americans who serve . . . in Vietnam and the Dominican Republic," as "the very best men that our country has ever produced," who were thereby entitled to "not just gratitude, but concrete help in getting a fresh start with educational assistance, with medical care, with guarantees that permitted them to buy homes to live in."[30]

Not far from Jimmy, Nathaniel (Nat) McLean, a native of Zebulon, North Carolina, and Leo Hinterlong, a 22-year-old from Cincinnati, sat in a bunker. They didn't talk much. A transistor radio was on. Nancy Sinatra's "These Boots Were Made for Walkin'" was playing. Nat was resting his head on his steel helmet trying to get some sleep, while Leo stood watch. Leo took out a letter from his best friend's girl. He had read it so much that the fold in the paper was soft and starting to tear. A reporter from the camp's weekly paper, *Tropic Lightning News*, had dropped in to do an interview with them. He wanted to talk about "bugs and bunker life," but he soon found out that time spent out on guard duty was more about loneliness. Seeing that Leo was reading a letter, the reporter asked if he had a girlfriend back home and if she wrote much, assuming that's whose letter he was reading. "Yes," he said. "Well, not that much . . . She wrote one time and told me she had found another boy friend." There was an awkward pause. The reporter then looked at Nat who quickly remarked, "I really get down in the dumps if I miss getting mail a day or two. I sure hope they have some mail for me tonight. I'm expecting some pictures from home. My wife has been keeping me up on my favorite TV shows."

The reporter had to stop the interview several times and wait until the artillery blasts ended. He often lost his train of thought between barrages. Nat repeated his question: "How long were we here before we saw our first action? Two hours. A guy went down to the river and the VC opened up. He couldn't get out." The sun started to sink into the rice paddies in the west. One of the company's squad leaders stuck his head into the bunker: "I want you boys to keep alert." Leo turned off his radio. "I'm glad I bought this thing," he said. "It's not too bad in here with this. It keeps us up with the world." "It can get real lonely here," Nat said. "You have so much time to think. You think about things you haven't thought about in 10 years. I thought about some girl I used to go with in grade school. She's probably married now and has a flock of kids."

There was no moon that night, and that always worried those on watch, especially if it was raining. "I've never seen anybody shoot at me yet," Leo claimed, "but I've had those bullets really hugging my head. The closest I've seen the enemy is when they capture one." When the darkness came, they talked in whispers. The silences between questions grew longer and longer. When they ran out of things to say, they all just listened to the sounds of the night and tried to keep still. Occasionally the reporter would rustle around and take swats at the mosquitoes on his neck. Then someone called in a high hushed voice, "Hey." Nat responded, "Who's there?" "It's Wherling," the voice replied. "What're you doing out there?" Nat asked. "Some of our sandbags fell in. I'm looking for the command post . . . " "Go behind the bunker," Nat growled. And then it was silent again. Leo went back on watch, and then it was Nat's turn. All of a sudden trip flares blazed about fifty yards from the bunker. Nat quickly grabbed his grenade launcher. The space in front of them was lit up in a deep orange glow. Each man narrowed his eyes, and with a fixed stare looked out into the distance. Nothing—no rattling of machine guns, no roar of artillery, no thudding mortars. It was strangely quiet. Then the light slowly disappeared and it was dark again.[31]

The short pause between missions did little to relieve Jimmy's anxieties and frustration. By early April, he had paid several visits to his unit's chaplain, Father Clarence Olszewski, who told him to be sure to come to Mass on Easter. Weary of the tension and increasing violence, Jimmy was beginning to seek a way out—even if for a short while—and again turned to home:

> *"Last night they let us see the movies again, guess what was playing (get yourself a college girl) . . . I have a little bad new's for you girl's, you to mom, I started smoking, not a whole lot, but every once in a while (almost 21 now so don't you all talk about me) remember I said I'll make PFC when I get here, well they told us all a lot of shit, you got to have 8 month's in so this is my 8th month now, so either*

> *this month or next's* [I should get a pay raise] . . . *If there was not a war here, it would be a great place to spend your army tour . . . I put in my leave the other day, you are allowed 7 day's, I think every 6 month's, I put down the Philippine's or Japan, (no I can't come home) because there are only 12 places were you can go, and Runnemede, New Jersey was not on the list, I asked for it in July . . . keep me in your prayers, and I will always pray for you people to . . . P.S. you should have seen me holding that gun to her head.*"

For Jimmy and many other soldiers, their growing disillusionment with the war made them a liability to themselves and their squad mates. The minute they began to think about what they were doing in Vietnam, they would move a little less quickly on patrol and pause before shooting.

By 1966 it had become clear that the war was taking an intolerable toll on the youth of America and the US intervention had failed to shake the determination of the youth of Vietnam to give up their fight for the full independence and the unification of Vietnam.

CHAPTER 6

The Price of Attrition

"The thing we value most deeply is not money, but men. We have multiplied the capability of our men [with firepower]. It's expensive in dollars, but cheap in life."

—ROBERT MCNAMARA QUOTED IN JAMES WILLIAM GIBSON, *The Perfect War: Technowar in Vietnam* (Boston: Atlantic Monthly, 1986).

"We as Americans, who considered ourselves the exceptions to history, showed ourselves to be as fallible as the rest of humanity; we could do evil as easily as we could do good. We were all too humanly arrogant in the hubris of our moments in the sun."

—NEIL SHEEHAN, *After the War Was Over: Hanoi and Saigon* (New York: Random House, 1992).

"History has proved and will continue to prove that the people's war is the most effective magic weapon in dealing with the American imperialist aggressor and its lackeys . . . The American imperialist charging everywhere like an unrestrained bull, will be burned to ashes by the very fire ignited by itself."

—LIN BIAO, Marshal of the People's Republic of China, translated from Chinese, 1965.

April was the deadliest month for B Company. May would not be much better. Jimmy would spend the next eight weeks almost entirely in the field. Each day a grind that chipped away, little by little, at his physical endurance and determination to succeed in carrying out his personal mission. And the nights, which left him alone with his thoughts, tested the limits of how much he could take before trying to escape from what would become the fiercest fighting he had yet to experience. The rapidly multiplying search and destroy missions carried out by Jimmy's Fifth Mechanized Infantry Regiment encapsulated the fatal flaws of General William Westmoreland's approach to the war. North Vietnamese and NLF strategists and fighters repeatedly exploited the openings provided by these miscalculations in their efforts to withstand the massive assaults unleashed by the global superpower. Although Westmoreland and the officers in his command had a better grasp of the military situation in country than the civilian leaders and Joint Chiefs who sought to manage US interventions from Washington, virtually no one at either level knew anything significant about Vietnamese history and culture. Even though they were readily available in English, neither Westmoreland nor most of his subordinate officers had bothered to study seriously Mao Zedong or Vo Nguyen Giap's seminal works on guerrilla warfare. Instead of drawing on Asian precedents, decisions about how to fight the Vietnamese communists were based on a mix of long-standing assumptions about the factors that had made for American success in past wars.

Surviving the Stalemate
April 1966

It was Easter Sunday. After Mass, Jimmy walked to the company assembly area where his commander, Ted Jagosz, held a meeting to introduce First Lieutenant Frank D'Amico who would take charge of B Company's Third Platoon. D'Amico was exhilarated to be on his first field operation in Vietnam. He had finally broken free of the boredom at Headquarters, or what was commonly called "the Puzzle Palace," where as a liaison officer he was in charge of emptying the "ash and trash." But having been trained as an airborne paratrooper, and stationed in Santo Domingo during the recent US intervention into the Dominican Republic's Civil War, D'Amico was well aware of the dangers of combat.[1]

Jimmy had the day off. He was killing time in his tent not far from the guard post. It wasn't long before Sanchez came by and started bragging about "how great of a lover he was," and how as soon as he got his pass, he was going right to Saigon to lay all the pretty girls. "If you want to have fun over here, you have to get in with the right guys," Jimmy wrote his father. But jokingly he admitted that he didn't have "what you could call a real class friend because he was afraid they would want to borrow money"—perhaps to use on whoring. It was "common knowledge" that "almost every girl fucks over here, from about 10 cents on up," Jimmy told his friend Gerry. "[But] I don't bother with any of them, I'll wait until I get home. . . . " His prudishness was also revealed in a letter to his mother, "I got Louise some real sexy night clothes, I felt kind of bad buying them. . . . "

A few days earlier Jimmy's girlfriend, Louise, had finally responded to his request for her to send him a "sexy photo" with her next letter. He wanted something to remember her by and to show off to the guys. When he opened the letter, he found a poem: "You are in my heart/so Please don't do anything to break it." She also included a photo of herself as a little girl at the beach in a bikini. He laughed, and told her she was a "real smart ass," and then hid the picture under the lid of his footlocker. It was where he kept his photos from home, his bible and a notepad, an old camera he had won in a card game, and a pair of boots for his brother to wear on hunting trips. He also managed to cram in a wool smoking jacket for his father, and two silk dresses—one yellow and the other pale blue—which he purchased a while back for his mother and Louise. He hadn't sent them home yet because he couldn't find the right paper to wrap them in.

Jimmy was worn down, as were so many of his squad mates, and he had trouble "finding things to talk about it" in his letters. He possibly felt that his stories were too gruesome and painful to write home about, such as a recent incident that involved several men from B Company who were caught raping a young Vietnamese captive behind an APC.[2] He was even reluctant to share combat stories with his friends. In a letter he'd written to Gerry on Easter, he focused mainly on past exploits, and tried to reassure his buddy that death would not come for him in Vietnam: "I really miss you and Louise. I get a little home sick when I think of the shore, and all the crazy times we put in together but it won't be long balls before we get back into action again, because it will take more than a VC to get me, or the weather, 110 to 130 [degrees] each day, I think it will be old age that will be my end . . . " But he lacked confidence in those claims—possibly thinking about the casualties in recent operations, especially Operation Circle Pines about which he said nothing more than "I have not written lately [because] we had to go out for 8 day's, I'll tell you all about it when I get home, I don't think I'll forget for a long time." He sought the reassurance of prayer, pleading, "Gerry, pray for me, because I sure need pray's."

The primary mission of Circle Pines was for the Seventh ARVN Regiment to push through the village of Phu Hoa Dong, while elements of the Fifth Mechanized Infantry set up ambushes in the heavily forested boundaries of the village. In the past, when the GIs raided the area the "VC would withdraw and exfiltrate" in small groups to safe regions in the Ho Bo Woods and the Iron Triangle. Then, to disrupt the Americans from immediately counterattacking, they would deploy sporadic sniper fire and set up booby traps along their lines of retreat. But this time, or so the planners of Circle Pines thought, the soldiers waiting in the jungle would be ready to block the guerrillas along their escape routes. The day before they set off, Jimmy's regimental commander briefed his men on the operation, and gave an order similar to the one made famous at the battle of Bunker Hill: "[no man will] shoot any VC unless [he is] close enough to see the whites of their eyes."

Phu Hoa Dong was not a small town. It would take days for ARVN troops to cover the terrain and, as one soldier noted, the Americans didn't have enough men in the battalion to properly contain all the houses and tunnels in a week's time. In order to get to Phu Hoa Dong, the US and ARVN forces had to cross over the Ben Muong River and through the hostile Filhol Rubber Plantation. As they advanced through the plantation, two APCs from C Company got stuck in the mud. Stranded, they came under attack, and one soldier was killed. At the same time Company A was ambushed. Two APCs hit makeshift mines recycled from unexploded US 175mm shells, which American artillerymen had lobbed into the area on the previous evening. The force of one explosion was so great that the twelve-ton track was flipped over, killing several GIs and severely wounding four. The other track was badly damaged, and three of the men onboard were bleeding profusely. One of the wounded was the platoon leader who kept shouting, "Call in a damn dust off!" But the helicopters never came. The landing zone was "too hot." So the survivors were left to tend to the wounded and pick up their dead and wait for relief. They counted each body—one was missing—placed them in rubber sacks, and stripped down the track to its shell, taking all the supplies and munitions that were salvageable so the VC couldn't get them. They then pulled back and sought cover. After nightfall the Vietnamese attacked them relentlessly. When morning came, the recovery vehicle sent from Cu Chi to tow in the wrecked APC finally showed up. That's when they found the cook, the missing man, crushed beneath the iron and steel, half sunk in oily mud.

On the following day, a track in B Company hit a mine. The explosion ignited the gas tanks and burned a man alive. During the firefight that followed, Jimmy's friend and squad mate, John "J.W." McGough, was struck by shrapnel. The next two days were equally as devastating. Seven men were badly burned when a mortar round accidently went off inside their track. Another four soldiers were killed and twenty were wounded in a fierce skirmish. When the helicopters delivered the broken bodies to the surgical unit in Bien Hoa, the doctors had them stripped, and the nurses pumped painkillers and plasma into their veins. Then they were sent to the shock and resuscitation ward where the amputations, skin-graphs, and probing for shards of metal began. When their burns were wrapped and their wounds stitched shut, they were placed in hospital beds and wheeled to the recovery room. Those who were severely wounded lay there with flushed faces and glazed looks in their eyes, and sometimes a medal would be pinned on their mattress. Some of the others, those who had only minor injuries, often demanded that they be discharged and returned to the field.

The Americans had some "success" during the mission. The Fifth Regiment's after action report recorded that forty VC were confirmed killed and estimated that fifty-seven were either dead or dying from their wounds. But the battalion as a whole had conflicting casualty totals. It had become apparent to the higher-ups at division headquarters that the reports reaching their desks were not accurate, and the field officers for the operation were reprimanded. To avoid further false information, and to ensure, as one soldier wrote, " . . . [that] some gung-ho [army] lifer would make a stupid promotion,"[3] some commanders of the Fifth Mechanized Regiment experimented with a policy that boiled desired outcomes down to the essential: "if a soldier killed a Viet Cong and his body and weapon were recovered, he was entitled to a three day pass to Saigon."[4] Division commanders also required that writers of after action reports provide specifics regarding the number of rounds, the caliber,

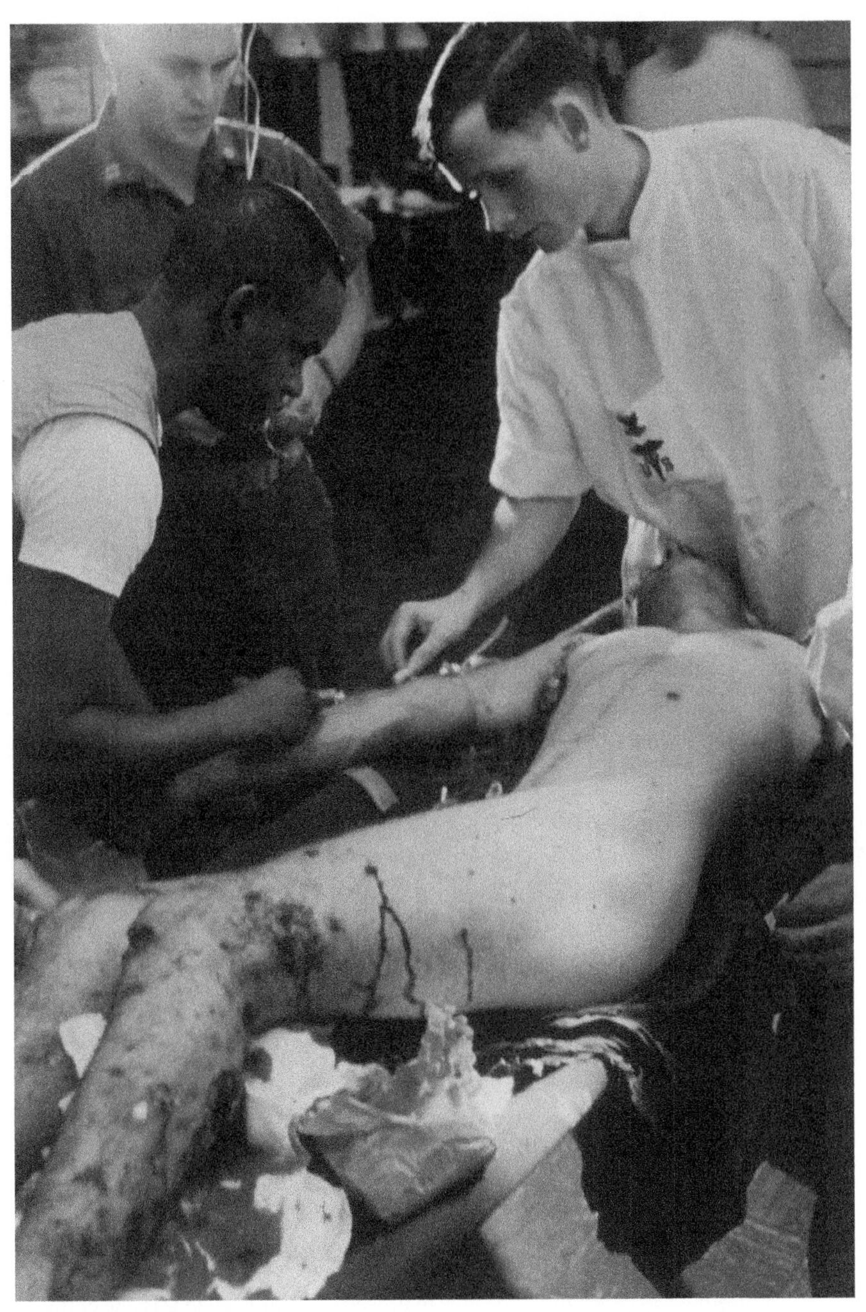

A soldier who has sustained heavy shrapnel wounds in his legs and chest is given treatment in the shock and resuscitation ward of a M.A.S.H. unit.

and the make and model of each weapon they confiscated. No longer was "small arms ammunition" sufficient. To mock the new order, some units took to reporting the capture of miscellaneous items, such as "2 bags of peanuts," "1 rubber sandal," "2 typewriters," and "a pair of gloves."

After Jimmy returned from Circle Pines, his platoon was immediately ordered back into the bush on April 7. Because he had not written to his parents in days, he jotted down a note that he managed to send home just hours before going back into action: "Mom. Dad. Not a lot of time, been very busy, will write when I get a chance, we were out in the jungle for almost 2 week's it was only suppose to be 2 day's, but we ran into trouble, let me know in your letter when you get my paycheck." As part of Operation Kahuku, Jimmy's unit was to conduct a reconnaissance patrol in the Filhol Rubber Plantation. Having recovered from his wounds, 27-year-old Captain Ellison Vickery, who would soon receive a second Silver Star for bravery, led B Company back into combat. On route to the Filhol, Vickery ordered the first platoon under Lieutenant Bob Whaley to stay behind at the village of Bao Cap and "seal off" the area at the same location he had previously been ordered to hold during Circle Pines. The lieutenant later recalled that his unit ambushed Viet Cong fighters "four or five times, [and] each encounter was with a small group, 2 to 4 individuals. Most would not surrender when challenged and although armed, would run and be shot. Each time we would take some branches and clean up the blood on the dusty trails and reset the ambush."[5]

On April 9, Vickery's two remaining platoons headed to a trench line on the northern edge of the plantation. He was using coordinates that a communist defector had given for the location of his former unit. Jimmy's platoon would be the spearhead of a frontal attack on the trench. Third Platoon, which was to the right of Jimmy's, was supposed to support the assault and block enemy troops from leaving the far side of the entrenchment. The defector's information was correct: the guerrillas were there, and they were heavily armed and well prepared. A thirty-five minute firefight ensued. "For the first twenty minutes," Jagosz wrote, "the [Vietnamese] forces whaled away . . . having machine guns, automatic rifles, and M-79 grenade launchers. Tens of thousands of rounds were exchanged" from both sides at a distance of no more than sixty-five feet.[6] As Jimmy's platoon neared the bunker, Third Platoon failed to move up in support. The VC made good use of their recoilless antitank guns at close range, forcing the Americans to fall back and regroup.

A meeting was called to decide how to proceed. Jimmy's squad was one of the few still intact. His platoon had started out with fifty-three men in February, and was now down to twenty-five. Despite the lack of manpower, a consensus was reached—they would assault the trench again up the middle. Most of the Vietnamese forces had retreated when B Company "bombed the hell" out of the enemy's defensive position on its second assault, with the Third Platoon still not moving in to support them. When Jimmy's squad reached the trench, they dismounted and began shooting into the dark passageways built into the fortification. The platoon pursued the attack all the way to the Saigon River, but it was soon bogged down by thickets and marshes along the waterway. One APC driver had underestimated the depth of a gully, flipped his track over, and it caught fire. The retreating enemy slipped away.

When Jimmy's company returned to the Cu Chi base camp, Jagosz questioned the leader of Third Platoon about his failure to support the assault on the earthworks. "I didn't see anything," the platoon leader said. But he had seen it; the whole skirmish had unfolded right in front of him. He heard it too: the gunfire, the explosions, the yelling. The mission marked his last days in the field. Jagosz later wrote, he had a case of the "'short timer' jitters."[7] He was worried about getting killed right before being promoted to a noncombat advisory role. When he left, Frank D'Amico took charge of Third Platoon.

Jimmy spent most of his Easter holiday sewing his clothes and writing to his "fan club." His "Easter Letters" set a pattern for what he would write about during the rest of his time in Vietnam. Getting to know his squad mates better led him to reflect on social issues at home, especially those relating to class, poverty, and discrimination. Several friends from the Deep South had grown up relatively poor, which was the reason why they volunteered or got drafted. They envied him when he talked about his family's business or described his "big house with a farm and a concrete swimming pool." They had trouble imagining a house with two bathrooms and a color television set. These guys think we're rich, he told his brother Georgie, but I haven't yet told them about the time "a few Easters ago you had to go to church first, come home, take the suit off, then I had to put it on and go." Jimmy came to realize that the war was being fought mainly by the poor and working classes, which led him to conclude that if you don't go to college, you go to Vietnam. But that conviction changed when Georgie received a draft notice. Jimmy told him that it must have been a mistake, and added half jokingly, "this place is for men not college boys."

He later wrote to his sisters explaining that the Vietnamese people were poor just like the soldiers he befriended. He reminded them, "We have a lot to be proud of and thankful for, you wont believe how some of my friends live, we really have something at home girls compared to what they got. . . . you always's think the grass is a lot greener on the other side, but then you find out it is not . . . so remember [that] before you [all] run away. . . . " Jimmy had also begun to question the racial divisions within the military, especially after he made friends with African Americans. Though he did not comment on this at length, he recognized that racism was wrong and something needed to be done. He even invited a black man from Brooklyn, Larry Van Clief, to visit his family after they were back in the States, an offer that he had also extended to his best friends from Ohio—John W. McGough and Samuel Harris.

Jimmy and his friend Larry Van Clief passing time in camp.

Jimmy often mentioned his "black friends" in his letters to his family, knowing that his remarks would not sit well with his father. In sending photos of them home, Jimmy made it clear that skin color was not an issue for him. In answering his father's questions about loneliness, he wondered if his "black friends" who didn't seem to have any one to write to "could become pen pals" with his sisters. The day before he set out on Operation Kalamazoo, Jimmy summed up what he had come to realize through serving with a diverse group of Americans: "Over here you learn to live with a lot of different people, white, black, yellow, pink, blue, etc, I found out it is not the color of a person's body, but how the person himself is . . . " His desire to learn more—or as he put it "giving it the old drop-out try"—was growing steadily, and he had begun to focus on the Vietnamese. He realized that intelligence could be measured in more ways than he had previously thought. He even considered reenlisting for a few more years so he could "see the world."

An Unwinnable War

William Westmoreland's stress on firepower meshed well with what had emerged in the US Civil War, and was more fully developed in the century that followed into what historian Russell Weigley dubbed "The American Way of War."[8] Weigley's formulation denoted combat strategies aimed at annihilating enemy forces by deploying a combination of advanced weaponry, war materiel, and logistical support, all of which were designed to be overwhelming by virtue of their sheer magnitude. Westmoreland's confidence in massive firepower as the essential component of success in military operations was bolstered just before he left for Vietnam in early 1964 by advice imparted by Douglas MacArthur, whose legendary career was forged commanding American forces against Asian adversaries in World War II and Korea. MacArthur emphasized that "the Oriental is terrified of artillery, if used properly, it was the best way to break his morale."[9]

As was apparent in the plan of battle for offensive operations in the Ia Drang valley, Westmoreland and his staff were determined to enhance the firepower delivered by high-tech weaponry. But this pivotal element of US military interventions proved to be counterproductive in a number of ways. In the sparsely populated central highlands and along the Cambodian border, it was difficult to target enemy forces moving through densely wooded terrain. When NLF guerrillas were spotted and drawn into close combat with US or ARVN forces, air support was often risky. On many occasions support from the air resulted in casualties due to friendly fire,[10] which over time contributed significantly to the demoralization of soldiers assigned to search and destroy patrols or larger operations against NVA regulars.

In addition, the quite reasonable US Army doctrine, which McNamara repeatedly insisted upon, and officers in the field regularly adhered to, that anti-insurgent combat operations emphasize "bullets not bodies,"[11] often worked to the advantage of enemy forces. When search and destroy parties made contact with guerrilla forces, for example, they would routinely pull back and call in air and artillery support. In many instances, this made it possible for guerrilla or NVA forces to retreat into fortified bunkers or withdraw entirely. In rainforest and plantation areas, the rampant natural cover for guerrilla ambushes and nighttime raids prompted Americans to fire their automatic weapons excessively, and randomly, at the slightest movement or sound.[12] Sidney Stone, an artilleryman also stationed in the Cu Chi area, recalled indiscriminate shelling leaving his unit with a profound sense of pointlessness, if not impotence:

> We were terribly frustrated because we were sitting in fire support bases and we were getting mortared periodically. In the ten months I was with the 13th Artillery, we had about three killed and 35 wounded. That was enough to get you really frustrated when you had all this firepower and didn't really have anything to release it on, and you couldn't really cut loose on someone. We were just firing in the dark too much, just shooting off our guns. We didn't know where to shoot or where to go. We had the punch but never really could throw it.[13]

The drawbacks of an emphasis on firepower-overkill were greatly magnified by aerial assaults and artillery barrages in the more densely populated coastal lowlands, in the districts surrounding Saigon, and further south in the Mekong Delta. Helicopters and a diverse array of jet and modified prop planes—all core components of Air Mobile warfare—obliterated entire villages flagged as enemy strongholds. The killing and maiming of peasants proved a major source of recruits for the NLF. This approach encapsulated the inexplicable perversity of American policy toward the civilian population that was also demonstrated by the Johnson administration's willingness to allow B-52 bombers to pulverize the forests and paddy fields of South Vietnam while prohibiting their use against North Vietnam.

The counterproductive nature of Westmoreland's emphasis on massive but indiscriminate firepower was directly connected to a range of misguided approaches to the war that contributed to America's defeat. Neither incessant bombing, nor innovations in weaponry that made possible ever greater killing power, nor innumerable search and destroy missions could offset the lack of an overall strategy. Remarkably, strategic issues were not even discussed in the pivotal meetings of American and South Vietnamese civilian and military leaders in Honolulu just as the US armed forces were taking control of the war in February 1966. Unable to come up with different, let alone appropriate, ways to reconcile the need to suppress the guerrilla resistance in the South and block incursions of regular North Vietnamese forces, American planners opted to wage conventional warfare against both.

As military and academic defenders of the conduct of the war have insisted in its aftermath, American forces prevailed in almost all of their major engagements with NVA and NLF adversaries. In several instances—Ia Drang, Khe Sanh, and the Tet uprisings—communist forces did in fact suffer heavy losses as a result of massed offensives against US fortified positions. But in most combat situations they relied on ambushes and hit-and-run firefights that were designed to allow rapid dispersal before the Americans could engage them in full-scale, decisive battles. The US military collected reams of statistics on everything from enemy casualties and defections to supplies confiscated, prisoners taken, and weapons captured to be fed into Robert McNamara's computers at the Defense Department. But meaningful metrics (ways of measuring progress or setbacks) in the war against communist forces were never agreed upon or officially adopted.

The NLF's skill in deploying guerrilla tactics and its long-term revolutionary approach to countering American interventions made traditional markers of victory irrelevant, such as territory or war materiel captured, prisoners taken, or the number of times enemy forces retreated from combat situations. By default, that left body counts—a gauge that was both morally reprehensible and callous, and proved impossible to sustain when deployed by the political and military leaders of a democratic society. Nonetheless, numbers of combatants killed became the single, consistent gauge of the success of the rapidly proliferating US operations launched against elusive communist forces and their well-concealed command centers. The reliance on the body count metric made the absence of a coherent strategy apparent, and resulted in unreliable estimates of the extent to which the war was being won or lost.

The policymakers who oversaw US interventions in the final stage of the Vietnamese wars for independence repeatedly stressed the importance of restoring Saigon's control over the peasantry and rural areas south of the 17th parallel. British counterinsurgency experts, who provided advice based on their successes in Malaya in the 1950s, stressed that winning the political allegiance of a majority of a country's people was as important as military victories. For well over a decade the necessity of securing the peasant base in "Third World" conflicts had been emphasized in US Army service manuals. But once the American military buildup was underway, pressure on the Saigon regime to develop constructive programs to counter widespread communist support at the village level receded beyond even the minimal, often ill-conceived efforts made during the Diem era. By 1969, for example, US expenditures for medical aid, which was desperately needed in war-torn South Vietnam, had shrunk by over 80 percent of the meager 5.9 million dollars allotted in 1967.[14] Overall, increasing shares of the funding that American aid agencies spent on projects for rural uplift were siphoned off by corrupt government officials and local power brokers, or diverted to special police and ARVN units. Little was done to introduce land reforms, provide education, or improve healthcare, which might have diminished the appeal of the revolutionary changes that the NLF promised and in many areas managed to implement.

Despite the neglect of the political and economic dimensions of counterinsurgent efforts, Westmoreland usually included the need for rural development in his assessments of what was needed to defeat the communists. In a briefing with Robert McNamara just before the US military buildup took off in mid-1965, Westmoreland warned that without a strong regime in Saigon that was seriously committed to improving the lives of the peasantry, American public opinion would soon turn decidedly against continuing support and the war would be lost. But after what he viewed as a resounding victory in the Ia Drang campaign, Westmoreland became increasingly fixed on winning the war through "big unit" battles against the threat posed by the infiltration of North Vietnamese regular forces into South Vietnam. His insistence on maximizing firepower, mobility, and what was fundamentally a conventional approach to the land war was strongly backed by the Joint Chiefs, influential civilian advisors in Washington, and Lyndon Johnson. The military's success in winning approval for a shift to full-scale, very expensive, high-tech warfare reduced US funding for development initiatives to "trifling"[15] levels that fell even below the estimated 10 percent of peasants benefitting from the assistance programs introduced in the Diem era.[16]

Since the years of the Truman administration, the lion's share of US funding provided to sustain South Vietnamese governments that had not been siphoned off by the bureaucracy was spent on weapons and training programs for ARVN contingents and local defense forces. As Westmoreland's big unit approach to the war gained momentum, civilian and military advisors who dared to speak out about the dangers of reductions in support for counterinsurgent operations and programs designed to raise the living standards of the peasantry were either removed from prominent positions in the Washington bureaucracy or forced out of the military. Already in the Kennedy years, Roger Hilsman and Michael Forrestal had risked their chances for promotions due to their outspoken criticism of the inadequate training of rank-and-file ARVN soldiers and the ineptitude of their officers in combatting guerrilla warfare. Forrestal concluded that US military escalation was becoming a "Greek tragedy, and that the curtain [was] slowly descending."[17] Refusing to be silenced in their opposition to the policies later being pursued by the Johnson administration, Hilsman and Forrestal were steadily marginalized. Hilsman, whom the president had long viewed as a "disloyal troublemaker," was soon replaced by William Bundy, Mac Bundy's brother. Both Hilsman and Forrestal eventually left government service.

Dissent in the military was more easily quashed than that expressed by civilian advisors. But John Paul Vann, who was widely considered one of the most knowledgeable and courageous of the American officers working with ARVN forces during the Diem era, was easily the most outspoken and influential critic of US approaches to the anti-communist crusade in Vietnam. As such, his frustration with the refusal on the part of most ARVN officers (for whom Vann was ostensibly an advisor, but actually a behind-the-scenes coordinator in combat situations) to comply with his orders turned him into an irrepressible critic of both the Diem regime and its US backers at the Military Assistance Command, Vietnam (MACV). Vann's scarcely concealed leaks to reporters, especially Neil Sheehan and David Halberstam, whose press releases became a major factor in domestic opposition to American support for the Saigon regime, infuriated Diem's most reliable ally, General Harkins, who headed up MACV.

During his tours of duty in the Kennedy era, and later during the years of the military escalations under Johnson, Vann scathingly condemned as a "cruel folly . . . the forced relocation"[18] of whole village communities and their confinement in poorly planned *agrovilles*, and later in sterile, prison-like strategic hamlets. He railed against bombing strikes that targeted highly populated, rebel-held areas. He also made no secret of his contempt for those (most infamously Samuel Huntington) who argued that the displacement of tens of thousands of peasants made homeless by US bombing raids was an effective way to deprive the NLF of their essential base of support among the peasantry and advance the process of "modernization" in Vietnam.[19] Although Harkins's attempts to discharge the disgruntled colonel from the army had been headed off by several staff officers who agreed with Vann's pessimistic assessments, his failure to get a hearing from the Joint Chiefs and other officials after returning to Washington led him to resign his commission and leave the military.

As Jonathan Schell's moving account of the destruction of the once-prosperous village of Ben Suc in early 1967 made abundantly clear, escalating US armed interventions and the policies adopted by military governments in Saigon had for the most part intensified the rural population's hostility and the peasants' determination to resist the American invaders and their "puppet" regime. Schell's narrative of the Cedar Falls Operation thirty miles north of Saigon chronicles the slaughter of farm animals, the brutalization and killing of civilians, and the displacement of whole communities. In that offensive, as in many others, the rainforests and rice paddies in the vicinity of heavily populated areas were bulldozed, napalmed, or defoliated. Once the surviving humans and animals had been removed, the houses, ancestral shrines, and local marketplaces were destroyed to ensure that the villagers would not try to return. In gestures aimed at placating the understandably distraught and angry villagers, the Americans brought in doctors, who noted on "the exceptional good health" of the peasants of Ben Suc. On the second day of the occupation of the village, a lunch featuring "hot dogs, Spam, and crackers, served with a fruit-flavored beverage called Keen," was also provided in a hastily constructed army mess tent.[20]

Aside from hungry children who regularly jostled for GI handouts, few of the villagers who hadn't fled or been killed bothered to sample the meager fare. The very notion that hot dogs and Spam could compensate for the obliteration of the once-thriving community of Ben Suc and the ruination of the livelihood of its old men, women, and children (young men had either fled, joined the resistance, or been taken prisoner) was absurd. It encapsulated the variable mixture of fear, contempt, and inability to consider their victims worthy of empathy which accounted for the responses of American infantrymen and—at times even more intensely—ARVN soldiers in their interactions with the Vietnamese peasantry. It also made possible the often brutal treatment that the arrival of search and destroy parties meant for village dwellers. The hundreds of Ben Suc "operations" conducted during the American phase of the Vietnam wars underscored just how debased US "development" schemes had become. The uprooted peasants and wasted villages exposed the dark underside of the vacuous modernization rhetoric that Walt Rostow and his ilk tirelessly intoned to provide a moral justification for the devastation of a land and its people.

Losing Hope
Mid-April–Early May 1966

The main objectives of Operation Kalamazoo were to hunt for tunnel entrances, provide security for local villagers, and check out reports that NVA regulars were moving into the Saigon area. B Company was heading north through the Ho Bo Woods when one of the four Patton tanks that was "buddied" with the tracks of the company hit a mine crossing a rice paddy. The big guns of the heavily armored vehicles were supposed to block counterattacks and help the mechanized infantry easily break through enemy bunkers. But in practice the tanks were a liability. For Jimmy, the seemingly counterproductive process by which the army operated had become more apparent than ever, and he soon lost count of how many times he had gone out into the bush. As Captain Michael O'Mera of the Twenty-Fifth Infantry Division's Tactical Operations Office testified, "When you send a man out every single day, a certain amount of fatigue sets in, he becomes careless, and all is [is] a walking target . . . [but] the division commander had no alternative because he was told to produce body counts, and the only way he could do it was to make their ground unit 'bait.'"[21] But the only numbers that mattered to Jimmy were the amount of days remaining until his R&R.

The odds were high that a lot of the devices and booby traps that Jimmy and his fellow soldiers would encounter in Operation Kalamazoo were designed—and even built—by To Van Duc, a self-taught explosives expert from the village of Cu Chi. The success of the farmer's cunning inventions strengthened his fellow revolutionaries' belief that determination and low-tech ingenuity could offset America's massive firepower. To Van Duc was also responsible for the strategic placement of booby traps and land mines. When farmers were forced to relocate, for instance, Viet Cong guerrillas buried explosives in abandoned rice paddies and let the sun dry the top layer of dirt. This fooled the Americans into believing that the ground was not only hard enough to accommodate their heavy machinery, but that it was also safe to cross. As one CIA report confirms, mines and booby traps, which contributed to twenty-six percent of all US casualties during the war, caused nearly half of the American deaths in populated areas similar to the one where Jimmy was deployed. Even more astounding: ninety percent of all the mines and booby traps used against GIs were either American-made or included US-manufactured parts.[22] Though guerrillas were successful in destroying the costly APCs and tanks, disabling them also proved to be an effective tactic because it divided American units, making them more susceptible to ambush.

Knowing that B Company could suddenly come under attack, Captain Vickery had his men remount quickly and continue the mission. A maintenance team was sent out from base camp to repair the tank. If an APC lost its caterpillar-like track, the troops being transported could usually push it back on. But fixing the wheels of a forty-ton M-48 tank was a more time-consuming procedure. Lieutenant Jagosz chose Jimmy's APC unit to guard the disabled vehicle, thereby reducing his platoon to less than seventy-five percent of its combat strength. When the repairs were complete, the squad had to catch up to the rest of the company alone. To make matters even worse, the APC and tank radios operated on different frequencies. In order for Vickery to talk to the tank crews, he first had to send all of his messages to the platoon leaders, who then relayed the commands through their portable radios. Jagosz did not like the way things were going. As the rest of B Company moved to the western end of the Ho Bo Woods, they encountered hardly any resistance, which was a problem for Jagosz, who later wrote, "you can't just find nothing. . . . It was a search and destroy mission, we [had to find] something to destroy. . . . "[23]

In early April, the "Iron and Steel" Division's 165th A Regiment of the NVA had begun to reinforce the battered Seventh Viet Cong Infantry Division. The reinforcements helped rebuild tunnels, boosted guerrilla recruitment, and secured areas in the Ho Bo Woods and Filhol Plantation as the future location for a new headquarters. Apparently oblivious to the buildup of enemy forces, General Westmoreland began taking units out of Cu Chi to strengthen bases in the Central Highlands, which left the forces under General Fred Weyand's command shorthanded. He was forced to improvise by combining US and ARVN units in order to eliminate the looming threat to Saigon. Though the Twenty-Fifth Infantry Division reported that during Operation Circle Pines 170 Vietnamese were killed and several tons of rice were confiscated, the combined forces had failed to draw out large communist units into a conventional fight. In order to secure the villages in the region, Weyand needed to push NVA regulars out of the area. But before launching a large-scale attack, he needed information as to their whereabouts. Smaller reconnaissance and task force missions, such as Operation Kalamazoo conducted on April 13, were necessary for gathering such intelligence.

During B Company's trek back to base camp, another tank was hit by a twelve-pound mine. Jagosz was again ordered to detach one of his squads to act as a security detail and safeguard the tank. He was left with half of his platoon. As the company neared an intersection, two groups of Viet Cong soldiers were spotted. One group continued down the road, and the other turned east in the direction of the Saigon River. Frank D'Amico's Third Platoon raced south to where the enemy soldiers entered a patch of rubber trees. As they moved through an open rice field, D'Amico saw that the tank attached to his platoon was stuck in the mud. Temporally halting the pursuit of the enemy, D'Amico dismounted to check on the armored crew. He was shot in the chest and fell. The four men who tried to drag his body behind the APC were also shot. When the medic finally arrived and bent down see if anyone had a pulse, he was shot twice in the head. Before the dust off arrived to take the bodies, Father Olszewski anointed them all. It didn't seem to matter that many of them weren't Catholic or even religious. When the Americans left, they "bombed the hell out of [everything]. I even saw a bicycle a VC had dropped on the trail. . . . I bombed that too," Jagosz wrote.[24]

Though Jimmy's squad hadn't been engaged in much of the fighting that day, they heard the voices screaming on the radio. They read the casualty reports. They listened to the debriefings. So it wasn't surprising that when Jimmy wrote to his parents the morning after he returned from the mission, he began with, "Thank God! The field problem only took two days." He then told everyone in the family that he was sending home all the presents that were stuffed in his footlocker. Perhaps he was worried that they might never get home if he didn't send them right away, or maybe he was losing his taste for consumption because material possessions seemed to no longer matter. What he needed now were only the bare necessities: "My birthday is coming soon, I'll be 21 year's old, can you believe it Mom, just a little boy Yesterday, and Today a man? I really could use (and I am not kidding), 5 or 6 sets of underwear, about the same in socks, also about 3 set's of fatigue's, could you dye the under clothes dark green when you send it, I also sent $150.00 home to you all but I might need some [money] soon for my pass." He then went on to respond to his mother's comment about his appearance in the photos he sent home: "In your letter Mom, you said who was I mad at, all combat soldier's have to look bad, like real killer's, if I would have a smile on my face, they would think I was a little boy or something so that is why I looked so mean, I'll have to get a better picture taken of myself."

Although he tried to portray himself as unchanged and unflinching, he was afraid and deeply disturbed by the war. It was clear that his good-will tour in the villages was failing, despite Weyand's new pacification strategy. And it didn't seem to matter "how many different things he told the new guys [replacements] that [he] had learned (good or bad)," they always ended up getting hurt. Many of the replacements who had been rushed through Advanced Infantry Training and sent to Vietnam, were required to take safety classes on booby traps and antipersonnel mines when they arrived at Cu Chi. During one of these classes, soldiers from B Company were priming a claymore mine inside an APC when it detonated.[25]

Pacifying the Cu Chi area was proving to be a tough assignment. Casualties for the Twenty-Fifth Infantry Division from January to April 1966 were ninety-one killed, 914 wounded, and twelve losses from non-battlefield deaths. Forty-one of the deaths were members of the Fifth Mechanized, and by the middle of May those numbers increased almost daily. "It's at the base camp that emotional things really hit you and hard," Ted Jagosz wrote. Two days after his friend Frank D'Amico was killed, Jagosz was beginning to question his Catholic beliefs and losing his moral bearings. "Trying to understand God's Providence is tough when you've lost so many good friends," he said. At one point he walked to the supply shed and hid behind the boxes and cried, "I didn't want anybody to see me doing it at 27 years old," he later admitted.[26] Lieutenant Brian Sullivan, who was stationed in Da Nang and had lost several members of his platoon, wrote home expressing feelings similar to those of Jagosz: "I'm so confused. At the services today they were talking about God protecting people and eternal life and I felt so desolate, so despairing. I know there is no reward waiting for them or any hope. I began to cry I felt so awful and hopeless, but somehow held it back and it just looked like I was sniffing from my cold. (See! How awful my ego and pride that I couldn't even let my self weep for those poor, poor kids.)"[27]

Many soldiers in Vietnam were aware of the absurdities of combat and the ways it forced them to realize the futility of war. In a series of moving written letters to his family in late 1966, Lieutenant Sandy Kempner explained how he felt trapped. He observed that no matter how hard someone tries to change things, some things just can't be changed: "This is not the place we would prefer to make this stand [and it is not the best] environment to utilize our standard armaments in which we have invested so much. But . . . we must fight where the confrontation is, despite [the war's] cost, infeasibility, and possible illegality, and physical and mental toll upon the participants. In short, we have no choice." In September, the young lieutenant addressed his aunt, describing to her the overwhelming sense of hopelessness that had come over him on a recent operation: "This morning, my platoon and I were finishing up a three-day patrol. Struggling over steep hills covered with hedgerows, trees, and generally impenetrable jungle, one of my men turned to me and pointed a hand, filled with cuts and scratches, at a rather distinguished-looking plant with soft red flowers waving gaily in the downpour and said, 'that is the first plant I have seen today which did not have a thorn on it'... [but] someday this hill will be burned by napalm, and the red flower will crackle up and die among the thorns. So what is the use of it living and being a beauty among the beasts, if it must, in the end, die because of them, and with them?" Three weeks later Kempner was killed by shrapnel from an exploding mine.[28]

Jimmy had undoubtedly begun to question his faith. But unlike those who completely shed their religion, or worse turned to drugs and alcohol, Jimmy sought the guidance of the brigade's chaplain. Though he did not write at length about his meetings with the priest, Jimmy did remark that after each session he "felt a little better for some reason (wonder why) . . . and would continue to go to Mass and pray for everyone." Though he later told his mother that he'd appreciate it if she "didn't go to church for [him] every day," he still continued to attend services at base camp and sometimes when on patrol a "Catholic priest would come and say mass in villages for the Vietnamese and GIs."

In May, he realized that he was powerless to prevent the worst atrocities from happening, and his determination to improve the lives of the farmers no longer mattered. Desertion was unthinkable. But regardless of the consequences, he decided to avoid going out on patrol whenever possible. Jimmy recognized that if he "got into trouble" he'd be put on Kitchen Patrol or ordered to clean the latrines. In a letter he mailed to his parents in late April, he set out his plan: "As you said my birthday is May 6 and I get freedom, but your wrong, I just woke up and found I have been free for a long time, I alway's wanted to be 21 year's old, now since I am just about, I would like to be little Joe's [his younger brother] age again, so Joe thinks he is in the army now, boy what a kid, I remember when I was small I alway's wanted to be a soldier or something, now since I am that something, I would rather just be that little boy who always got into trouble in school than a GI, but I can get into trouble here to, so maybe I'll give it a try."

Confounding the Colossus

When US military interventions in Vietnam rapidly escalated in the mid-1960s, they were directed against both the communist regime in the North and the allied guerrilla movement in the South. Both were deeply committed to the national unification of the Vietnamese people and revolutionary transformations in a land ravaged by decades of occupation and repression. Although prone at times to forced development schemes, the charismatic, reformed-minded leadership of the communists, personified by Ho Chi Minh and Vo Nguyen Giap, had been able to retain the support of the vast majority of the Vietnamese people. By contrast, neither the Americans nor successive governments in Saigon could come up with effective ways of dealing with the underlying political and economic sources of South Vietnam's civil strife. Their failure to provide security and better living conditions in the countryside gave them little chance of winning over the peasant population that the NLF guerrilla movement depended on for survival. Abortive and underfunded development programs, combined with Westmoreland's emphasis on defeating the regular NVA forces, enabled the communists to take advantage of an impressive range of strategic and tactical opportunities that were critical for their remarkable victory over the American colossus.

In addition to the many lessons learned about combating conventional Euro-American armies in the French phase of the wars of liberation, the Vietnamese proved adept at adapting Maoist stratagems for organizing and deploying guerrilla *and* conventional forces. NLF operatives were also able to reinvent age-old modes of resistance that Vietnamese rebels deployed to offset America's intimidating technological advantages. Sanctuaries, for example, became even more indispensable for NLF fighters and NVA soldiers than they traditionally had been for social bandits, rebellious peasants, slaves, or laborers. The Johnson administration's prohibition of all but clandestine raids into Cambodia and Laos frustrated American commanders seeking to pursue and destroy adversary forces throughout the late 1960s. The vast rainforests of the Southeast Asian highlands and the luxuriant undergrowth of the Mekong Delta swamplands proved critical to the success of the ruses communist operatives improvised to foil the high-tech surveillance devices that American air and ground forces had developed to track enemy troop movements. The use of toxic chemicals to defoliate densely forested areas brazenly violated international law and devastated the very environment, including the abundant wildlife, of the country that US officials claimed they were seeking to rescue from communist totalitarianism. Chemical warfare killed, maimed, and deformed (for generations) the children of peasants as well as shifting cultivators in the hill country who lived in targeted areas. It also ensured that those who were not already hostile to the Saigon regime and the American invaders would become supporters of the communist resistance.

NVA and NLF technicians found ways to fool or evade even the most sophisticated American surveillance technologies. Some of these were designed to interdict the flow of supplies and soldiers moving along Ho Chi Minh trail network. No detection system—or single technological complex for that matter—exceeded that of the Infiltration Surveillance Center (ISC) at Nakhon Phanom in Thailand that served as the command center for a top secret Air Force operation, implausibly dubbed Igloo White. At a cost of $5 billion (over 37 billion dollars in FY 2016), it housed IBM computers and display panels that monitored signals from tens of thousands of sensor devices, which had been airdropped into heavily forested areas that concealed enemy pathways through southern Laos into South Vietnam. The sensors, which were disguised as innocuous natural substances—from broken branches to piles of dung—relayed signals emitted by sound (motorcycle engines), smell (exhaust fumes, human sweat), or motion (a squad of weapons carriers passing by) to the computer screens at the ISC. Once the location of the intercept was plotted, the coordinates of suspected enemy activities were transmitted to Phantom jets that would then bomb the targeted areas.

The statistics Air Force spokesmen provided to hype the great success of the operation were impossibly inflated, as was made clear by the fact that the 35,000 trucks allegedly destroyed "greatly exceed[ed] the number of trucks believed by the Embassy to be in all of North Vietnam."[29] Equally sobering was the calculation that, even if the official estimate was reliable, it would have "put the cost of interdiction in the neighborhood of $100,000 for each truck destroyed [and] 73 tons of bombs to kill one North Vietnamese soldier marching down the Ho Chi Minh trail."[30] Bad statistics could not disguise the cost-effective ways the Vietnamese devised to fool the sensors, such as tossing feces along the trails or running decrepit vehicles through rainforest pathways. Many types of sensors could also be set-off by heavy thunder or wind gusts, earth tremors, and low-flying US aircraft. Once the Phantom jets had finished their bombing runs—more often than not in areas evacuated by NVA forces—soldiers and supply units would continue to trek into South Vietnam at rates more than sufficient to support communist forces there for the duration of the war.

The ingenuity that the communists displayed in limiting American attempts to prevent the infiltration of North Vietnamese troops and supplies to the South was paralleled by their responses to the massive bombing campaign against the Democratic Republic of Vietnam itself. In addition to the dearth of targets, such as major industrial complexes and military installations, the US air offensive was bedeviled from the start by adverse weather conditions, particularly during the monsoon season. Inclement weather often delayed bombing raids, giving the Vietnamese time to disperse machinery, weapons, and skilled workers to remote, well-camouflaged locations. In the first years of the Rolling Thunder campaign, Lyndon Johnson and his team of micromanagers designated Hanoi off limits, despite the fact that the city had the highest concentration of factories, oil storage facilities, and power plants in North Vietnam. Bombing runs against Hanoi's seaport of Haiphong were also prohibited, even though it was the main conduit for arms and supplies shipped from the Russians and their Warsaw Pact allies. Fearing that bombing the densely populated capital and main harbor would bring Communist China directly into the war, civilian planners repeatedly overruled the Joint Chiefs who opposed the constraints placed on conventional air operations. In response to the damage inflicted on roads, railways, and bridges beyond the Hanoi-Haiphong area, the North Vietnamese government mobilized hundreds of thousands of workers—both men and women—to repair bombed out communications networks and electrical grids. If the damage inflicted was severe, alternate roads were upgraded and pontoon bridges afforded temporary river crossings.

Particularly in the early stages of the bombing campaign against North Vietnam, the size and speed of American aircraft, which were designed for anti-Soviet missions at high altitudes over the vast plains of northern Europe, proved a major liability in the reduced air space over North Vietnam. In addition to their rapidly improving antiaircraft weaponry, which the Vietnamese both obtained from communist suppliers and manufactured themselves, the smaller, more maneuverable MIG fighter planes provided by China and the Soviet Union inflicted a heavy toll on American assault aircraft. The introduction of Soviet SAM missiles in 1965 posed an additional threat, which peaked in the number of planes shot down in the mid 1960s. By the time of the US withdrawal in 1972, over nine hundred aircraft had been lost over North Vietnam. These totals underscore the critical, often overlooked ways in which advanced weapons, from MIG fighters to AK-47 assault rifles—as well as specialists to train Vietnamese gun crews and pilots—provided by communist backers contributed to North Vietnam's ability to withstand the onslaught of the American military. From a global perspective, the scale of support the United States and its communist rivals provided each side in the conflict reminds us that it was also a proxy war. In the broader context of the cold war standoff, it could not have been otherwise.

The vital contributions that China and the Soviet bloc provided to ensure the survival of the government in North Vietnam contrasted sharply with the failure of successive Saigon regimes to make effective use of American assistance. In the decades following the 1954 Geneva settlement, US presidents and policymakers had insisted that unless Diem and his military successors put together a viable political alternative to Hanoi, American efforts to prevent a communist takeover of South Vietnam were bound to fail. Because no president or top advisor had followed up on threats of major cutbacks or a US withdrawal, the successive governments in Saigon continued to squander American aid and exploit Westmoreland's willingness to allow US forces to supply the resources and a lion's share of the manpower needed to fight the war.[31]

There were South Vietnamese politicians, intellectuals, and military leaders who genuinely aspired to build a government committed to social reform and increasing political participation. But as Truong Nhu Tang stresses in his account of his decision to join the NLF resistance, he—along with many other activists and intellectuals who "would have been willing to accept almost any regime that could achieve real independence and that had the welfare of the people at heart"—was harassed, tortured, and imprisoned by the regime's secret police force with little protest from its American backers.[32] Though constrained by war and party ideologues in the upper reaches of the government hierarchy, Saigon's communist adversaries not only offered the promise of revolutionary transformations, they actively strove to improve the lives of the peasantry. By stressing its opposition to the "subservience to foreigners"[33] of the Saigon regime, the NLF was also able to appeal to the deeply ingrained Vietnamese longing for independence and unity. The fact that promises of democracy and development touted by American politicians and advisors in country had yielded little more than rigged elections, blatant corruption, and repression gave the beleaguered peasantry scant reason to rally to the defense of any of the dictatorial regimes in Saigon.

Political dysfunction inevitably undermined the effectiveness and morale of the Army of the Republic of Vietnam, which was ostensibly the main defender of the South Vietnamese regime. From its inception, ARVN was riddled by divisions and ill-prepared to take on its communist rivals. Because rank-and-file soldiers were drafted by a dictatorial regime propped up by a foreign power, they had limited, and at best reluctant, support from the population they claimed to defend. Though all males between the ages of eighteen and thirty-seven were subject to the draft, sons of elite families and government officials were usually able to acquire exemptions or be inducted into the officer corps. Partly as a result of this favoritism, ARVN's top military leaders, with some exceptions, were notoriously inept, corrupt, and reluctant to take on NLF forces.[34] American advisors, most stridently John Paul Vann, were appalled by South Vietnamese officers who focused their units' operations on areas where intelligence reports indicated no guerrillas were active, and who avoided combat when enemy forces were unexpectedly encountered.

Equally disturbing was the fact that the ARVN command and South Vietnamese society more generally were infiltrated with communist agents who provided advance notice of military offensives and regularly sabotaged communications and military materiel. The superior intelligence provided by spies as well as ordinary villagers, including women and adolescents, proved to be a major advantage for both NLF guerrillas and regular NVA units throughout the war. Little wonder that induction into the armed forces by the Government of South Vietnam had come to be widely viewed as a death sentence, and this perception was a major factor accounting for the high and steadily growing numbers of defections. Often abetted by NLF propaganda, desertions peaked at 34,000 in 1964, and averaged an estimated 21 percent of ARVN forces throughout the half-decade of the American phase of the Vietnam wars. By contrast, less than 1 percent of NVA soldiers defected in the same period.[35]

With the arrival of American contingents in the mid-1960s, ARVN soldiers were mainly deployed in support of US operations. Nonetheless, they were often routed in clashes with the more committed and better-led soldiers of the NVA. These setbacks reinforced Westmoreland's conviction that "South Vietnamese forces are not ample enough to cope with main-force units throughout the country . . . " and his determination to Americanize the conventional war against the North Vietnamese.[36] At the same time, it was decided to concentrate ARVN units in renewed efforts to "pacify" and protect the rural population. As their previous history made clear, however, that was an assignment they were not prepared to carry out. In crucial ways, responsibility for ARVN's failures in counterinsurgency can be traced to the late 1950s and early 1960s, when American advisors took the lead in training Diem's armed forces and supplying them with US weapons.

Neither the Joint Chiefs in Washington nor U.S. Army officers working with South Vietnamese draftees in country gave much thought to the threat that the revival of guerrilla resistance posed for the regime. They convinced Diem that he needed an American-style, big-unit army to defend against a conventional military offensive from the North. But communist strategists in Hanoi had no intention of invading the South or fighting the kind of war that US advisors and the Saigon government wanted them to wage. Once the NLF had rallied resistance forces in the South, ARVN units proved to be no match for dedicated and resourceful guerrilla fighters. Even though total ARVN forces were on average ten times more numerous than those of the NLF throughout the 1960s,[37] they repeatedly suffered humiliating defeats inflicted by guerrilla insurgents. These setbacks opened the way for communist control of the greater portion of the heavily populated rural areas in the Mekong delta, along the coast, and even in the vicinity of the capital itself by the time of the first direct US military interventions in 1965.

The arrogance and brutal policing methods of ARVN soldiers frequently turned peasant communities against the Saigon government and drove them to cooperate with the NLF. According to a 1968 survey of Viet Cong prisoners, 28 percent decided to join the resistance due to the bullying, pilfering, and public humiliation of parents and community elders by government soldiers.[38] ARVN intelligence personnel often took the lead in interrogations, which invariably involved beatings and torture of suspected guerrillas or villagers thought to be cooperating with local NLF operatives. ARVN troops were also placed in charge of relocating village populations. In carrying out these deeply resented transfers, they were not above raping outspoken peasant women and young girls or randomly slaughtering invaluable farm animals.[39] As a result, they conceded the space beyond their fortified encampments as well as the hours from dusk to dawn to guerrillas moving freely in the unoccupied zones, infiltrating villages for supplies and recruitment, transporting weapons, and preparing ambushes and minefields.

Of the many contradictions associated with the conduct of America's crusade to prevent a communist takeover of South Vietnam, perhaps the most unsettling was the immense high-tech violence visited on the land and people whose rescue

Children of peasant families were very often the victims of ARVN operations.

was alleged to be the overriding purpose of US interventions. Policymakers in Washington and advisors in country sought to reconcile their democracy and development rhetoric with the reality of the devastation that counterinsurgency operations were inflicting by stressing the evils inherent in guerrilla warfare. It was, of course, routine for those who denounced communist violence against the South Vietnamese peasantry to allege that it was predictable, given the brutal and tyrannical nature of the system the NLF and Hanoi were attempting to impose on a resistant, democratic nation. It was certainly true that, because NLF and NVA forces were technologically inferior to the American superpower on the basis of every imaginable conventional criterion, it was critical for them to maintain control over the rural population. Though there were excesses and innocent victims, the uneven odds insurgents faced go far to account for the often brutal communist reprisals that mainly targeted suspected government collaborators, ranging from local headmen and double agents to peasant communities siding with Saigon in the civil war. But because guerrilla fighters were embedded within local communities, overt violence against civilians was usually contained and selective.

The NLF and NVA's ability to withstand the American onslaught came to depend on finding ways to counteract a steady stream of ever more advanced US weaponry. The incremental introduction of these innovations gave communist adversaries in the North and South time to find ways to neutralize them, or at least greatly diminish their impact on both their guerrilla and conventional forces. Helicopters and heavily armored vehicles proved particularly susceptible to guerrilla tactics. Loud, bulky, and prone to bog down in South Vietnam's dense rainforests, swampy or paddy-laden lowlands, and shell-pitted dirt roads, APCs and tanks were highly vulnerable to Russian and Chinese armor-piercing grenade launchers and mobile artillery ordinance. Mines—often fashioned from recycled casings from unexploded American artillery or bomb shells—also took a heavy toll on both mechanized units and infantrymen searching for or engaging guerrilla forces. To warn of approaching assault helicopters, spotters were stationed in the canopy of the rainforest near NLF bases or encampments set up by units on the move. Landing zones for US helicopters transporting mobile combat troops were favored ambush sites for guerrillas armed with grenade launchers and an array of machine guns and mortars.

In terms of their pervasiveness and everyday psychological impact on American soldiers, no weapons in the communist arsenal exceeded the minefields and booby traps that guarded communist sanctuaries and disrupted routinized US patrols and full-scale offensive operations. Sharpened punji stakes placed in pits covered with foliage had been used for centuries against invading armies and domestic rivals. Other booby traps involved turning American garbage, including tin cans, discarded bottles, and the powder from dud shells, into deadly explosives buried in forests, paths along paddy fields, hanging from trees, and spread across the approaches to guerrilla bunkers. Some of the more ingenious were a blend of old and new antipersonnel explosives, including the gunpowder-filled sugar cane stalks devised by To Van Duc that were hidden in

Ordinary peasants, such as To Van Duc – here demonstrating how to assemble his anti-helicopter mine – contributed significantly to the arsenal of booby traps that proved deadly to US search and destroy operations and raids on suspected enemy-held villages.

tree branches and triggered by the forcible down draft of landing helicopters. No writer has more poignantly captured the relentless tension and traumatic sense of loss that these low-tech devices inflicted than Tim O'Brien in *The Things They Carried*:

> In the mountains that day, I watched Lemon turn sideways. He laughed and said something to Rat Kiley. Then he took a peculiar half step, moving from shade into bright sunlight, and the booby-trapped 105 round blew him into a tree. The parts were just hanging there, so Dave Jensen and I were ordered to shinny up and peel him off. I remember the white bone of an arm. I remember pieces of skin and something wet and yellow that must've been the intestines. The gore was horrible, and stays with me. But what wakes me up twenty years later is Dave Jensen singing 'Lemon Tree' as we threw down the parts.[40]

Jimmy Gilch's disillusionment, which was shared by growing numbers of ordinary infantrymen and line officers, was fed by the search and destroy missions that brought US soldiers into regular, direct contact with peasant communities. From the outset these encounters were hostile, and they became increasingly lethal. The failure of ARVN and local militias to clear and then secure villages compelled the staff at MACV to increase American counterinsurgency operations against guerrilla forces that were deeply entrenched in local peasant society. By the middle of June 1967, 86 percent of American units were engaged in search and destroy missions, reflecting the refusal of NVA and NLF commanders to fight the big-unit war that Westmoreland assumed would bring victory.[41]

Because most American infantrymen were taught in training almost nothing reliable about the Vietnamese people and their culture, changing their mission to focus on winning over the civilian population was a misjudgment at best. Information sessions stressed the underdeveloped condition of the country and the poverty and filth of the peoples' dwellings and bodies. The instruction trainees received purposefully or ignorantly disregarded two thousand years of civilized attainments and an East Asian predilection for personal cleanliness, thereby reducing the Vietnamese to subhuman status. Thus what little information inductees were given only reinforced their contempt for the peasantry. Jimmy and other inductees were predisposed to see the Vietnamese as devious, untrustworthy, and prone to violence. These racial stereotypes were, of course, deeply embedded in American society and history, and were readily internalized by the mostly young, often poorly educated males consigned to infantry service in Vietnam.

Although veterans of the Vietnam conflict frequently acknowledged the bravery and determination of both guerrilla fighters and NVA regulars (often referred to as "Charlie" when positive qualities were acknowledged), they and the civilian population as a whole were usually lumped together as "gooks," "slants," "chinks," or "dinks." When degrading stereotypes were linked to warnings about the dangers posed to outsiders by the deceitful, backstabbing Vietnamese civilians, the admonition to shoot first and make excuses for civilian deaths afterward became deeply fixed in the minds of infantrymen sent into the Vietnam quagmire. As Jonathan Schell documented early in the American phase of the conflict, even soldiers who lived for extended periods among the peasantry felt little remorse for civilians killed in raids or bombing runs. One sergeant emphatically declared that, even though "I've worked, eaten, and slept with those villagers for six months, and I want to tell you I have no sympathy for those people. I really don't." Another sergeant engaged in the destruction of Ben Suc laughed when Schell raised questions about the civilians killed in the operation, and remarked, "What does it matter? They are all Vietnamese."[42]

The need to inflate body counts inevitably contributed to appalling levels of victimization of peasants in villages that became targets of "fix and clear" operations or were simply suspected of support for guerrilla forces. High rates of civilian casualties and dismembered bodies that allowed for double or triple counting, and field officers' guesstimates recorded as accurate totals in after action reports made for bloated body counts. Though not official army policy, officers serving in Vietnam had good reason to believe that advances in rank depended heavily on the totals of communists killed in action by the soldiers under their command. That obscene incentive for ambitious officers was further compromised by the fact that it was also used at times to determine the number and difficulty of the missions to which different units were assigned.[43]

The army commanders' decision to wage a war of attrition (which Marine Corps commanders consistently opposed) also required American casualties to be constantly compared (invariably positively) to the number of guerrillas or NVA regulars presumed killed or captured in each engagement. The protagonist of Philip Caputo's memoir, *A Rumor of War*, who is assigned to count the dead on both sides and calculate the ratios, viscerally captures the contempt increasing numbers of American infantrymen felt for the single statistical measure that the military consistently applied to gauge the success or failure of their missions: "I had acquired a hatred for the scoreboard, for the very sight of it. It symbolized everything I despised about the staff, the obsession with statistics, the indifference towards the tragedy of death; and because I was on the staff, I despised myself."[44]

The combination of increasing emphasis on search and destroy operations in heavily populated rural areas and the elevation of body counts as the defining measure of the success or failure of US and allied military operations steadily eroded the cohesion and morale of American forces fighting in Vietnam. Having committed to a war of attrition that they were confident America's superior technology was sure to win, policymakers in Washington and military planners in country proved incapable of seriously considering better options. Following their setbacks at Ia Drang, the communists took control of the kind of war that would be waged, when and where combat would occur, and how long firefights would last. McNamara's computer team calculated that in the late-1960s, NLF or NVA units initiated nearly four-fifths of the armed clashes.[45] In the great majority of instances, they managed to terminate them before US air and artillery forces could unleash their potentially decisive firepower. The communist strategy of avoidance also meant there was no need to pay the high price of capturing and holding territory, no battles that had to be won, or front lines to hold and convoys to protect. For the Americans there were no decisive victories that the military could cite to mollify the growing chorus of critics of the conduct of the war back in the States, and few heroes to demonstrate the courage and resolve of their armed services fighting for a noble cause in a far-off land.

The search and destroy missions that became the centerpiece of Westmoreland's war of attrition were in essence expanded versions of scouting and patrolling parties that had long been standard procedure for conventional armies. Designed primarily to locate and fight holding actions with enemy forces and positions, the routinized—hence predictable—nature of these small unit forays into rainforests and paddy fields made them susceptible to both ambush and evasion on the part of guerrilla or NVA forces. But because communist commanders chose when and where a majority of firefights or larger engagements occurred, contacts with significant concentrations of enemy forces were exasperatingly infrequent. In most cases deadly clashes were "inconclusive at best." Eric Bergerud tersely captured the sense of futility expressed by many of the soldiers he interviewed who served with the Twenty-Fifth Division in the Cu Chi region where American infantrymen suffered higher casualty rates than in any other combat zone in Vietnam: "Enemy units were never encircled and wiped out in large numbers, and our [US] casualties were painfully high. A good 'kill ratio' did not sound like victory to the American people."[46] Even in situations where communist troops were trapped and decimated or driven from target areas, American forces were usually ordered to withdraw from the positions captured, which were soon reoccupied by guerrilla or regular NVA soldiers.

As Jimmy and increasing numbers of foot soldiers came to realize, this was not the war they assumed they were drafted or recruited to fight. In addition to coping with elusive enemy forces, they found themselves policing, bullying, and basically at war with the South Vietnamese peasantry. Prodded by the military brass, they were repeatedly forced into situations that induced tension, bursts of anger, aggression, and remorse—and tested their most basic ethical values. For Jimmy and his compatriots the campaign to "win hearts and minds" rapidly devolved into seemingly endless slogs in enervating heat and humidity, through insect-and vermin-infested rainforests, scrublands, swamps, and flooded paddy fields. These ordeals bred resentment towards the officers who issued orders from distant air-conditioned trailers or helicopters high above the contested terrain. Varying responses to peasant distrust, truculence, and scarcely disguised antagonism also intensified personal and ethnic tensions and open hostility, at times leading to death threats within the ranks of the "grunts," who were locked in the standoff with the peasant population.

The cohesion of army units was undermined from the outset of American military interventions by recurring changes in the composition of combat forces due to the twelve-month (thirteen for those in the Marine Corps) limit on the length of service time for infantrymen and the six-month rotation of field officers. Nonetheless, in firefights with guerrillas or NVA regulars, American soldiers usually closed ranks. In situations where enemy fire was coming from nearby villages, search and destroy parties promptly called for artillery barrages or F-4 Phantom jet assaults. In addition, a range of explosives, napalm, white phosphorous, and ever more savage antipersonnel bombs were deployed to obliterate entire villages in NLF-controlled areas or those in contested zones believed to have sheltered or supplied guerrilla fighters. Jeff Yushta, a young Marine, described what remained of the peasants of the hamlet of Le Bac 2 after one of hundreds of assaults on defenseless civilians:

> One of my vivid memories was a stack of some thirty-some bodies that other marines and other people after us had just thrown into a pile. It was just a jumble of arms and legs. I can still see it. There was a kid in the pile and there was no way for me to tell whether he was killed by small-arms fire or the air strike or whatever.

Yushta admitted that the carnage left him "battling some real conflicting thoughts," which were shared by other infantrymen. Like so many of them, he shifted the blame for the killings to the enemy and the gullible peasants:

> " . . . I can't make any sense out of why these people were involved in this. It was one of the things that made you hate the Viet Cong. They involved what we would call innocent people. Nobody was innocent there, I guess."

It was true that the guerrilla insurgents sometimes purposely shot at American patrols from villages in order to draw artillery fire or strafing by US support forces against communities suspected of supporting the government and its American backers. But in this case, as Yushta explained, the hamlet was in a free-fire zone—where by official decree, any Vietnamese was fair game. So he and the Fifth Marines "were doing a job that [he] still felt had to be done."[47] And that "job" left an estimated 300,000 civilians killed or wounded in the free-fire zones.[48]

Civilians were also victimized when army patrols "swept" villages suspected of sheltering or supplying NLF forces. Exhausted by tension-filled days of futile hunts for enemy forces or enraged by friends killed or maimed by booby traps or shot by unseen snipers, American patrols "had to take [their] frustration out on something. Sometimes when we'd be on operations, [we'd] burn down villages. They were made of grass, and all it would take was a match and the whole village would be in flames."[49] In these situations, burning hooches and shooting pigs, chickens, and even precious water buffaloes became standard procedure. But, especially when reporters or TV crews were absent, angry soldiers—having been told in mission briefings that anyone found in the area of operations was either a guerrilla or a "Viet Cong" sympathizer—turned their fire on the terrified villagers. On the pretext that they were flushing out guerrilla fighters, they lobbed grenades into the makeshift shelters where old men, women, and children sought refuge, and shot those who tried to flee and even those who had been herded into captive clusters. Very often the perpetrators of the atrocities raped, looted, defiled ancestral shrines, and torched the "ville" as they departed.[50]

"Wasting the locals" often led to quarrels and tense standoffs within the companies or battalions involved. One of the more horrific confrontations centered on a baby boy whom Yoshia Chee (who admitted he and his Special Forces squad were high on Methedrine) held by his ankles and threatened to shoot unless his mother told him where the VC were. When the mother refused, he realized he couldn't do it, that shooting a baby point blank wasn't "going to be on [his] conscience." Chee froze, and his commanding officer, angered by his insubordination, "shot *it* [italics ours]. He shot the baby. I almost shot him." Chee was also reluctant to join in destroying the village, but worried that the CO would see to it that he and the squad would "be in deep shit" when they returned to base. But the major was killed in a firefight with guerrillas shortly afterward, and Chee was badly wounded.[51]

As psychological studies would lead one to expect, soldiers who witnessed but refused to participate in violent assaults on defenseless Vietnamese civilians or to become involved in the altercations that followed often stood by stunned and afraid to speak out. Individuals who objected and made it clear that they intended to report soldiers who had committed criminal acts were very likely to be threatened by those who had participated in the atrocities. If they made it back to base, whistleblowers were usually transferred to other units, and the reports based on their testimony usually shelved, and very often "lost" in the years following the war.[52] Some soldiers, such as the deservedly famous Hugh Thompson, Jr., a reconnaissance helicopter pilot who repeatedly risked his life to rescue women and children during the infamous massacre at My Lai in March 1968,[53] directly challenged those committing atrocities and succeeded in reducing or stopping the killing. Others, including Jimmy Gilch, sought both to avoid missions where abuses against the peasants were likely to occur and to find ways of compensating, such as insisting that the wounded receive treatment or that orphaned children be fed and sheltered. But given the ambiguities of official regulations concerning war crimes, atrocities often went unreported and unpunished.

Although symptoms of the breakdown of US forces deployed in the land war were as yet vague and little heeded during the time of Jimmy Gilch's service in Vietnam, there was a sense of futility and loss of purpose. The surprisingly early views of some of Jimmy's field officers that the war was unwinnable captured this mood and confirmed the conviction of leaders in Hanoi and NLF commanders that the daunting firepower assaults of American armed forces would prove counterproductive. The indiscriminate slaughter and suffering inflicted on the civilian population of North and South alienated the majority of the Vietnamese people from the "puppet" Saigon regime and its "imperialist" allies, and solidified support for the communist revolutionary, nationalist alternative. Unrestricted coverage by American and foreign reporters and television crews energized mass protest movements across the United States and throughout Europe, the communist bloc, and the nations of the developing world. The appalling losses and immense sacrifices that the Vietnamese people endured to overcome the aggression of the American superpower made it intolerable for them to even consider surrender or a compromised peace.

Waiting for Leave
June–July 1966

Nearly fifty tons of ammunition hauled by helicopter and vehicle convoy arrived daily at the Cu Chi base camp. Major Edmund K. S. Chine, chief division ammunition officer, estimated that his largest stockpiles consisted of buckshot, mortar bombs, artillery shells, claymore mines, and M-16 rifle rounds, all of which required sixty vehicles to transport. Soldiers of the Twenty-Fifth Infantry Division fired on average 1.5 million rifle rounds a month. By May, the U.S. Military Assistance Command issued a warning to all American servicemen to "exercise care in their contacts with the Vietnamese people during combat operations." The authors of the report cautioned against "the unnecessary killing of livestock, a practice which [alienated] noncombatant Vietnamese against the American military mission." Although it was necessary to prevent buildings and property from falling into the hands of the Viet Cong, the report mentioned that, "care should be taken to insure that the property of friendly civilians is not destroyed in the process."[54]

To accommodate the massive influx of weapons and supplies, the base camp was continuously expanding. Warehouses were built to safeguard the food and medical supplies donated to Weyand's civic action programs. Widows of Vietnamese soldiers—"hungry and homeless"—regularly arrived at the US camp "beaming with smiles" when they left with "bundles of clothing, cans of juice and salad oil and boxes of rolled wheat."[55] An outdoor stage was also erected to house concerts performed by visiting entertainers. Beer halls and baseball fields were built, the PX was expanded, and the camp was now fully electrified, allowing Jimmy to use "the electrical shaver Louise gave [him] for [his] birthday." Some tents at headquarters had air-conditioning units, fully stocked bars, and refrigerators with icemakers. There were even plans to build a swimming pool and a patio area with a barbecue pit.

The newly constructed buildings and enlisted men's clubs excited Jimmy, but in ways that had little relation to their intended purpose. Even though he did frequent the beer hall, his enthusiasm for the expansion projects was mainly because he could now "pull over more KP duty." One disgruntled soldier, who was later accused of fragging, explained, "I volunteered for KP, trash run and other nasty details, like burning human waste in a barrel while my company went out on a four-day mission."[56] Jimmy also began volunteering for miscellaneous jobs around camp so he could avoid combat: "Well the ambush went well off real good, just before we were going to leave, they said a man had to stay back at camp, and go out in the morning with the track driver, so guess who that lucky person was? So me and the track driver left about 9 am, so I had a full nights sleep just about, well anyway, the company done good, because by the time we got out there, they had killed 7, a possible 3 or 4, and also captured 7 weapons, so it turned out to be very good in all, so today we are just sitting around cleaning our weapons, telling jokes, and having a few cold drinks."

It was during the down time that false reports were concocted and spread around camp, which led Jimmy to write, "I heard I might be coming home in 150 days!" When these proved false, he was angered by what he called "the usual barber shop stories," and was further irritated when he discovered that the army had been cheating him (due to a clerical mistake) out of twenty-five dollars every month since he arrived in country. His growing frustration was clear in his letter: "I just don't trust these people anymore, especially with my money, I'll just send it home by money order." As the numbers of men increased so too did the rat population, and on days when there was no breeze, the smell of burning shit and oil was stifling. Aside from having to fill steel drums with human waste and wash pots in the mess hall, Jimmy also spent most of his nights in the orderly room answering telephones and taking messages. It was an alternative to guard duty. The time alone allowed him to reply to his parents, whose letters kept piling up:

> *Dear Mom and Dad: I always think when I am doing something, like eating dinner, that* [you] *are doing the same, but I know your really not, but I just like to believe it. . . . I got two letters from Barbara and one from Alice and Kathy, two from Louise, and one from Gerry yesterday, I could not write right back because I was on KP* [Kitchen Patrol] *all day, so I guess I didn't really miss anything by not getting the* [colonel's aide] *position and staying at Ft. Dix because they all left there anyway and ended up here* [in Cu Chi] *. . . I am really glad the station continues to get busy, but remember Dad, don't lose your head when Georgie takes to long for lunch because. . . . I remember when you use to*

say Jim, I'll be right back and then you go and eat lunch, and the next time I would see you was to relieve me for dinner, so just remember do unto others as you want them to do for you . . . I am glad everyone is fine at home, I hope every thing stays that way until I get home to raise hell, then you all can say Jimmy has not changed a bit then I'll say I guess [you're] *right and laugh as I am leaving with the car and leaving Georgie down the station to* [work alone], *and of course my room will also be dirty and I'll tell a few lie's here and there, but nothing to big . . . Georgie about not looking bad in the those Army* [boots] *I sent, maybe you might want to keep them because it wont be long, at least I hope not, until I get home to see your face when you leave for Fort Dix . . .*

When he finished the letter, he slipped the life insurance policy he had taken out into the envelope and added, "You'll never get the chance to collect it because I'll be home February 5, 1967."

Aside from receiving mail from family and friends, Jimmy also received letters from strangers, one of whom was a woman from Illinois he thought must be a "nut [because she] mailed the whole entire company." The division's newspaper began publishing some of the more well written and encouraging letters that were simply addressed to "any American soldier in Vietnam." Massive amounts of mail came in daily from all sections of the United States. One writer—possibly the woman who wrote to Jimmy—had sent several letters explaining that she was just "lonely" and wanted someone to "please write." Topics ranged from religious devotion and patriotic support to antiwar sentiment. One of the most widely circulated was written by a female high school student from the Bronx. Though she was against the administration's policy in Vietnam, she wanted the soldiers to know that "even those of us who are anti-war haven't forgotten you. . . . Tomorrow, I'm cutting school and going on a protest march to Albany. . ."

Elementary school students also began writing to American soldiers serving in Vietnam, including a fourth-grade class in the Yorkship School in Camden, New Jersey, which adopted a platoon of soldiers as pen pals. The Camden students were mostly unaffected by the war's brutality. Death was unimaginable, so it came as a great shock when the teacher broke the news to the class that one of the pen pals had died. Some of the children began to cry. The war for the nine-and-ten-year-olds became more personal. Some student pen pals from other schools mentioned how jealous they were of the soldiers. Douglas Crawford, a twelve-year-old from Richmond, West Virginia, said he was proud of American accomplishments in Vietnam: "I really envy you guys because you guys at least get to fight for what you want but us we can't fight the school so we have to go."[57]

Through most of May and June, Jimmy was able to avoid fighting in Operations Maili and Wahiawa, for which General Weyand committed all six of his battalions to wipe out NVA units in the Ho Bo and Boi Loi Woods. Weyand and his staff felt that because the planting season in Cu Chi stretched from June through August, guerrilla fighters would be working in the rice paddies, providing GIs with a relatively safe way to capture suspected enemy soldiers. Despite what proved to be meager results, Weyand pushed back against his critics by arguing that "no one should expect spectacular results or large VC losses" because pacification was intended to win over the local population— not destroy it. Working in tandem with South Vietnamese Special Police forces and medical crews, infantrymen were ordered to search every house and check the credentials and health of every man, woman, and child they came across.

Meanwhile, the U.S. Army's Psychological Ops team dumped billions of leaflets onto the small towns and villages inside the Iron Triangle. The flyers were intended to inform the peasantry about both bombing schedules and US medical programs. Some leaflets didn't mince words, and like a satirical skit from Monty Python, ordered occupants of villages to "leave their area or you will be struck again and again" from planes that fly "too high to be seen" which will "rain death upon you again without warning." Aside from propaganda posters, the Army broadcast thousands of hours of taped messages from loudspeakers attached to airplanes that informed those on the ground to evacuate their homes or, if they were Viet Cong, to give up fighting. The army even went so far as disguising roughly 3,000 Vietnamese intelligence agents as actors who traveled from village to village performing folk songs, magic shows, dances, and dramatic plays that were intended to give the peasantry a "better understanding of [US] Government policies."[58]

The communists left propaganda leaflets of their own along trails or in tunnels for the Americans to find. Following Vo Nguyen Giap and Ho Chi Minh's cardinal principles of political warfare, "Do not attempt to overthrow the enemy but try to win him over and make use of him," the Viet Cong became masters of the art of propaganda, which they used to bolster both domestic and foreign support. Because they lacked heavy paper and colored ink, most Viet Cong flyers were printed from hand-carved wooden or rubber blocks that were stamped on transparent rice paper. Designers of the leaflets sought to convince GIs that they and the American people were being exploited by their leaders and wealthy capitalists. They also tried to create racial divisions within the ranks by printing comics and handouts that depicted African Americans as "cannon fodder."

For the most part Jimmy was unaware of these propaganda efforts, but he became obsessed with collecting leaflets and trying to translate them, paying close attention to the accent marks and punctuation. In June he befriended a young ARVN soldier who had begun to teach him Vietnamese. Sharing his enthusiasm with his parents, he wrote, "I really found out a lot of new words to speak, and not just curse words, I found a really good friend who is a South Viet Nam soldier name Lê Vaň Tân, I will send you his picture, he is 19 years old and has helped me a lot as far as learning to speak . . . time is flying though, I don't think I will have a chance to do and learn everything I had planned on, but one thing I really want to do is learn how to speak Vietnamese."

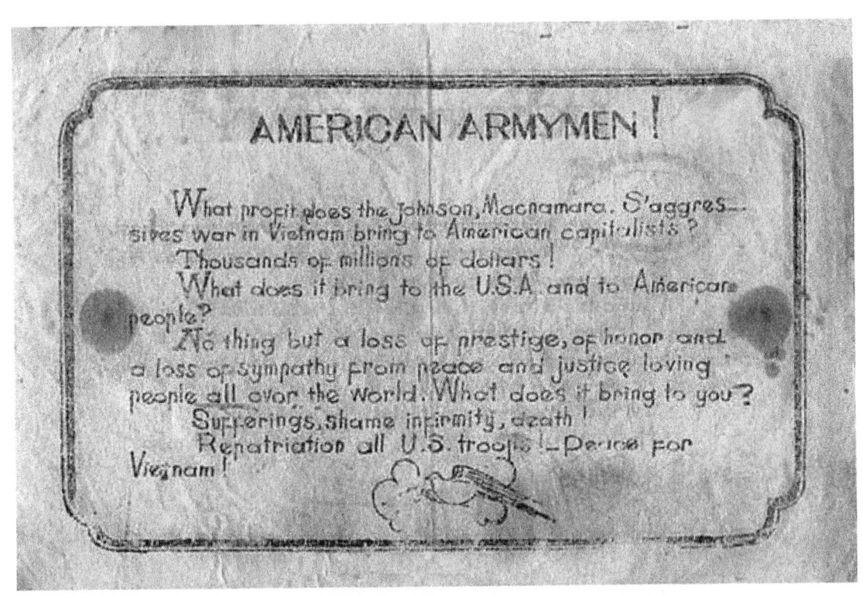
AMERICAN ARMYMEN!

What profit does the Johnson, Macnamara. S'aggres-sives war in Vietnam bring to American capitalists?
Thousands of millions of dollars!
What does it bring to the U.S.A and to American people?
No thing but a loss of prestige, of honor and a loss of sympathy from peace and justice loving people all over the world. What does it bring to you?
Sufferings, shame infirmity, death!
Repatriation all U.S. troops! – Peace for Vietnam!

Two examples of communist propaganda leaflets intended to (the first) convince GIs that they had been manipulated by the US government into fighting an unjust war, and (the second) to persuade African American soldiers that they were victimized because they were regularly given the most dangerous combat assignments.

Lê Vaň Tân

Although most American infantrymen held soldiers in the South Vietnamese Army in contempt, Jimmy began to appreciate their culture and enjoyed their company. Not only was skin color becoming a non-issue for him, he also had come to respect the South Vietnamese fighters at a time when relations between the two armies were becoming increasingly tense. Many GIs thought their "allies" were lazy, thieves, and by some accounts, possibly spies for the NVA and Viet Cong. Marine colonel Robert Tschan, for example, explained why he had a low opinion of Vietnamese troops after a firefight with the guerrillas: "They [ARVN soldiers] would not come out of their bunkers to help with the medevacs, but while Sergeant Green and I were loading the medevacs on the choppers, the bastards came out, went into our two bunkers and stole everything we owned, personal property, clothes, food, cigarettes, personal gear of our dead and wounded, and two radios. Our sole purpose is to help them with air power, naval gunfire, artillery, and advice—and this is our reward?"[59] In this context, perhaps Jimmy tried to find a way, however modest, to make up for American killing and destruction by learning the Vietnamese language and forging a friendship that ran against typical army practice, and even the inclinations of his fellow grunts.

By the middle of June, Jimmy's letters home became less and less frequent. Early in his tour of duty he had written once, even twice a day, but now he seemed to be more concerned with avoiding combat and hanging out with his old friends from Fort Dix. As had been the case with most soldiers, Jimmy turned to friends to ease the trauma of combat. Though most of them were clerks, many had been previously stationed in the field so he was able to relate to them better than his family. In talking with the desk duty officers, he found out that because the ground was too wet, his unit would not go out on patrol until the monsoon season was over. But again the report was false. As the rest of the company prepared for an operation slated to begin on June 25, Jimmy was confident he would find a way out of the mission. The time away from the field had changed his mood for the better, and a recent note from his father explaining that his paychecks were to be used to make a down payment on a new flatbed tow truck gave Jimmy the sense of purpose that he joined the military to acquire.

> *Dad, I got your letter and I was real glad to hear from you, I think it was real good idea about the flat bed truck. . . . In fact, I have a hard time sleeping at night thinking of the [truck], we are really going to have a good business now, you know I never did know much about cars, just knew where the gas tank was at, Dad, do you remember the time I towed the big truck in and you got so made at me, after you think about it, it was kind of funny. I feel real good and I really think I look a lot better now than before because I was always skinny but now my weight is just about right, and I always stand up (straigt) straight now too, I am getting back to my old self again, I change clothes every night, the whole works, my bill for getting them cleaned is getting high, but I feel better wearing clean clothes . . .*

It wasn't long after he wrote to his father that he sent another letter home: "I just got done [with] KP, so I thought I would write a letter home. Two more guys in the squad got their leave, so I am next." But by the time the letter reached home, he was already leaving on Operation Coco Palms. He was unable to escape the mission, and wrote home explaining that "a lot of Viet Nam girls are working in our company area and they will pull our KP for us." Several days after the operation was terminated, Second Platoon returned to Cu Chi down one man. The company as a whole suffered two deaths and eighteen wounded. Jimmy didn't write home that night, or for the next couple nights. His friend Gerald Rolf had been killed, and his sense of loss had become oppressive.

On July 19, the Twenty-Fifth Infantry Division conducted another pacification mission in the Hau Nghia Province. Operation Mokuleia was implausibly named after a strip of coastline in Hawaii called Slaughterhouse Beach. Several platoons of the Twenty-Seventh Infantry, nicknamed the "Wolfhounds," were helicoptered into the target area and almost immediately ambushed by NVA soldiers. Jimmy's unit was placed on stand-by. In just three hours, the Wolfhounds had sustained over forty casualties, and of the twenty-five dead, sixteen were left behind during their chaotic retreat. Jimmy could hear the sound of outgoing artillery that was clearing the landing zones as he sat in his APC. While he waited in the motor pool to lead a counterattack and recover the missing American dead, he wrote a letter to his sister Maureen that captured his unease: "I received your letter from July 13th last night . . . My leave is coming up soon, I don't know where I will go, but it does not make a big difference because if it was hell and back again I would take it . . . I'll have so much to tell you when I get home, [and] I know you will be proud me . . . " His letters were filled with anxiety, and he developed a kind of "tunnel vision" that blocked out the rest of the world, while he focused on family, his narrowly conceived future, and R&R.

Jimmy's mindset came to be categorized by army psychiatrists as "Short Time Syndrome."[60] It developed in soldiers who got nervous and worried about getting killed just before going home or on leave. Anticipating downtime on R&R often reduced the effectiveness of soldiers who were left with no choice but to return to the bush. With their thoughts still centered on leave, they were vulnerable to being "wasted." Just returning from R&R could be unsettling. Specialist Bob Leahy explains: " . . . A man [came] back from R&R and everyone [was] looking at the pictures he took and joking with him. He [then] looks around and [says], 'Where is Monte?' The joking stops and there is silence. Finally someone says, 'Monte died two weeks ago, a 105 booby trap.' Then everyone sorta drifts away to let the returning man grieve alone."[61]

When the GIs who longed for leave finally received their wish, many refused to go because they were worried they might come back to find all their friends . . . dead. Lieutenant James Simmen, succinctly captured this response, "I feel like a crudball leaving my men."[62] Yet, as Private Ken Bagby countered, sometimes seeing a friend die was worse. He recalled, "On Monday morning, the 15th of November, my friend [Dan Davis] died in my arms of two bullet wounds in the chest. He said, 'Ken, I can't breathe.' There was nothing I could do. . . . The odor of blood and decayed bodies, I will never forget . . . I will never, never, never, be the same. If I have to go into battle again, if I am not killed, I will come out insane."[63] GIs who witnessed buddies killed when they had little time left in country were deeply traumatized. This often led them to commit unnecessary, yet sometimes heroic, acts toward the end of their tours of duty that cost them their lives or left them permanently injured. Aware of these demoralizing breakdowns, a group of American soldiers of the 196th Light Infantry Brigade (attached to the Twenty-Fifth Infantry Division) wrote President Nixon in 1969 asking that troops be assigned to jobs in the rear for the last three or four months of their tour, or be excused from patrols when they were close to R&R. The president never responded. [64]

In collections of letters from soldiers in Vietnam, it is well documented that combat infantrymen "would rather take permanent KP or burn human waste on a fire support base than spend another night in the field" so close to their departure.[65] This was exactly what Jimmy was doing, and at times he even purposely got into trouble to avoid another day in combat. But he could not avoid the operation to search for enemy forces in the Filhol Plantation, even though he was physically and mentally shutting down. His letters became stream of conscious assertions about how he was "OK"—when he wasn't. Those assurances led to questions about his family. He never wrote about combat. But he often told them when he was "going down to see his friends."

On the morning of July 20, the men of B Company found the bodies that had been left behind arranged in a neat row on their backs. They were all clothed, but stripped of their equipment and weapons. It was a horrifying sight. Once the bodies were transported back to base, B Company began a sweep of the area, but met no resistance. Interrogations of peasants on the following day indicated that the NVA soldiers had moved north. The information seemed to check out. Aside from capturing several Viet Cong tax collectors, the company found no sign of the enemy's presence. It didn't even look like a battle had been fought there. So they turned around and headed back to base. On their return they passed a downed helicopter. The charred body of the door gunner was still clutching his M-60 machine gun.

In a rainforest clearing an NLF officer (partially hidden by a tree and using a burnt-out U.S. Armored Personnel Carrier as a blackboard) instructs guerrilla fighters about the types of American explosives that would likely be deployed against them in combat.

CHAPTER 7

Return to Filhol, Late July, 1966

Men who died were never referred to as killed. They were simply "wasted" or "zapped." They were casualties, not deaths. Only the enemy was "killed." Gerald Rolf was "wasted". If a man was shot through the guts and bled to death, he was never reported as having suffered "penetrating abdominal trauma." Instead, the army registered the cause of death as a "GSW" (gunshot wound). If a man died from voluntarily taking a dangerous risk, the army labeled his death as "unnatural" or "misadventure"—the same category it reserved for suicide or homicide victims. Rolf's death certificate simply reported, "ground casualty, small arms fire." Even the word certificate seemed unfair. That was supposed to be something good, like winning an award or completing school. Sadly, Rolf's only certificate was a death notice. He wasn't present for the seven guns that fired three times in salute—nor was he there to accept his purple heart. He had become just another number.

On the night of July 20th, six days after the army terminated Operation Coco Palms, B Company was exhausted when they returned to Cu Chi. Nonetheless, it was again ordered back into the Filhol Rubber Plantation. Jimmy's squad would head out the next morning. He managed to mail a letter to his parents in which he scribbled: "Not much time to talk." Complaints were muttered that evening as several men, including Jimmy, had bad feelings about a return to the plantation—and the mission itself. The Filhol and the Ho Bo Woods had an eeriness and a dangerous beauty that were all too familiar to them. The men of B Company tried to rest that night, but the constant throb of helicopters, outgoing mortars, and sniper fire allowed only restless sleep and unsettling dreams.

The next morning B Company was ordered to start packing their APCs with C-4 explosives and antipersonnel mines. Throughout the 1960s and '70s, the United States was the world's leading producer and exporter of landmines. Of the 340 types available, the M14 was a favorite of American soldiers for protecting perimeters at night. It was small enough to place into a shallow hole or under leaves, and would detonate if stepped on. The explosive charge in the mine was cone-shaped, which forced much of the blast upwards, increasing its destructive effects. In situations where M14 victims were barefoot or wearing sandals, much of the front foot was blown away, so the device was dubbed the "toe popper." Claymore mines were similar in their destructive power. They were remotely detonated and packed with hundreds of steel pellets and a few additional pounds of C-4 explosive. When the mine was set off, the expanding gases of the C-4 sent steel shot flying through the air at 26,000 feet per second. Philip Caputo calculated, "that terrific force made the explosion of a command-detonated mine equivalent to the simultaneous firing of seventy twelve-gauge shotguns loaded with double-0 buckshot."[1] Anyone hit at close range by the explosive was made unrecognizable.

As usual, B Company's mission was to search for the enemy and destroy anything in the target area. The Filhol plantation was reported to be the site of a newly built VC training camp. In the week before the mission, Vietnamese soldiers were sighted south of the town of Ap Ben Do. They were recruiting guerrilla fighters, in some cases visiting their families, and making sure the village would be able to supply food and resources to local Viet Cong units. Additional communist forces were also spotted operating just outside the town of Cu Chi collecting taxes, repairing tunnels, and planting explosives. These devices were responsible for many of the shrapnel wounds that the U.S. Army called "multiple fragment lacerations" or "MFLs." They were also the chief cause of a much more gruesome injury, dismemberment. The military's term for this was "traumatic amputation," even though a soldier's body was hit with such explosive force, it did not break cleanly apart. Second Lieutenant Robert C. "Mike" Ransom, Jr, commander of a tank platoon in the Eleventh Light Infantry Brigade, wrote home describing what a mine was capable of doing to the human body: "The tracks were returning to where we would stay overnight. When we reached our spot we jumped off the tracks, and one of my men jumped right onto a mine. Both his feet were blown off, both his legs were torn to shreds – his entire groin area was completely blown away. It was the most horrible sight I've ever seen. I am now filled with both respect and hate for the VC and the Vietnamese."[2]

Jimmy and B Company left base camp at 0900, and entered the Filhol by late morning. They were headed in the same direction where in early April they had lost Frank D'Amico. They were hyper-alert as they continued into the Ho Bo Woods and around the village of Phu My Hung, which was a well-known, well-secured area that held two enemy hospitals, a fortified headquarters, and a training depot—all mostly underground. The Filhol area was notorious for hidden enemy entrenchments and snipers, who climbed high into the trees and hid in the foliage. The GIs in B Company expected to be ambushed, so they breathed a sigh of relief as the APCs maneuvered past ground that had claimed many of their friends.

The Filhol rubber plantation was immense. It stretched north of the town of Cu Chi, along the Saigon River facing the Iron Triangle. When the French abandoned the area during the First Indochina War, the plantation's regimented lines of rubber trees became a Viet Cong sanctuary. In the early months of 1965, the local Forty-Ninth ARVN unit had secured a small outpost in the area, but because they struggled to hold it, American forces were called in to keep the area free of communist infiltration.

After a search of the preselected objectives on July 21, by early afternoon B Company had found and destroyed only one bunker near where the Ho Bo Woods and Filhol plantation met. The places targeted by the high-ranking officers at headquarters appeared to be based on faulty intelligence, so not much was found. Late in the afternoon—relieved that there had been little action—the Company headed back to Cu Chi. But on the return trip, guerrilla forces ambushed B Company in the same place where earlier that afternoon they had dismounted their APCs and demolished an enemy entrenchment.[3] The ambush began with small weapons fire from the earthworks one hundred meters away. An ammo box inside Lieutenant Jagosz's APC was struck and exploded. Jagosz was knocked unconscious and pinned to the floor by falling ammo boxes. His driver was hit in the face by shrapnel and slumped over the gears, sending the track into reverse.

The VC had placed command-detonated mines all around the area. They also hung recycled US howitzer shells from low-lying tree branches, which they shot down on the approaching Americans. Shrapnel and large wooden splinters wounded several men, including Captain Vanneman, who had been returning fire from the exposed overhead hatch of his APC. In an effort to flank the enemy, Jimmy and his third squad mates took it upon themselves to move their APC around the enemy trench line to support the units that were pinned down under fire. They were hoping their flanking maneuver would disrupt the enemy's ambush long enough for A Company to arrive and repel the guerrilla's assault. As their track moved across the trench, it was hit by a command-detonated mine. The blast set off several pounds of explosives stored in the overhead compartments. The hood covering their engine, weighing several tons, flew at supersonic speed through the air. The only thing left of the APC was the floorboard and the driver's steering sticks. All seven soldiers aboard were killed instantly.[4] The shattering and fragmenting effects from high explosives made for great difficulty in recovering their remains as several body parts were mixed together in and around the rubble. Others were never found. It was noted in Jimmy's medical evaluation report that a careful search for human remains should be made if tactically possible whenever a soldier was mutilated beyond recognition. In cases where the injuries of men who died together were so severe that the bodies could not be distinguished, dental records would be needed to assist in positive identifications.

Epilogue

"If the needs of this country are not met by middle-of-the-road progressivism, the problems won't be met, and the time will come when only extremist solutions are possible."

– UNITED STATES SENATOR CLIFFORD P. CASE, 1956.

A green Oldsmobile decorated with white stars exited the New Jersey Turnpike and went north on the Black Horse Pike. After several miles the car turned around and headed south towards Runnemede. The driver was lost. He pulled into the first gas station he came across to get directions. When the gas jockey came up, the army officers asked for directions to Davis Road. The attendant was hesitant to respond. He was a longtime friend of the Gilches, and didn't think it was a coincidence that the family who lived on that street had a son serving in Vietnam. The service attendant gave the officers directions, and after the car sped away he ran to the office in the towing garage to find his boss, George.

When the officers drove through town, the locals who spotted them knew they were the bearers of bad news. During the early years of the Vietnam War, the government issued death notices that were delivered by Western Union often arrived before the U.S. Army's scheduled in-person visits. Although the CNOs (Casualty Notification Officers) who were going to the Gilches had arrived ahead of the telegram, they were not sufficiently prepared to deal with the anguish that their presence would provoke. "They train us as warriors. [But] they don't teach us how to take the pain away," one CNO remarked. Another recounted, "I remember every single one. I remember every single phone call at 4:30 in the morning. I remember driving to every single house. I remember once going to a place in what would have been an idyllic, Robert Frost snowfall in Southern New Hampshire and knowing that on this beautiful day I was going to be destroying some family's lives."[1]

When the gas attendant finally got ahold of him, George asked what was wrong. The young man's face was flushed. He had carefully planned what he was going to say to his boss, but he was so nervous about George's reaction that he just told him that he ought to go home right away. Then the phone rang. It was Kate. She was crying. The officers had found the house, but because army regulations required it, they refused to break the news to the family without the father being present. George was confused. He could barely understand his wife over the phone. He quickly ran out the door, and raced away in his car, driving on the shoulder at times to get around the traffic on the Pike. It wasn't until he pulled into the driveway that he realized Jimmy was dead.

The officers broke the bad news, but refused to discuss the circumstances of Jimmy's death. Though it could only have added to the shock and sorrow of his parents and siblings, they did mention that Jimmy had received "multiple fragment lacerations" to his body. Perhaps hoping to correct for that disturbing revelation, one of the CNOs quickly added: "Sir, there are medals involved. Your son James has been awarded the Bronze Star for bravery." George looked up, blurry-eyed but angry. His persisting guilt that he hadn't pressed harder to convince Jimmy to join the National Guard intensified his grief. He suddenly lashed out against President Johnson. Knowing that the president's daughter Luci was to be married that August, George blurted out, "Pin the damn medals on the Johnson wedding cake!"

Months later on a cold night in a ceremony at Fort Dix, Jimmy was posthumously awarded the Purple Heart. At his mother's insistence, his younger brother Joey received the medal in his honor. After the ribbon was pinned to his oversized coat, Joey walked up the wooden bleachers, sat down and cried. In the year that followed, the town built a memorial in the high school courtyard and dedicated it to Jimmy and seven other former students who were killed in Vietnam. Though the small monument stands as a testament to the town's local history, it also commemorates the sense of loss and disorientation felt by all American families who lost loved ones.

Tens of thousands of American families had CNO visits similar to the one that transformed the lives of the Gilches. As of 2008, the most accurate count of U.S. servicemen killed in Vietnam had reached 58,220, of whom 40,934 died in combat with enemy forces, and 5,299 died of wounds after being evacuated from battle sites. Another 382 died of self-inflicted wounds. A total of 9,107 died of "accidents," but it is not clear what percentage was due to friendly fire. In addition, 236 were homicides, 938 died of disease, and 123 were presumed dead because they were MIAs.[2] Though estimates vary, over 300,000 American servicemen were wounded. The high survival rate for the wounded was largely due to Medevac helicopters that allowed for rapid evacuation from the often remote battlefields of the war. As postwar novels and memoirs attest, by 1967–1968 the Veterans Administration was all but overwhelmed by the number of wartime casualties. Long delays and misguided or inadequate medical care meant that many wounded veterans, including those diagnosed with Posttraumatic Stress Disorder (PTSD), were often left to struggle with lifetime disabilities that might have been remediable.[3] As Robert Jay Lifton's analysis of returned combatants' accounts of their experiences in the war suggests, perhaps a majority suffered

severe psychological aftereffects due to what they witnessed or did during their time in country.[4]

In 1969, at the height of US engagement, there were approximately 542,000 American military personnel in Vietnam, but most were assigned to logistical, clerical, and other operational support roles. Even if they were not combatants, when soldiers returned home to a country where there was widespread opposition to the war, many were vilified as war criminals, though reports that they were spat upon and physically harassed were wildly exaggerated. Once reunited with their families, the majority found peacetime jobs, which were still quite abundant and provided a decent standard of living. In far too many instances, however, discharged servicemen, particularly those with war-inflicted disabilities, were unable to find regular employment or struggled to support themselves in low-paying, menial jobs. Other veterans found themselves among the homeless population that soared in the postwar decades.[5] Encouraged by opposition to the war at home, thousands of veterans joined the protest movement. In April 1967, a small group of the most active returning soldiers founded the Vietnam Veterans Against the War to publicize both the intolerable dilemmas an attrition strategy had posed for combatants, and the treatment of both wounded and discharged veterans after they returned home. As its numbers increased into the tens of thousands, the VVAW became a major factor in the domestic demonstrations that finally ended America's military interventions in Southeast Asia.

An Anti-Vietnam War Demonstration in Washington, D.C., 1967.

Of the many localized antiwar protests, one of the most resonant was directed against Jimmy Gilch's local draft board. As the death toll of New Jersey GIs approached one thousand in August 1971, a group of leftist Catholic activists, lead by Father Michael Doyle, raided the U.S. Army's Selective Service headquarters in Camden, New Jersey. Their aim was to destroy draft files. They were arrested and tried, but were acquitted by a jury "after being permitted to give their moral arguments in court regarding why they committed the act of civil disobedience."[6]

Buoyed by widespread public outrage against the Nixon administration's approval of ground offensives into Cambodia in April 1970, the VVAW reached the peak of its influence in the early months of 1971. Despite an initial media boycott, its January 31 to February 2 Winter Soldier Investigation of American soldiers' war crimes in Vietnam was subsequently widely publicized. The moving and informed testimony provided by Lieutenant John Kerry at the forum led to an opportunity for him to address the Senate Committee on Foreign Relations on April 22, 1971. Kerry's influence was enhanced by his extended and courageous service in Vietnam from August 1966 to January 1970, for which he received numerous honors, including Silver and Bronze Stars, three Purple Heart medals, and a Combat V award for "heroic achievement." Some veterans then and decades later supported often spurious efforts to discredit his war record, Congressional testimony, and antiwar activities. But Kerry's firsthand accounts of military mismanagement and atrocities committed by GIs against Vietnamese civilians contributed significantly to the last wave of public protest that influenced the decisions to withdraw US combat forces from South Vietnam.

In the decades that followed, other veterans, who already had or were able to gain the literary skills to make their voices heard, went on to write some of the most powerful novels, poetry, and memoirs in 20th-century American literature. Despite pushback from hawkish politicians and veterans, who insisted that the war was fought well and for a noble cause, these dissident authors have shaped the dominant image of America's interventions in Vietnam as unnecessary, misguided, and sources of immense human misery for all who were caught up in the conflict.

Although American casualties were without question sobering in terms of the numbers of mostly young lives lost and devastated, the number of Vietnamese killed on both sides of the conflict was at least fifty times higher than the 58,000 plus American soldiers who died. Civilian casualties accounted for a substantial percentage of the Vietnamese total. The patient registers of wartime South Vietnamese hospitals provide one of the few reliable gauges of noncombatant victims. They show that one-third of the wounded were women and nearly a fourth were children under the age of thirteen.[7] These losses meant that in addition to the sons, brothers, and fathers lost to families like the Gilches, and tens of thousands of other American families, the Vietnamese mourned daughters, sisters, mothers, as well as grandparents and grandchildren. In part, the internecine conflict that pitted communist insurgents in the South and NVA soldiers from the North against forces loyal to the Saigon regime accounts for the vastly greater numbers of Vietnamese dead and wounded. The counterinsurgent responses to guerrilla warfare in the South also predictably resulted in high civilian casualties. But above all, the differential in wealth and power between the American interventionists and the Vietnamese nationalist-revolutionaries was responsible for the great disparity in the levels of killing and destruction inflicted by the two main adversaries in the final phase of the decades of conflict.

Guerrilla warfare has been a recurring mode of resistance since ancient times,[8] but never has an insurgent movement faced an adversary with weapons systems, surveillance technologies, logistical support networks, and military forces—with the capacity to strike from the air, land, and sea—that could even begin to match those deployed by the United States. A war-ravaged former colony of approximately thirty-four million people in 1950, in an area roughly the size of California, refused to back down in the face of ultimatums and then military aggression by a transcontinental, industrial superpower with a population of over 150 million. The Vietnamese victory was all the more remarkable given decades of struggle from the 1930s into the 1960s, first in local rebellions and then through the decades of the communist-led revolutionary resistance against French colonizers, Japanese occupiers, a massive wartime famine, and the American-backed Diem regime. The guerrilla war the Maoists waged against the Guomindang in China was concurrent with the early decades of the Vietnamese resistance to the French and Japanese. That conflict was also far larger in scale. But the Vietnamese revolution continued for nearly a quarter of a century longer than the Chinese, and the greatest devastation and loss of life came during the half decade of direct US military intervention.

The covert nature of guerrilla resistance invariably made for imprecise casualty counts and understated cost estimates. But without question the total of dead and wounded, both civilian and military, in China's civil war and resistance to the Japanese invasion was by far the highest in any human conflict in which guerrilla forces played a major role. As a percentage of a much smaller population, however, Vietnamese losses, particularly among the civilian population, very likely exceeded even the levels documented for revolutionary China.

American and European estimates of Vietnamese killed on all sides of the war from 1965 to 1974 range from Charles Hirschman's (1995) conservative calculation of nearly 900,000 to a more recent 2008 total reported in the *British Medical Journal* of 1.7 million. The British computation was almost doubled to over 3 million by both the government of Vietnam's postwar count and the combined analysis of researchers at the Harvard Medical School and the University of Washington's Institute for Health Metrics and Evaluation. The official Vietnamese total includes almost two million civilians and 300,000 military MIAs for just NVA and NLF forces. The number of soldiers and civilians wounded, permanently maimed, and missing was almost certainly a good deal higher. But civilian casualties are impossible to determine with any accuracy because their deaths were often listed by the American military as "guerrillas killed," and in many instances no one was counting at all. These levels of death and injury resulted from one of the most relentless and massive assaults leveled against a land and people in all of human history. The scale of bombing alone is difficult to justify, especially when the size and underdeveloped state of the targeted areas is taken into account. In the decade between 1964 and 1973, the United States Air Force as well as Navy and Marine squadrons dropped 7,662,000 tons of explosives on Indochina. More than 90 percent hit targets in Vietnam (rather than Cambodia and Laos), and a substantial portion battered the villages and rice paddies of the southern half of Vietnam that American leaders claimed they were trying to save from oppressive communist rule. These bombing totals dwarfed the tonnage dropped by American forces on *all* fronts in World War II and the Korean War combined.[9]

When the determination and resilience of the communist resistance thwarted American expectations of a quick victory, a whole range of antipersonnel weapons were deployed. Many were specifically concocted for assaults on guerrilla forces and peasant communities supporting them. The most publicized during the war was napalm, an incendiary bomb that combined petrol and viscous chemicals. When detonated, it ejected sticky fireballs (at temperatures as high as 3,632 degrees Fahrenheit) that seared the skin of humans and animals within the range of the blast.[10] Introduced during World War II, napalm was considered a "conventional" weapon at the time of the Vietnam War, in contrast to several other incendiaries. These include white phosphorus and magnesium that burned deeply into the victim's flesh and ate away her or his bones at temperatures from 3,632 to 7,052 degrees Fahrenheit. The carbon monoxide produced by these weapons could asphyxiate soldiers or civilians within the range of the explosions, or leave the survivors with poisoned livers, kidneys, and severe nervous disorders. Phosphorous is especially horrific. It burrows inside the wounds the explosive inflicts, and can burn for weeks giving off a greenish light in hospital wards where victims are treated.

In addition to chemical weapons, the American military deployed several types of fragmentation bombs developed by the technicians at Honeywell and other US weapons manufacturers. These were also specifically designed to kill and maim people, and were often deployed in densely populated areas. Steel pellet (CBU46s) and related "pineapple" and "guava" cluster bombs exploded before hitting the ground, releasing hundreds of steel balls or needlelike spikes that literally shredded guerrilla fighters as well as villagers and their livestock.

The explosive impact of the "daisy cutter" bomb was so powerful that its shock waves annihilated all plant, animal, and human life within a 3,200-foot radius.[11] "Spider mines" were often dropped along with fragmentation bombs. As their name suggests, the mines shot out nylon threads when they hit the ground and exploded if peasants or guerrilla fighters passing by tripped the well-disguised, faux tentacles. More conventional bombing runs, especially those flown by American B-52 pilots, which carried the most powerful explosives, also led to high levels of civilian casualties and turned forests and paddy fields into desiccated wastelands. The B-52's contribution to the war on the Vietnamese ecosystem also included craterization, which consisted of large holes that could reach

Bomb craters scarred the landscape over many districts of South Vietnam.

30–40 feet in diameter and 40–50 feet in depth, carved out by exploding bombs. By 1972, when the United States officially ended its military interventions, more than ten million craters pockmarked the South Vietnamese landscape. They not only left an area the size of Connecticut a patchwork of fields and forests unfit for cultivation or logging, but the tens of thousands of craters became breeding ponds for malarial mosquitos and other disease-spreading insects in the monsoon season.

Because antipersonnel and environmental weapons were usually launched from high above the areas targeted, the American servicemen who delivered them were distanced from the nightmarish slaughter they unleashed. Consistent with the "trial runs" and "experimentation" with ever more nefarious killing and polluting devices, this distancing exemplified General Maxwell Taylor's notion that South Vietnam was a "laboratory" where the United States could test its "equipment requirements" for defeating guerrilla warfare.[12] The notion of a lab to test counterinsurgency responses, which was an analogy also favored by a number of other war planners, blatantly dehumanized the Vietnamese who were the objects of the experiments. This mode of justifying mass killing and destruction was nothing less than a cynical revival of the racist denigration that has justified the massacres and subjugation of non-European peoples throughout history.

Some advocates of these indiscriminate assault weapons lauded the fact that they often wounded rather than killed their victims because this meant that the enemy would be forced to devote time and scarce resources to injured survivors. In South Vietnam, where it was estimated that there was only one doctor for every 16,000 people, and three-fourths of the MDs available were assigned to the military,[13] this extreme shortage meant horrific suffering for those who survived. Tens of thousands of children were either malformed at birth or suffered from chronic illnesses in the generations that followed. Because children made up a considerable percentage of the casualties, it is fitting that the plight of Luan, an eight-year-old boy wounded in a napalm strike, serves to capture the ordeals inflicted on Vietnamese civilians. As one of the "lucky ones," Luan was eventually flown to England for treatment:

> "He came off the plane with a muslin bag over what had been his face. His parents had been burned alive. His chin had melted into his throat, so that he could not close his mouth. He had no eyelids. After the injury, he had no treatment at all – none whatsoever – for four months. It will take years for Luan to be given a new face."[14]

Even in the rare instances where victims were taken to hospitals, there were often no anesthetics, or even Vaseline, to treat burns.

The failed attempts by well-meaning American assistance personnel to compensate for these atrocities—a recurring pattern throughout U.S. history—were perhaps best captured by a confrontation recounted by Neil Sheehan in *A Bright Shining Lie*.[15] In January 1966, Doug Ramsey, who was attempting to deliver food to refugees in the Trung Lap camp near a big rubber plantation in the Cu Chi District, was asked by one of the peasants what agency he worked for. When Ramsey responded "AID," (the U.S. Agency for International Development), the peasant exclaimed, "AID! Look about you," as he pointed to the charred remains of the abandoned homes of what had once been a thriving village community. "Here is your AID!" And he spat on the ground and walked away.

In 1962, several years before direct US military intervention, American advisors to the Diem regime launched yet another sort of war in South Vietnam. They provided herbicides that were sprayed on areas designated as NLF strongholds to deny communist forces refuge and food supplies. Each defoliant (orange, blue, and white) was a variant of acid or arsenic compounds mixed with diesel fuel. They were systematically deployed to destroy the crops on which the Vietnamese people depended for their livelihood, and huge swaths of the rainforests that covered so much of their verdant land. Though commonly lumped together under the label Agent Orange, all of the defoliants were prohibited in the United States

Helicopter spraying rice paddies in South Vietnam.

and banned as forms of bacteriological warfare by the terms of the Geneva Protocol. Agent Blue was used to poison rice crops and other Vietnamese staple foods. Between 1963 and 1969, Operation Ranch Hand was responsible for the defoliation of 4,500,000 acres of forest (an area slightly smaller than Massachusetts) and the destruction of 510,000 acres of farmland.[16]

Spraying croplands and forested areas proved devastating for several other of Vietnam's leading economic sectors, including timber production, rubber plantations, and the fishing industry. Among the most sobering longer-term consequences of the chemical assault on South Vietnam's agricultural and raw material sectors were chronic food shortages that were responsible for widespread malnutrition and uncounted numbers of children with kwashiorkor, which can lead to permanent brain damage. By one estimate, the mortality rate of South Vietnamese children under the age of five had soared to 50 percent by 1970. Another measure of the catastrophic effects of chemical warfare on the region's vital agricultural sector was the fact that a country that had once been one of the world's three main rice-exporting areas was importing tons of rice from California by the mid-1960s.

Despite decades of denial on the part of the American government, many of the servicemen involved in the Ranch Hand operations paid a very high price in chronic illnesses that resulted from exposure to the chemical substances they handled and dumped in massive doses on Vietnam. But often the military personnel who were able to avoid contamination distanced themselves from the human suffering and permanent environmental damage they were inflicting. Some did this in rather cynical ways by painting obscene mottos in bold letters on their planes and helicopters. Perhaps the most callous was "Only We Can Prevent Forests," which was a corruption of the then pervasive motto of Smokey the Bear. But official American policy for compensating civilians whose deaths were deemed "collateral damage" could also be appallingly obscene. For the loss of a civilian who had no apparent affiliation with the insurgency, the US government paid his or her family $34. For the destruction of a rubber tree, the rate of compensation was $87.

In constant FY 2011 dollars, the $738 billion spent on the American military interventions in Vietnam made it the most expensive war to that point in time in United States history with the exception of World War II, which cost an estimated $4.104 trillion.[17] Given this outsized expenditure and the unprecedented sophistication, killing power, and indiscriminate nature of the weaponry deployed in Vietnam, incredulity is the only reasonable response to Admiral U.S.G. Sharp's frequently iterated contention that America failed in Vietnam because its military forces were ordered to fight "with one arm tied behind their backs."[18] What more harm could possibly have been done if the other arm was freed to strike? Some of the more hawkish proponents of further escalations at the time called for an invasion of the North, or more radically, the use of tactical nuclear weapons. But those actually shaping policy on the civilian side, and some in the military, were convinced that either response would very likely bring China into the war and turn world and domestic opinion decisively against American military interventions. It was also clear to opponents of these extreme measures that nuclear weaponry was ill-suited to cope with guerrilla insurgencies that would inevitably bog down invading armies north of the 17th parallel. The possibility of bombing the dikes and flooding the heavily populated Red River delta was broached on occasion, but again less impetuous and more foresighted war planners warned that the catastrophic loss of civilian lives and ecological devastation that followed would at the very least spark outrage across the globe and risk alienating even America's closest allies.

Sharp's preoccupation with how the war ought to have been conducted obscures more fundamental questions relating to whether the war should have been fought in the first place. Kennedy, McNamara, Ball, and other key policymakers realized that decisions to intervene militarily in response to internal political strife in Vietnam ought *not* be seen as a major security concern of the United States. Neither Vietnam's resources and market potential nor its location made it strategically vital to America's global interests. And never—despite decades of American meddling and then direct and unrestrained aggression—did the communist leadership even consider a Vietnamese strike at the US homeland. In fact, the reverse was true. For nearly a decade during which they fought against the Japanese alongside American and allied forces, and then during the war of independence from French colonial rule, Ho Chi Minh and like-minded Vietnamese leaders openly sought—despite repeated rebuffs—to stress the nationalist side of their revolution and enlist American aid in the postwar development of their country.[19] A neutral communist state similar to Marshal Tito's Yugoslavia was a very real possibility. But American interventionism, as George Ball and even Lyndon Johnson's friends in Congress argued, had far less to do with Vietnam than a national obsession with cold war competition with the Soviet Union and Communist China.

An inexplicable ignorance of Vietnam's history and nationalist movement on the part of virtually all of the major policymakers in US administrations from Truman to Nixon goes a long way to explain their refusal to jettison the conviction that Vietnam was a pawn of Russia or China. The notion that the Vietnamese would acquiesce to control by yet another great power after fighting for decades to rid themselves of French and Japanese domination proved to be one of the most fateful false assumptions of the decades of sorry diplomacy that led to the Vietnam debacle. However remotely it may have affected specific decisions for escalation, the implausible analogy of falling dominos also provided impetus for those advocating ever more costly commitments to the moribund regime in Saigon. Laos had already been lost with negligible impact on the global balance of power. American offensives into Cambodia, not the communist victory in Vietnam they were intended to thwart, were directly responsible for the overthrow of Norodom Sihanouk, a popular and neutral leader, and the installation of a weak government in Phnom Penh beholden to the United States. Thus American attacks on that neutral nation destabilized a domino that soon fell to the communist Khmer Rouge and the homicidal Pol Pot. Once in power, that fanatical regime proceeded to carry out one of the most thorough and vicious genocides of a century replete with them.

Underlying the cold war rationales that American policymakers offered to justify intervening militarily in Vietnam was their presumption that the United States not only had the power to shape the historical trajectories of other, especially underdeveloped, societies, its historic mission obligated it to do so. In the post–World War II decades, this interventionist mandate was repeatedly invoked in situations where vulnerable new nations were threatened by communist takeovers. The belief that communist governments were inherently despotic, oppressive, and evil, which McCarthyite ideologues fiercely proselytized in the 1950s, had come to be widely accepted by American policymakers and the broader public. Fear of communist expansionism prompted the Gilch family and tens of thousands of others families to heed John F. Kennedy's inaugural exhortation to "pay any price, bear any burden, meet any hardship" including the loss of their sons, husbands, and fathers, to prevent communist "takeovers." That hubristic rallying cry would soon make a target of the distant, hitherto little-noticed country of Vietnam.

Although we cannot know for certain what Vietnam's first decades of full independence would have been like if the United States had abstained from entering the war on the side of the Saigon regime, it is clear that a great deal of human suffering and environmental degradation would have been avoided. If the signatory parties to the Geneva Accords and American leaders, whose predecessors had refused to sign them, had insisted that the elections pledged for 1956 be held under the supervision of neutral observers, there is little question that Ho Chi Minh and the communists would have won a decisive victory. Violent resistance might well have been mounted by a coalition of the fragmented parties that lost the election, particularly in Saigon and the southern districts as well as pockets where Catholics and followers of the religious sects were concentrated. But NVA and NLF forces, had the capacity to suppress dissent, and very likely without prolonged warfare.

Undoubtedly, scores would have been settled and "thought correction" facilities would have multiplied. The government of the united country would definitely not have resembled anything like American democracy, but then none of the American-backed Saigon regimes had even considered transitioning to that mode of governance. Ultimately though definitely brutal at times and adversely affecting hundreds of thousands of Vietnamese who had sided with the Saigon regime, compared to the retribution and massive purges carried out when other revolutionary movements have come to power (consider, for example, French, Russian and Chinese predecessors), the transition to communist rule in unified Vietnam was less lethal and prolonged. It also brought to power a government able to establish with remarkable rapidity the political and economic stability essential for efforts to raise living standards and restore normalcy to the everyday lives of ordinary citizens.

Rather than seeking to spread communism in neighboring countries as American proponents of intervention relentlessly predicted, the Socialist Republic of Vietnam, which was established in 1975, became embroiled in border disputes with the People's Republic of China. These confrontations were in part linked to the Vietnamese invasion and temporary occupation of Cambodia in order to overthrow the rogue communist Khmer Rouge regime and put an end to its horrific genocide. Equally remarkably, despite decades of US-imposed trading sanctions against Vietnam, and efforts to block funding from the World Bank and the IMF, internal restrictions and state regulation have been steadily loosened. By the 1990s, the country was well on its way to becoming a significant force in the global economy. As those familiar with their history anticipated, the Vietnamese have proved very able competitors, and increasingly partners, with other emerging, market-oriented Asian and Western nations. Beginning in the late 1980s, the United States provided Vietnam with small sums of funds for development, and in the 1990s lifted the trade embargo and established diplomatic relations.

Ho Chi Minh did not live to celebrate victory in the long struggle of the Vietnamese people for liberation and unification. But by the time of his death in September 1969, fittingly on the anniversary of the founding of the Democratic Republic of Vietnam, he was widely considered one of the most revered of a remarkable cohort of world leaders that emerged in the early decades of the twentieth century. General Vo Nguyen Giap, who was the main strategist and commander of the Viet Minh and later communist-led forces that defeated Japanese, French, and American occupiers, remained an influential, though often controversial, political leader into the early 1990s. He died in 2013 at the age of 102, and has been widely considered one of the most successful military commanders of the late twentieth century. The contrast between the fate of these pivotal Vietnamese leaders and the two Americans most responsible for the failed military interventions in Indochina has been pronounced and certainly warranted.

If he had not led the United States into the Vietnam quagmire, Lyndon Baines Johnson would likely have been elected for a second term and subsequently ranked among the nation's most effective chief executives of the twentieth century. As Johnson realized well before his stunning announcement on March 31, 1968 that he would not run for a second term, the cost in lives and treasure of his administration's commitment to containing communism in Vietnam would undermine the Great Society and War on Poverty programs. It was also clear that his insistence on "staying the course" of a war that America could neither win nor retreat from "with honor" had aroused mass domestic protest and personal vilification of a chief executive on a scale not seen since the Great Depression. Equally ominously, continuing the war had deeply divided the Democratic Party, and would in the longer term discredit the activist social engineering that had been the hallmark of the dominant progressive wing of the party since Franklin Roosevelt's long tenure in the White House. In the years that followed, "liberal" became a pejorative label associated with do-gooder advocates of bloated government who were sneeringly derided by Republican politicians, most advantageously Ronald Reagan and George H.W. Bush.

Secretary of Defense Robert McNamara alone in meeting room.

With the possible exception of W.W. Rostow, no high-ranking presidential advisor personified aspirations to Americanize emerging nations overseas through programs for socioeconomic development more confidently than Robert McNamara. His widely publicized brilliance, legendary aptitude for solving problems, and copious computer-generated "facts" allowed him to exert extraordinary influence in the formulation of foreign policy in both the Kennedy and Johnson administrations. Without Robert Kennedy to counterbalance him, McNamara's ability to translate his views into policy prescriptions peaked from mid-1964 through late 1965—the span of months when the critical decisions to escalate radically the military buildup in Vietnam were made. Though he had played a major part in all of the decisions to commit to war, by the end of 1965 he had become increasingly convinced that it was unwinnable.

After two more years of increasing estrangement from the president due to his attempts (in private) to make the case for a negotiated retreat, in early 1968 McNamara resigned his position as Secretary of State to become the president of the World Bank. Though he served ably as head of the bank for thirteen years, McNamara was tormented until the end of his life by his role in the Vietnam debacle, which took a heavy toll on his wife's frail health and led to his son's estrangement. His eventual public admission in a 1995 book that the decisions for escalation that he advocated were "wrong, terribly wrong"[20] was seen by some commentators at the time as an act of courage, but many others, especially those who had fought in the war, angrily denounced it as too little, too late. Neither his impressive achievements before or after the years he was one of the main architects of arguably America's greatest foreign policy disaster until the beginning of the twentieth-first century could assuage his sense of guilt and failure.

> Despite strong, enduring support from friends and family in the years after Jimmy's death, and the many letters of commiseration sent by his commanding officers, the president, and New Jersey notables, such as U.S. Senator Clifford Case, George was never reconciled to the loss of his son in what he believed to be an unnecessary war. His anger only intensified over the years as he railed against the war and told friends that, given the opportunity, he would kill the president. In 1967, fearing George might try to follow through on his death threat, the state police placed him under house arrest during the days of Lyndon Johnson's meetings with Soviet Premier Alexei Kosygin at Glassboro State College, not far from Runnemede. For several days afterward a trooper was assigned to stand watch over the house. That same year George sold the gas station, and in 1972 he put his last tow trucks up for sale. He had become a heavy smoker and drinker, and three years later died of a massive heart attack. He was 62. If he had lived a few more years to see his youngest son graduate from high school, he would have been even more outraged by a cruel irony: Joe's first job was to demolish a Newark chemical factory whose smoke stacks had once spewed pollutants in the production of Agent Orange.

Timeline

1802–1858: Nguyen Anh unifies Vietnam as the Gia Long Emperor of the Nguyen Dynasty; reigns until French annexations begin in the late 1840s

1850s–1907: Successive stages of French colonization of Vietnam, Cambodia, and Laos, which are combined as French Indochina

1880s–1896: Early "Restore the Emperor" movements against French

1913–1917: Localized nationalist risings and agitation against the French

1930: Communist Party (initially the Revolutionary Youth League) founded

1927–1931: Major revolts by the Nationalist VNQDD and Communists (Nghe-Tinh)

1940: Japanese occupy French Indochina

1941: The Viet Minh (League for Vietnamese Independence) founded

1945: Massive famine kills hundreds of thousands in North and Central Vietnam

1941–1945: World War II in the Pacific, Vietnam under Japanese-French rule

August 1945: Japanese surrender ends the Second World War; French begin to recolonize Indochina; United States enters a period of unparalleled prosperity

September 1945: Ho Chi Minh proclaims the establishment of the Democratic Republic of Vietnam (DRV), beginning the liquidation of the French empire in Indochina; French forcibly attempt to reoccupy Vietnam, sparking Vietnamese resistance and the onset of the French-Indochina War

1947: George Kennan introduces the notion of "containment" to stop the spread of Communism; the United States funds the Marshall Plan for European recovery; India and Pakistan are freed from British colonial rule

1949: NATO is formed, Chinese Communists defeat Kuomindang and rule mainland China

1950: North Korea's invasion of the South marks the onset of the Korean War with America backing the South; Truman begins US military aid to the French in Vietnam

1953: Armistice agreement reached in Korea; Joseph Stalin dies; French forces build a fortress at Dien Bien Phu

1954: Decisive French defeat at Dien Bien Phu; accords signed at an international conference at Geneva divides Vietnam at the 17th parallel; SEATO established; Ngo Dinh Diem returns from exile to become prime minister of South Vietnam

1955: American aid begins to be funneled to the Diem regime in Vietnam; Diem crushes sectarian and Binh Xuyen rivals; Viet Minh operatives migrate to North Vietnam; Ho Chi Minh solicits aid from the Soviet Union; Diem rejects the Geneva Accords and promised Vietnam-wide elections, instead proclaiming the Republic of Vietnam (RVN) in the South

1956: Diem moves to eliminate leftist parties; Suez Crisis in the Middle East; Soviets crush uprisings in Hungary and Poland

1957–1959: Government repression and communist resistance spreads across South Vietnam; Hanoi government decides to back armed struggle against Diem; Charles de Gaulle takes power in France, opposes American intervention in Vietnam

1960: National Liberation Front (NLF) formed in South Vietnam with backing from Hanoi; leftists seize power in Laos escalating civil war; John F. Kennedy elected in the United States; coup against Diem fails; Saigon officials dub communist forces the "Viet Cong"

1961: Khrushchev prioritizes guerrilla war to spread Communism given the nuclear standoff; Failure of the Bay of Pigs invasion in Cuba, straining U.S.-Soviet relations; Lyndon Johnson begins visits of top American officials to South Vietnam; American aid, including military and development advisors, increases substantially

1962: Cuban Missile Crisis; Strategic Hamlet program replaces Diem-devised "agrovilles" scheme as key to peasant uplift in South Vietnam; U.S. Military Assistance Command (MACV) set up in South Vietnam; over 11,000 American personnel in country; US pilots initiate spraying of Agent Orange and other herbicides over extensive areas of forests and farmlands in South Vietnam

1963: Widespread protests led by Buddhists in South Vietnam; Diem and his brother Nhu killed in a military coup; Kennedy assassinated; Lyndon Johnson becomes president of the United States

1964: United States begins secret operations against North Vietnam, Disputed North Vietnamese naval assaults on American vessels in the Gulf of Tonkin enables Johnson to get a carte blanche resolution from Congress to wage war; Johnson is reelected; North Vietnamese regular armed forces infiltrate into the highlands of South Vietnam; NLF guerrillas attack US military bases

1965: Operation Flaming Dart inaugurates over a half decade of US aerial assaults on North Vietnam; Rolling Thunder expands the bombing campaign; Marine units land at Da Nang; Nguyen Cao Ky takes command in Saigon as Prime Minister, Lyndon Johnson and his advisors approve of successive increases in American military forces, which reach nearly 200,000 by year's end; America and Vietnamese clash in one of the biggest battles in the war in the Ia Drang valley in October

1966: Johnson and Defense Secretary Robert McNamara meet with South Vietnamese leaders in Honolulu; Buddhist-led protests against the Saigon regime continue; French President de Gaulle calls for America to withdraw its military forces from Vietnam; the number of American forces in country reaches 400,000

1967: Nguyen Van Thieu elected president of South Vietnam; American military operations, including Cedar Falls and Junction City, fail to curb NLF advances and determination to topple the Saigon regime; Lyndon Johnson's meeting with Soviet Prime Minister Kosygin does little to curb the growing conflict in Vietnam; major battle at Khe Sanh begins; antiwar demonstrations in the United States and Europe expand and spread; North Vietnamese plan a major offensive for the coming year

1968: Siege of Khe Sanh peaks; Tet offensive by NLF and North Vietnamese forces begins throughout South Vietnam; American and South Vietnamese units put down the Tet risings; Eugene McCarthy and Robert Kennedy challenge Lyndon Johnson for the nomination of the Democratic Party; My Lai massacre is exposed; LBJ announces he will not to run for a second term; officials at the Pentagon opt for the "Vietnamization" of the war; US–North Vietnamese peace talks begin in Paris; Creighton Abrams replaces William Westmoreland as US commander in Vietnam; Rolling Thunder bombings are suspended; Richard Nixon is elected president; American forces in Vietnam just short of 500,000

1969: U.S. begins secret bombings of Vietnamese targets in neutral Cambodia; antiwar demonstrations multiply; first US troop withdrawal; Ho Chi Minh dies in Hanoi

1970: Prince Sihanouk deposed by a US-backed coup in Cambodia; Nixon orders an invasion of Cambodia; four student protesters are killed at Kent State University; US troops withdrawn from Cambodia

1971–1972: Nixon begins détente with China; William Calley found guilty of murders in My Lai; Khmer Rouge becomes a major force in Cambodia; NVA offensives throughout Vietnam; "Linebacker" bombing raids of North Vietnam culminate in Christmas bombings

1973–1976: Paris Peace Accords signed; United States promises to withdraw all troops within two months; last American troops withdrawn from Vietnam; Case-Church amendment forbids further US military interventions in Southeast Asia; Nixon resigns due to Watergate scandal; NVA invasion and capture of the South ends the Vietnam wars for independence and unity; Phnom Penh occupied by the Khmer Rouge, genocidal purges begin; Vietnam united under communist rule as the Socialist Republic of Vietnam

✳

Jimmy Gilch's Letters

Altogether Jimmy Gilch wrote 72 letters to his parents and siblings, as well as additional ones to several to other family members, his best friend Gerry Shields, and his girlfriend Louise during the six months he served in Vietnam. Only three of the letters to Gerry have survived, and none of those to Louise. Counting just the letters that remain, Jimmy wrote approximately every two days – and on some days he wrote twice. He wrote at all hours, but usually indicated that he was on guard duty, spending downtime in camp, or on a search and destroy mission. All of the letters to his family were addressed to his parents, except one, the last, which was addressed to his sister Maureen. The letters were posted at his base camp in Cu Chi, taken by convoy trucks to Tran Son Nhut airbase near Saigon, flown across the Pacific by the Army Air Force to San Francisco, and from there transported to Runnemede, his home town. The process usually took about a week.

From the outset Jimmy was aware of his poor grammar and spelling. His mistakes repeatedly prompted regrets that he had not taken his schoolwork seriously and listened to his parents when they warned that his indifference would limit his career options. Soon after arriving in Vietnam, Jimmy asked them to send a dictionary, and over time his writing improved somewhat. But he continued to add an apostrophe to plural nouns and write in what can best be described as a raw, stream-of-conscious mode. Despite Jimmy's stylistic shortcomings, he also wrote letters for several members of his platoon. Presumably like his own letters, they were written in pen on white lined paper or soiled army stationary. Similar to those of most soldiers in country, substantial portions of many of Jimmy's letters were focused on responses to reports of what was happening at home and plans for his future once he returned to New Jersey. Those concerns, as well as anticipating his mid-tour of duty leave time in Japan, intensified in the weeks before he was killed in action. He frequently offered advice to his sisters, at times devoting several sentences or more to each one. He was intent on teaching them to learn from his mistakes.

Although Jimmy became increasingly reluctant to write at length about his combat experiences, he did so in considerable detail during the first weeks after his arrival in Vietnam and periodically in the months that followed. From our perspective these portions of letters were critical for our efforts to provide a historical narrative that focused not just on a single US infantryman's experiences in combat, but also the broader contours of the war and on its impact on the soldiers on all sides as well as the Vietnamese civilian population. Jimmy recognized in his infrequent initial letters during basic training that he was gaining a sense of discipline and direction that he had lacked, and he also had little hesitation at that point about discussing the lessons he was given in the many ways to kill in a hand to hand fight (see the letter from boot camp, written in late October, 1965). Nonetheless, he had already begun to doubt that service in the army would make for a fulfilling career. As his letter of April 16, 1966 conveys, once he was he was sent to fight in Vietnam, Jimmy wonders how, when he was a boy, he could have been so determined to become a soldier when he grew up. After arriving in Vietnam, most of his letters are critical of the sergeants ordering him about, and express – most fully in his letter of February 10, 1966 (though he misdates as 1965) – dismay at the poverty of the people in the countryside and the backwardness of Vietnam more generally. Early on he was a reliable – if contentious (see, for example, the P.S. to the boot camp letter from late October) – soldier, who like so many GIs at the time, sought to emulate the style and courage in combat that John Wayne projected in his highly popular films.

Roughly midway through his tour of duty, a number of key encounters with the Vietnamese peasantry led him to become more and more disillusioned with American military interventions due to their devastating effects on civilian population, particularly women and children (see, for example, the letter dated March 20, 1966). Those contacts and a budding friendship with an ARVN soldier also fostered a growing appreciation of Vietnamese society and culture, which was reflected in his efforts to learn the language and communicate with the peasants he encountered during military operations. Though there is no single letter in which Jimmy sums up his negative assessments of the war effort, in his last letter home, written on July 19, 1966, in a response to a question by his sister Maureen regarding where he would like to go on leave, he replied that he didn't much care, but he'd rather go to hell and back than be at war in Vietnam.

Despite Jimmy's disillusionment and personal attempts to mitigate the damage done by the war, the medals he earned and numerous posthumous letters sent to his parents, including those from New Jersey Senator Clifford Case and Jimmy's company commander Captain E.B. Vickery that are included here, make it clear that he remained a good soldier and loyal friend to the GIs he served with in Vietnam.

BEFOR READING IT
I all ready know words
are spelled wrong

thursday
Feb 10, 1965

The United States Army Training Center, Infantry
~~Fort Dix, New Jersey~~

I DON'T KNOW THE NAME
of the town I am in, but
it is in southern Viet Nam

Dear Mom and Dad

How are you, well I got here all right, there is so much to tell you, I just don't no where to start, I am not going to the 1st CAV like I told you, my order's were changed. I am supposed to go to the 25th Inf. that is Located in Southern Viet Nam, so far I like it here the (~~whe~~) weather is very hot during the day, and (~~[illegible]~~) fairly kool at night, maybe something is wrong with me but I think it is pretty funie there every body try's to hind from detail's all day, but there is so much work to be done, they get you sooner or later, the way thing's are here, is very hard to belive, the way they live, and even dress, every family has 9 or 10 kid's you can't tell one from the other, it is just like a war story you see on TV, a little kid running after you while you are marching and saying GI do you have candy, if you give him a peace your the greatest, but if you don't, you name it and he will call it to you and it will all be in English, it took 22 hour's to get here, there are 12 hour's different in time, VN is 12 hour's ahead of the East coast, USA

February 10, 1966 – South Vietnam

continued

they sell silk clothes ceap here, every thing is a lot
ceaper here than the states, when I get paid I
will send some clothes home for the kid's and I'll
give you 5 ¢ in Viet Nam money so you can see it.
the food is not real bad, but it could be bettet
guess what kind of hat I were, a cowboy hat, just
like the Rangers wear, I will get a picture taken
soon, so you can see me in it. In a way it is like
the shore, the ~~hot~~ weather, & and the girl's that
is all you see here, they all work for the government of the
U.S., in the PX, taylor's etc, they have the men working
here to, laying pipe, for water, but they sleep most
of the time, the people here are living way better
now, than ever before, because they all work now
they say the Viet Nam people are not afraid to die
I guess not, they ~~n~~ don't have any thing to live for
all of them live like pig's, the men are only about
5'6 in at the most about 135 or 140 lbs, they wear all
GI clothes, boot's even, every Sgt has a girl's friend
here are some word's for you, (PUT UP YOUR HANDS ~~ON YOUR HEAD~~)
DUA TAY LÊN

(HALT)
DỪNG LẠI
(I WILL SEARCH YOU)
TÔI KHÁM ÔNG

I don't no how to say them, I copyed them from
a card, tell George to take my clothes
because they won't fit me a year from now,
tell my body I said hello. I will write again in a couple
of day's, don't write until I tell you because I won't
get the mail, until I get to the 25th Inf, then you can
write,

Love
Jimmy or the Love GI

(1)

Dear family + George jr too

How are you, well I got a little time to my self so I through I would drop a line to all of you, well I got just 10 day's left here and than after that, well it will be up to Uncle Sam, but I will tell him what I want, the Weather is getting cold, and I got one too, but I think I will be all right I am going to drop out for sick call tomorrow just to get checked out right, did you hear from Kathy, maybe I should have joined with her, we could have gone in as a team but I think the army needs me, we learn more about hand to hand combat, boy you can really hurt a guy if you want too, but what they are teaching is nothing to play around with, it doesn't take much to hurt a person no matter what the size or weight, if you have good speed and fast moves it is hard to be beat, but I know the other guy

October 25, 1965 – Fort Dix, New Jersey

continued

is not just standing there singing ②
if you are slow when you come in contact
with him, you don't have to worry no more
because you will never be slow again, once
you get him on the ground you try to smash
his head into the ground 7 or 8 in, with your
heel of you foot, than you decide how to ~~[illegible]~~
depose of him, that's were the fun starts
I have not ~~[illegible]~~ figure out which one
I like the best, there are 10 or 12 different
types of position's you can use, I will show
the girl's what they are, so they can take care
of them self's, and you to Mom so when George
and BoB start up you can quick double them
up, we take a P.T. test thursday, and
all of next week we go to pro-park-
for our last test, they say it will be real
hard, but if Billy Bollard done it, I know
any body can do it (-I hope)

OVER

③

so I got to get ready for bed, I will
do my boots tomorrow *if* I feel like it,
so I will call in a couple of day's, so tell
every body hi, so good bye for now

Love
Jimmy

P.S.
my Sgt had me
doing push-up's
last night for talking
back to him, I don't think
I like him any more, I will
have to do some hard to land
on him, and if that don't work
I will try to out *run* him the *other way*
because he is pretty big, (Mom, he is picking on me
write to our congress
and tell him, b
know I alway's
so I will a

March 20, 66

Dad + Mommy

Well, I am back again, today is sunday, we got back last night so it was about 6 day we stayed out, so much happen in those 6 day's, I could write a book for each day, let me tell you a little bit on what happen, the first day we rod on the trank, the second day we walk, anyway while walking we had to cross river's and lake's I had to swim over water, way over my head, I guess we marched 10 to 12 miles, most of it was through water and rice fields, after crossing a couple of river's, we would start burning up all the house, we could find, and about 2 or 3 in the evening the VC set up a ambush on us just as we were crossing a river every body quick hit the ground

March 20, 1966 – Cu Chi, South Vietnam

and started to fire back, we all
got up, and started to run across
the rice field's, which were full
of water, if it was not for Sgt Bennett
I guess we would have been in a
lot of trouble, it was his idea that
we ran across the field, to get
away from the heavy VC attack,
so that was it, for that day,
the next couple of day's, we went
into small town's, my job was to
go into the house, & get the people
out side, what a feeling it is to
hold a gun on a person, & you are
telling him what you want him to
do, and he is telling you to, but
either one of us can understand
what one is saying to the another, I had
to hold this girl at gun point, I
held it right at her head, because
she was a VC and she could shoot
a rifle just like a man,

continued

we were eating lunch along the road, while eating all of the little kid's would come out, I just could not eat in front of them, At first I could, but one little girl looked like our Barbara, then I thought this could be one of them so I gave them everything, and I had to go early in the morning to this house, to see if any young men lived there, there was just a little old lady there, she wanted me to stay and eat with her, so I had a couple cup's of tea and left, we went in to a lot of houses while there, of course we ran out of water to, I might go out again soon, for 30 day's, that is what I hear, well what has happen lately anything I got a little letter from Kathy again,

I got you letter Maureen and Post card
also you's to George & tina, I was
glad to see you were still together?
I got the radio today it play's pretty
good, I can listen to all of the
VC station's now, I can find out
what they are doing, here is what I think
about the war coming to an end,
over ~~here~~, here, the CO told us thing's
are no better now than 3 year's ago
but people back in the states are
getting mad, so the newspaper put
in what they think sounds good,
but never tell you the little thing's
that happen, I get paid in 10 day's
so I'll send the same amount home
again, so you should get it sometime
in april, well I'll let you all go now
girl's be good, and do what you are told

P.S you should have seen me Helen holding to her dol girl head.

Love
Jimmy

April 16, 66

Dear Mom and Dad

I received your two letters Mom,
and one from little Chris, I was
real glad to hear from you Mom
Louise wrote me to, In her letter
she said Maureen called her on Easter
sunday, she said Mommy was worried
because I did not write in a week,
when I don't write, don't worry about
a thing because I am on a field
problem, and when I get back off
of one, I always write home that thing
But sometimes they don't tell us
we are leaving until the last
min. therefore I can't write and
tell you, that I can't write for
a while, so Please don't worry about
your boy, about Easter I went to
Mass and after. I talked with the

April 16, 1966 – Cu Chi, South Vietnam

priest, I feel a lot better for some
reason (now, (Wonder Why) also thanks
for going to Mass for me, but I would
like it more, if you don't go every
day for me, because it is Hard Mom
getting up early every day, so Please just
go when you can, OK, In your
other letter you said you got the
money and picture's that's good
so daddy went fishing, what shape was
he in when he came back, every
time he goes fishing, he alway's gets
drunk, (Right Pop) about Chocalate
Candy it will not hold up over here
in the Heat tell aunt Emily also aunt
Lil, because she tried it already,
you said my ~~birthday~~ birthday is May 6TH
and I get freedom, your wrong I just
woke up, and found I have been free
for a long time, I alway's wanted to
be 21 year's old, now since I am just

continued

about, I would like to be Joe's age
again, so Joe thinks he's in the
army now, boy what a kid, I remember
when I was small I alway's wanted to
be a soldier or something now since I
am that something, I would rather just
~~be~~ be that little boy who always
got in trouble in school, than a
GI, but I can get in to trouble
in here to, so maybe I'll give it
a try,

Chris,

So Helen told Gale Hurst
off the other day, (good girl Hel)
and you also like my bed, and dad
you say Joe is making a fuss again
(the goof Joe) and Joey stop yelling for
Mommy every Morning like Chris told
me, because Army men don't yell
for their Mother's, unless they need

Money, so like I said before don't
worry, when you don't get mail from
me, some of our field problem's might
last 3 weeks or more, we were going out
for 3 weeks in april, but something happen
and we are not, maybe May or June
and on field problems, you just don't
have time to write, so how did
you like the picture's, I smiled
just for you Mom, (did you really see bear
cans) well folks be good, I got to
write Louise, Jerry got today, if
I can, I'll write later today so
be good, and don't worry about J.G.-OK
no fighting girl's, and Mom take care of
yourself, and Dad, make sure she obeys,
George Jr. does the nice ▬ looking
— still walk around the station,
Tina - I'll tell you later OK
(what a fight I started)
or did Tina just laugh,

Love Jimmy

July 19, 66

Dear Maureen

I received your letter from July 13 last night, I know about the airlines being on strike and realize the mail will take time getting here so Dad broke down and got a house down the shore (the 1 summer I won't be at home and he gets a place down the shore) so that means wow, only kidding I hope you and the rest of the family have a real nice and enjoyable time down there, My Leave should being coming up soon I don't know where I will go but it does not make a big difference because

July 19, 1966 – Cu Chi, South Vietnam

if it was to hell and
back again, I would take
it, things are really not
that bad over here but
you know how I get sometimes
just don't know what I want
I'll have so much to tell
you when I get home
and I think you will be
very proud of me because
I have done so good over-here
(even if I say so my-self
so you will be driving soon?
I guess business will pick
up a lot than, tow wise
so Aunt Mae is coming to
the Christmas make sure you
say hi to her for me
because she has wrote me
alot and has been very nice
also, there not a whole
lot to talk about today

continued

Maureen so I'll let you
get back to the TV set
alright? tell Daddy & Mom
I said hello and the
rest of the peons and by
the way I have a job
for you, you know how
I worry about money so
after each pay day would
you write and tell me
if my allotment check
got home alright, I don't
know wheather you got the
check for June or not
so please let me know
the reason I did not address
the letter to Mom & Dad
is because I thought I
will give you a thrill of
receiving a letter from me
Ha-Ha

Love
Jimmy

United States Senate
WASHINGTON, D.C.

July 29, 1966

Dear Mr. and Mrs. Gilch:

There is no grief more poignant than that of a parent who has lost a son. While there are no words that I know of to assuage your pain, I do want to say that your son served his country well and those of us who have not been called upon to sacrifice as he did are forever in his debt.

With deepest sympathy, I am

Sincerely,

Clifford P. Case

Clifford P. Case
U. S. Senator

CPC/bw

Mr. and Mrs. George Gilch, Sr.
2961 Davis Road
Runnemede, New Jersey

July 29, 1966 – Runnemede, NJ

COMPANY B
1ST BATTALION (MECH) 5TH INFANTRY
APO San Francisco 96225

24 Aug 1966

Mr. George Gilch
2961 Davis Road
Runnemede, New Jersey

Dear Mr. Gilch:

It is with deepest regret that I inform you of the death of your son Private First Class (E-3) James X. Gilch, US51569003, on the evening of 21 July 1966.

James was involved in a search and destroy operation with his squad near Cu Chi, Republic of Vietnam, when he was killed instantaneously as the vehicle he was riding was hit by a hostile command detonated mine.

James was undoubtedly one of the finest soldiers in Company B. His devotion to duty and concern for the welfare of others was a constant source of strength to all those of us who knew him. Your son's death comes as a distinct shock to us as I am sure it does to you. I trust, however, that you may find some consolation in the knowledge that we, his friends and associates, share your grief.

The officers and men of Company B extend to you our most profound sympathy in this time of bereavement.

Sincerely yours,

Robert G. Vanneman
ROBERT G. VANNEMAN
Captain, Infantry
Commanding

August 24, 1966 – Runnemede, NJ

Acronyms and Key Terms

17th Parallel The latitude agreed upon by the great powers at the Geneva Conference in 1954 that arbitrarily divided the emerging nation of the Vietnamese people approximately in half.

After-action reports Official retrospective analyses of military operations conducted to serve as aids in performance evaluation and improvement of search and destroy operations.

Agrovilles Peasant villages set up by the Diem government in the late 1950s to resettle Catholic peasant migrants from North Vietnam, and transfer villagers from heavily populated areas in South Vietnam to the Mekong Delta and highland regions that were only sparsely settled.

Annam The central coastal area of Vietnam, which was carved into an independent colonial enclave by the French.

APCs (Armored Personnel Carriers or M113) Fully tracked, moderately amphibious aluminum armored troop transport vehicles that are most commonly fitted with a single .50 caliber machine gun.

ARVN The acronym for the regular Army of the Republic of South Vietnam.

Ia Drang Key early battle between American and NVA regular forces along the Ia Drang River in the highlands of Vietnam. It set in place the basic combat patterns for conventional engagements during six years of war.

Cochin China The southern third of the present nation of Vietnam, which is dominated by the Mekong River Delta and the major urban center of Saigon. The French ruled it as a separate colony.

COSVIN (Central Office for South Vietnam) The main NLF command center for guerrilla operations in South Vietnam, which was located in the areas just over the Cambodian border.

Cu Chi District A major stronghold of the Viet Minh and later the NLF during the Vietnamese wars of liberation that was renowned for its tunnel networks.

Dien Bien Phu The Viet Minh victory in this decisive battle forced the French to negotiate the withdrawal of their forces, ending their failed attempt to recolonize Vietnam after the end of World War II.

DRV (Democratic Republic of Vietnam) The communist-led nation established in North Vietnam after the armistice signed at the Geneva Conference in the summer of 1954.

Dust Off GI term for the evacuation of wounded and dead soldiers from combat areas.

Filhol Name of a French rubber plantation in the Cu Chi region that became a battleground for French and later American forces against Viet Minh and later NLF guerrillas.

Friendly Fire The accidental killing of soldiers fighting on the same side by forces intending to fire on enemy positions or advancing units.

Geneva Conference and Accords An international conference and agreement in 1954 in which the end of the French phase of the Vietnam wars was negotiated and the great powers forced the Vietnamese to accept a (promised) temporary division of their country.

Haiphong The main port of North Vietnam's capital at Hanoi.

Hanoi The capital and largest city of North Vietnam.

Ho Bo Woods Heavily forested region in the Cu Chi district of South Vietnam that in both the French and American phases of the wars of liberation was a major center of NLF military control and resistance.

Ho Chi Minh Trail The shifting network of paths, roads, fordable rivers, and bridges that ran through Laos and Cambodia which were the main conduits of troops and supplies between North Vietnam and guerrilla forces in the South.

In Country Term used by American military, advisors, and reporters for Americans stationed or fighting in South Vietnam.

Indochina A French designation for eastern, mainland Southeast Asia—including Laos, Cambodia, and Vietnam—which was between India and China.

Iron Triangle An area of forests and plantations northeast of Saigon that was a major center of guerrilla resistance in both the French and American phases of the Vietnamese wars of liberation.

MACV (US) Military Assistance Command Vietnam The American military operations headquarters that was set up in South Vietnam after Vietnam as a whole was divided by the Geneva Accords in 1954.

NLF (National Liberation Front) Officially the National Front for the Liberation of Vietnam, a communist-dominated organization that was established in December 1960 to overthrow the government of Ngo Dinh Diem and unify Vietnam.

NVA (North Vietnamese Army) Abbreviation for the regular army of the Democratic Republic of (North) Vietnam, also often referred to as PAVN (The Peoples' Army of Vietnam).

Politburo A council appointed by the members of the Central Committee, which is elected by the National Congress, the highest governing body of the Democratic Republic of Vietnam, and later the Socialist Democratic Republic of Vietnam.

Red River The major river system of the Tonkin region or North Vietnam, which was the original heartland of the Vietnamese people.

RVN (Republic of Vietnam) Established after the ratification of the Geneva Accords in 1954, it was made up of the parts of Vietnam south of the 17th parallel, and lasted until the conquest and the unification of all of Vietnam by the communists in 1975.

RPG (rocket-propelled grenade) A recoilless shoulder-fired, anti-tank weapon that fires rockets equipped with an explosive warhead.

Rolling Thunder Campaign A sustained US-conducted bombing campaign against North Vietnam begun in March of 1965, and finally ended in November 1968.

Saigon The largest city in South Vietnam and capital of the Republic of South Vietnam from 1954 until 1975.

Search and Destroy The U.S. Army's designation for the main approach to the counterinsurgency against NLF guerrillas, which involved inserting ground forces into hostile territory to locate enemy units, engage them in combat, call in artillery and air support, and withdraw afterward.

Strategic Hamlets Fortified villages set up with major American assistance in South Vietnam during and after the decade of the Diem regime to prevent communist control of the peasant population.

Tonkin The northern third of Vietnam, dominated by the Red River system and ruled as a separate colonial enclave by the French.

VC (Viet Cong) A derogatory designation for communist guerrillas that opposed the Diem regime and later US forces in South Vietnam from the late 1950s until 1975.

Viet Minh The communist-led, but multiparty political and military organization formed in May 1941 to end French colonial rule and establish a united Vietnamese nation.

VVAW (Vietnam Veterans Against the War) As its name suggests, the VVAW was an anti–Vietnam War organization founded by GIs returning from the conflict in 1967. It joined in the widespread protests against the war that continued into the early 1970s.

Notes

Prologue

1. Described by Rick Eilert, in Terrence Maitland and Peter McInerney, *A Contagion of War* (Boston, MA: Boston Publishing Company, 1981), 151.
2. Randy Kethcart, in "Bobcats: First Battalion (Mechanized), Fifth Infantry, Twenty-fifth Infantry Division in the Viet Nam War 1966–1971." Compiled by First Battalion, Fifth Infantry Division of Vietnam Combat Veterans, 2000.
3. Billy Heflin, in "First Kill," directed by Coco Schrijber. Lemming Film. The Netherlands: IKON Television, 2001.
4. From the account of Vo Thi Mo's remarkable exploits in the resistance in Tom Mangold and John Penycate, *The Tunnels of Cu Chi* (New York: Random House, 1985), 228–240.

Introduction

1. George Herring's *America's Longest War* (NY: McGraw-Hill, 1979) provides the most concise political-diplomatic narrative. Marilyn Young's *The Vietnam Wars, 1945–1990* (New York: HarperCollins, 1991) is both a cogent critique of the French and US interventions and ground breaking in its detailed attention to the Vietnamese side of the wars.
2. Among the best accounts in this regard, we include Michael Lee Lanning and Dan Craig, *Inside the VC and the NVA: The Real Story of North Vietnam's Armed Forces* (New York: Fawcett, 1992); Lt. General Harold G. Moore and Joseph Galloway, *We Were Soldiers Once and Young: Ia Drang, The Battle That Changed the War in Vietnam* (New York: Random House, 1992); and Andrew F. Krepinevich, Jr., *The Army and Vietnam* (Baltimore, MD: Johns Hopkins University Press, 1986).
3. An important exception to the absence of Vietnamese voices in works of fiction by American writers is Robert Olen Butler's *A Good Scent from a Strange Mountain* (NY: Henry Holt, 1992), which treats mainly refugee South Vietnamese responses to the conflict and its aftermath with a great deal of imagination and sensitivity. Translations from Vietnamese writers and American authors from Vietnamese-American families have also made major contributions to the rich literature on the war and its aftermath, most recently Viet Thanh Nguyen, *The Sympathizer* (New York: Grove Press, 2015).

4. Of particular value for broader insights into American soldier's responses in the moment are the introductory essays to *Dear America: Letters Home From Vietnam*, edited by Bernard Edelman (New York: Norton, 1985). See also the Vietnam War portions of Andrew Carroll, ed., *War Letters* (New York: Scribner, 2001); and Bill Adler, ed., *Letters from Vietnam* (New York: Presidio, 2003).
5. The fullest and most insightful analysis of these patterns remains Christian G. Appy's *Working Class War: American Combat Soldiers and Vietnam* (Chapel Hill: University of North Carolina Press, 1993), especially chapter 2.
6. Ibid., 28–38.
7. Robert Jay Lifton, *Home From the War: Vietnam Veterans, Neither Victims nor Executioners* (New York: Simon and Schuster, 1973), 37–58.

Chapter 1

1. *The Observer* [newspaper], Blackwood, NJ, August 1945, quoted in William Leap, *The History of Runnemede New Jersey 1626–1976* (Borough of Runnemede, New Jersey: self-published, 1981).
2. William L. O'Neill, *American High* (New York: The Free Press, 1986), 25–26.
3. John Keats, *The Insolent Chariots* (Philadelphia: J.B. Lippincott Company, 1958), 10.
4. For information on the 1944 famine see: Fredrik Logevall, *Embers of War: The Fall of an Empire and the Making of America's Vietnam* (New York: Random House, 2012), 79–82.
5. For an insightful discussion of the historical setting of Ho Chi Minh's speech and the different ways his inclusion of passages of the American Declaration of Independence and revolution were interpreted by American, French, and Vietnamese observers, see Mark Philip Bradley, *Imagining Vietnam and America: The Making of Postcolonial Vietnam, 1919–1950* (Chapel Hill: University of North Carolina Press, 2000), 3–7, 33–37.
6. David Biggs, *Quagmire: Nation-Building and Nature in the Mekong Delta* (Seattle: University of Washington Press, 2010). Chapters 1–3 include a detailed analysis of French transport and hydraulic projects in southern Vietnam and their detrimental effects on the peasant population and the environment of the Mekong Delta region.
7. Lloyd C. Gardner, *Approaching Vietnam: From World War II through Dien Bien Phu* (New York: Norton, 1988), 49.
8. James M. Carter, *Inventing Vietnam: The United States and State Building, 1954–1968* (New York: Cambridge University Press, 2008), chapters 2 and 4.
9. For cold war shifts in US strategic policy see especially, John Gaddis, *Strategies of Containment: A Critical Appraisal of Postwar American National Security Policy* (New York: Oxford University Press, 1984).
10. For the most detailed (and lively) account of one of the most decisive battles of the postwar decades, see Jules Roy, *The Battle of Dienbienphu*, translated by Robert Baldick (New York: Harper and Row, 1965).
11. For population numbers of New Jersey's municipalities and counties, see The State of New Jersey, Department of Workforce and Labor Development, "New Jersey Resident Population by Municipality: 1930–1990," *The United State Census Bureau*, http://lwd.dol.state.nj.us/labor/lpa/census/1990/poptrd6.htm.
12. W. H. Auden, *The Dyer's Hand and Other Essays* (New York: Vintage, 1989), 83.
13. O'Neill, *American High*, 331.
14. Ibid., 79; see also Martin Halliwell, "Film and Television," in *American Culture in the 1950s*, by Martin Halliwell, (Edinburgh: Edinburgh University Press, 2007), 147–166.
15. Vance Packard, *The Hidden Persuaders* (Brooklyn, NY: IG Publishing, 2007).

16. For popular television shows in the 1950s and 60s, see David Marc, *Demographic Vistas: Television in American Culture* (Philadelphia: University of Pennsylvania Press, 1984), 135–147.
17. Michael T. Bertrand, *Race, Rock, and Elvis* (Champaign-Urbana: University of Illinois Press, 2000). For music of the era, see Marcel Danesi, *Cool: The Signs and Meanings of Adolescence* (Toronto: University of Toronto Press, 1994), and *Forever Young: The "Teen-Aging" of Modern Culture* (Toronto: University of Toronto Press, 2003). For further information on the emerging youth culture in the 50s and 60s, see Dick Pountain and David Robins *Cool Rules* (London: Reaktion, 2000).
18. For a general overview of Americans and religion see R. Stephen Warner, *A Church of Our Own* (New Brunswick, NJ: Rutgers University Press, 2005).
19. Dwight D. Eisenhower, "Address at the Freedoms Foundation, Waldorf-Astoria, New York City, New York [12/22/52]"; *The Eisenhower Presidential Library, Museum, and Boyhood Home*; Presidential Libraries System, National Archives and Records Administration, Abilene, Kansas.
20. Will Herberg, *Protestant-Catholic-Jew: An Essay in American Religious Sociology* (Chicago: University of Chicago Press, 1994), 285.

Chapter 2

1. Frederik Logevall, *Embers of War: The Fall of an Empire and the Making of America's Vietnam* (New York: Random House, 2012), 609.
2. Lloyd C. Gardner, *Approaching Vietnam: From World War II Through Dien Bien Phu, 1941–1954* (New York: Norton, 1988), 316.
3. Key works on the intertwined strands of Marxism and patriotism in Vietnamese anticolonial struggles include Huỳnh Kim Khánh, *Vietnamese Communism 1925–1945* (Ithaca, NY: Cornell University Press, 1982); William Duiker, *The Rise of Nationalism in Vietnam, 1900–1941* (Ithaca, NY: Cornell University Press, 1976); and David Marr, *Vietnamese Anticolonialism,1885–1925* (Berkeley: University of California Press, 1971).
4. Khánh, 63-89.
5. Quoted in James Zumwalt, *Bare Feet, Iron Will* (Jacksonville, FL: Fortis, 2010), 211.
6. Our account of Diem's ambitions and maneuvers to establish himself as the president of an independent state in South Vietnam has relied heavily on Edward Miller's thoroughly researched and cogent reassessments in *Misalliance: Ngo Dinh Diem, the United States, and the Fate of South Vietnam* (Cambridge, MA: Harvard University Press, 2013), esp. chapters 1–2.
7. Figures for military spending from 1948 to 1959 are computed from nominal-dollar purchases and GNP deflator in the "Council of Economic Advisors, Annual Report" (Washington, DC.: Government Printing Office, 1987), 245–248.
8. Michael Harrington, *The Other America* (New York: Simon and Schuster, 1997), 5.
9. Dwight D. Eisenhower, "Telephone Broadcast to the AFL-CIO Merger Meeting in New York City," December 5, 1955. Quoted in *The American Presidency Project,* Gerhard Peters and John T. Woolley, eds. (Santa Barbara, CA: University of California Press, 1999–2016).
10. Dwight D. Eisenhower, "Address in Detroit at the National Automobile Show Industry Dinner," October 17, 1960. Quoted in *American Presidency Project*.
11. John Kenneth Galbraith, "How Much Should a Country Consume?" in *Perspectives on Conservation,* edited by Henry Jarrett (Baltimore: Johns Hopkins University Press, 1958), 90.
12. For a comprehensive study on American consumerism and the rise of suburban communities, especially in New Jersey, see Lizabeth Cohen, *A Consumer's Republic* (New York: Vintage, 2003).

13 Andrew Jamison and Ron Eyerman, *Seeds of the Sixties* (Berkeley: University of California Press, 1994), 33.
14. Michael Adas, *Dominance by Design: Technological Imperatives and America's Civilizing Mission* (Cambridge, MA: Harvard University Press, 2006), 219–256.
15. Harrington, 199.
16. Miller, *Misalliance*, chapter 5.
17. For a detailed, yet succinct, critique of the strategic hamlet program see, Michael E. Latham, *Modernization as Ideology: American Social Science and "Nation Building" in the Kennedy Era* (Chapel Hill: The University of North Carolina Press, 2000), chapter 5.
18. James M. Carter, *Inventing Vietnam: The United States and State Building 1954–1968* (New York: Cambridge University Press, 2008) chapters 4-6.
19. For teenage culture of the 1950s and 60s, see Grace Palladino, *Teenagers* (New York: Basic Books, 1996), 96–115, and Thomas Frank, *The Conquest of Cool* (Chicago: University of Chicago Press, 1997), 74–88.
20. John F. Kennedy, "Special Message to the Congress on Education," February 20, 1961, *Public Papers of the Presidents, John F. Kennedy, 1961* (Washington, DC, 1962), 107. See also Robert Hamlett Bremner, ed., "Education and Reform: A Federal Initiative to Support Public Education" in *Children and Youth in America: A Documentary History*, Vol. 3 (Cambridge, MA: Harvard University Press, 1974), 1974.
21. James B. Conant, *Education in a Divided World; The Function of the Public Schools in Our Unique Society* (Cambridge, MA: Harvard University Press, 1948), 2–4, 203; "Scientific Education of the Layman," *Yale Review* 36 (September 1946): 15–36, and Wayne J. Urban, *American Education: A History* (New York: Routledge, 2008), 369–373.
22. For a historiography of science education in the United States during the post-war era see, Michael Aaron Dennis, "Historiography of Science: An American Perspective, in *Science in the Twentieth Century*, ed. John Krige (New York, NY: Routledge, 2013), 1-26.

Chapter 3

1. Christian G. Appy *Working-Class War: American Combat Soldiers in Vietnam* (Chapel Hill: University of North Carolina Press, 1993), 31.
2. Marine Corps Private First Class Reginald "Malik" Edwards' recounting of the Cam Ne operation in a collection of oral interviews of African American soldiers edited by Terry Wallace, *Bloods: An Oral History of the Vietnam War by Black Veterans* (New York: Ballantine, 1992), 3–5.
3. Lt. Col. Verle E. Ludwig, First Battalion, Ninth Marines, Da Nang, RVN, 050800 August 1965, after action report Number 1-65. For a narrative of the operation, see Major H.A. Hatch's account, Apex C-1 - C-5. (United States Marine Corp, 1 Bn, Ninth Marines, Unclassified).
4. Morley Safer, *Flashbacks: On Returning to Vietnam* (New York: Random House, 1990), 89–95. Also see *From Reporting America at War: An Oral History*, compiled by Michelle Ferrari, with commentary by James Tobin (New York: Hyperion, 2003), 211–222. For more on news reporting and the media during the war, see Daniel C. Hallin, *The "Uncensored War": The Media and Vietnam* (Berkeley: University of California Press, 1989).
5. Quoted in Tom Engelhardt, *The End of Victory Culture: Cold War America and the Disillusioning of a Generation* (New York: Basic Books, 1995), 190.
6. The draft motivation for the National Guard and reserves enlistment is discussed in Lawrence M. Baskir and William A. Strauss, *Chance and Circumstance: The Draft, the War, and the Vietnam Generation* (New York: Alfred Knopf, 1978), 50–52; George H.

Walton, *The Tarnished Shield: A Report on Today's Army* (New York: Dodd, Mead & Company, 1973), 180–181; and William L. Hauser, *America's Army in Crisis: A Study in Civil-Military Relations* (Baltimore: Johns Hopkins University Press, 1974), 155.

7. New York Times Editorial Board, "In Honor of Fighting Frank Farley", *The New York Times*, April 11, 1977, 40; and Edward Thomas Ellson, *Lords of Corruption* (Bloomington, IN: Xlibris Publishing, 2002), 144.
8. Quoted in William Westmoreland, *A Soldier Reports* (New York: Doubleday, 1976), 161.
9. George W. Ball, *The Past Has Another Pattern: Memoirs* (New York: Norton, 1982).
10. Department of the Army, "Army Regulations and Personnel Processing: Processing Procedures at U.S. Army Reception Stations," Army Regulation 612-10 (Washington, D.C: United States Army War Office, Headquarters, Pentagon Printing Office, August 1965).
11. Lamont Steptoe, "Before Going," *From Both Sides Now: The Poetry of Vietnam and its Aftermath*, edited by Phillip Mahony (New York: Scribner, 1998), 36.
12. James Gilch was undergoing Advanced Infantry Training at Fort Dix while reporter John Sack was spending time at the New Jersey base camp conducting interviews for his article, "M: The True Story of M Company from Fort Dix to Vietnam," which was first published in *Esquire* in 1966 and later reproduced in book form by New American Library (1967). Sack later told Eric Schroeder: "I wanted to go to a camp that I thought would represent a cross-section of the army population; I thought that I would have to go to a camp in the South. But the Pentagon said, 'They're all cross-sections, and Fort Dix is as much of a cross-section as any.' I even went down to the Pentagon to assure myself of this. And, in fact, in order to maintain this feeling of generality, I never mention Fort Dix in the book, nor do I mention the name of the division or the battalion or where they are in Vietnam." For the full interview: Eric Schroeder, *Vietnam, We've All Been There: Interviews with American Authors* (Westport, CT: Praeger, 1992).
13. For a report on the U.S. Army's physical fitness program see Department of the Army, "Personnel, General: Army Physical Fitness Program," Army Regulation 600-9 (Washington, DC: United States Army War Office, Headquarters, Pentagon Printing Office, January 1965).
14. Photographs of the billboards appear in *The Vietnam Experience: A Contagion of War* edited by Terrence Maitland and Peter McInerney (Boston: Boston Publishing Company, 1983), 30. The Fort Dix sign is described in Ronald V. Dellums and The Citizens' Commission of Inquiry, *The Dellums' Committee Hearings On War Crimes in Vietnam: An Inquiry into Command Responsibility in Southeast Asia* (New York: Vintage Books, 1972), 161.
15. For a detailed report of the purpose and objectives of the U.S. Army's Character Guidance Program see the Department of the Army, "Personnel, General: Character Guidance Program," Army Regulation 600-30 (Washington, D.C: United States Army War Office, Headquarters, Pentagon Printing Office, March 1965).
16. For statistics on suicide rates at Fort Dix see Appy, *Working-Class War*, 92, and Peter Barnes, *Pawns: The Plight of the Citizen Soldier* (New York: Alfred Knopf, 1972), 105–111. The study on stress and basic training was conducted by William Datel and Stephen T. Lifrak, "Expectations, Affects Change, and Military Performance in the Army Recruit," *Psychological Reports*, June 1969.
17. The graphic portions of the "rabbit lesson" come from Robert Lifton, *Home From the War, Vietnam Veterans: Neither Victims nor Executioners* (New York: Simon and Schuster, 1973), 43, and the partial quote comes from Martin Gershen, *Destroy or Die: The True Story of Mylai* (New Rochelle, NY: Arlington House, 1971), 186.

18. The heavy load carried by a US infantryman is thoroughly detailed by Michael Clodfelter, *Vietnam in Military Statistics: A History of the Indochina Wars, 1772–1991* (Jefferson, NC: McFarland & Company Publishers, 1995), 76. The soldiers' gear is also discussed in Gordon L. Rottman, *U.S. Army Infantryman in Vietnam, 1965–73* (Oxford: Osprey, 2005), 27–29.
19. The general process of duty assignment that frames our discussion of Jimmy's experiences is based on John Sack's detailed account of boot camp at Fort Dix in *M*, and Schroeder, "Vietnam, We've All Been There: Interviews with American Authors," in which Sack revealed: "I went to the Pentagon to see the process by which the members of the company were chosen to go or not to go to Vietnam." On the use of computers for tour assignments see Baskir and Strauss, *Chance and Circumstance*, 55–56; Andrew J. Glass, "Defense Report: Draftees Shoulder Burden of Fighting and Dying in Vietnam," *National Journal*, August 1970.
20. Major General Charles E. Beauchamp, *The United States Army Basic Training, Yearbook of the United States Army Training Center: Infantry, Fort Dix, New Jersey* (Topeka, KS: Jostens Military Publications, 1965), 5.
21. Tra and Ba's accounts of their wartime experiences are included in the excellent collection of Vietnamese oral interviews edited by David Chanoff and Doan Van Toai, "*Vietnam*" *A Portrait of Its People at War* (London: Tauris Parke, 2009), 27–34, 152–158.
22. William J. Duiker, *Sacred War: Nationalism and Revolution In A Divided Vietnam* (NY: McGraw-Hill, 1995), 110–137. Ngoc-Luu Nguyen "Peasants, Party and Revolution: The Politics of Agrarian Transformation in Northern Vietnam, 1930–1975," PhD diss., Amsterdam: University of Amsterdam, 1987, chapter 5.
23. For the fullest and best documented account of the political machinations behind Hanoi's shift to active military engagement in the South, see Lien-Hang T. Nguyen, *Hanoi's War: An International History of the War for Peace in Vietnam* (Chapel Hill: The University of North Carolina Press, 2012), 48-68.
24. Truong Nhu Tang, A Viet Cong Memoir (NY: Vintage, 1985), 158.
25. Chanoff and Toai, *Portrait of People at War*, 151.
26. Ibid, 113.
27. Ibid, 152–154.

Chapter 4

1. John Morrocco, *Thunder from Above* (Boston: Boston Publishing Company, 1984), 100.
2. *The Pentagon Papers, Gravel edition* (Boston: Beacon, 1971), 4: 27.
3. For numbers, figures, and direct quotes, see *Pentagon Papers*, 3:439, for a discussion of the entire buildup, see 433–485; also see David Kaiser, *American Tragedy: Kennedy, Johnson, and the Origins of the Vietnam War* (Cambridge, MA: Harvard University Press, 2000), 440–441.
4. George Ball's June 18, 1965 memo to Lyndon Johnson, "Keeping the Power of Decision in the South Viet-Nam Crisis," can be found in David M. Barrett, ed. *Lyndon Johnson's Vietnam Papers: A Documentary Collection* (College Station, TX: Texas A&M University Press, 1997), 172–176.
5. The LBJ Tapes, Lyndon Johnson and Robert McNamara, June 10, 1965. Parts of the transcript are quoted from George C. Herring, *The War Bells Have Rung: The LBJ Tapes and the Americanization of the Vietnam War* (Charlottesville: University of Virginia Press, 2015).
6. Quoted in David Kaiser, *American Tragedy*, 445.
7. Ibid., 478–483.
8. Quoted in Brian VanDeMark, *Into the Quagmire: Lyndon Johnson and the Escalation of the Vietnam War* (New York: Oxford University Press, 1991), 181.

9. Lyndon Johnson to Dwight Eisenhower, quoted in VanDeMark, *Into the Quagmire*, (A.J. Goodpaster's Memorandum of Meeting with General Eisenhower, June 16, 1965, "President Eisenhower," NF, Box 3, NSF, LBJL.), 163.
10. Johnson's words of January 27 are taken from a draft of the letter found in his diary dated January 25, 1966. For a transcription of the letter see Barrett, *Lyndon Johnson's Vietnam Papers*, 322–323.
11. See VanDeMark, *Into the Quagmire*, 179. The meeting between Robert McNamara, Nguyen Van Thieu and Nguyen Cao Ky is ably described in Bui Diem, *In the Jaws of History* (Bloomington: Indiana University Press, 1987), 152.
12. Quoted in T. Christopher Jespersen, "The Challenge of Revolutions and the Emergence of Nation-States: British Reactions and American Responses," in *America, the Vietnam War, and the World: Comparative and International Perspectives*, ed. Lloyd C. Gardner et al. (Cambridge, MA: Cambridge University Press, 2003), 80.
13. For the fullest account of the critical decisions to go to war made by the Johnson Administration in 1965 see Kaiser, *American Tragedy*, chapters 14–15.
14. Quoted in Lawrence M. Baskir, *Chance and Circumstance: The Draft, the War, and the Vietnam Generation* (New York: Alfred A. Knopf, 1978), 126.
15. Galbraith letter quoted in VanDeMark, *Into the Quagmire*, 205–206.
16. Lyndon B. Johnson: "The President's News Conference," July 28, 1965. Online by Gerhard Peters and John T. Woolley, *The American Presidency Project*.
17. Quoted in VanDeMark, *Into the Quagmire*, 213.
18. In the Diem era and during the American occupation, NLF resistance fighters were pejoratively labeled Viet Cong, short for Vietnamese Communists. In the literature on the war, the term has been so widely applied that it has lost its negative connotations. We have used it sparingly as an alternative designation for guerrilla fighters of the National Liberation Front, but retained it in sections dealing with American soldiers' responses to the Vietnamese.
19. Quoted in Tom Mangold and John Penycate's, definitive account of *The Tunnels of Cu Chi* (New York: Random House, 1985), 68–69.
20. Some of the tunnels were retained by the US military for training selected soldiers—dubbed "tunnel rats"—how to navigate and engage the enemy in their underground labyrinth.
21. Richard L. Snider, *Delta Six: Soldier Surgeon* (Berwyn Heights, MD: Heritage, 2003), 25.
22. See Mangold and Penycate, *Tunnels of Cu Chi*, 72.

Chapter 5

1 Lt. Gen. Harold G. Moore & Joseph L. Galloway, *We Were Soldiers Once . . . and Young* (New York: Harper, 1992), 277–278.
2 Morley Safer, Narrator, *CBS News Special Report on The Battle of Ia Drang Valley*, 1965.
3 Donn Starry, *Mounted Combat in Vietnam* (Department of the Army, Washington, DC, 1989), 85.
4 Quoted in Stanley Karnow, *Vietnam: A History* (New York: Viking, 1983), 512.
5. Quoted in Gregory Daddis, *No Sure Victory: Measuring U.S. Army Effectiveness and Progress in the Vietnam War* (Oxford: Oxford University Press, 2011), 149.
6. Ibid, 172.
7. "2D BDE Operations," in *Tropic Lightning News* 1, No. 1 (March 4, 1966), 4; "Brigades Continue to Pound V.C.," in *Tropic Lightning News* 1, No. 2 (March 11, 1966), 1.
8. George Olsen, "Dear Red", August 31, 1969, as quoted by Bernard Edelman editor of *Dear America: Letters Home From Vietnam* (New York: W.W. Norton & Company, 1985), 118.
9. Lt. Brian Sullivan, "Darling", March 2, 1969, as quoted in *Dear America*, 132.

10. "NCO's Active Imagination Becomes All Too Real," in *Tropic Lightning News* 1, No. 10 (May 11, 1966), 5. Also see "Bobcats, The 1/5th (Mech) History," eds., Randy Keithcart and the 1st Bn(M) Fifth Infantry Society of Vietnam Combat Veterans, 7.
11. Terry Wallace, *Bloods* (NY: Ballantine, 1984), 15.
12. Tim O'Brien comments on the ways a similar incident captured key aspects of the nature of the war in Vietnam, graphically describing a squad killing a water buffalo in *The Things They Carried* (NY: Penguin, 1991), 78–80.
13. 1st Lt. James Simmen, "Hi Vern", March 12, 1968, *Dear America*, 94–95.
14. Michael Herr, *Dispatches* (New York: Avon, 1968), 90–92, and Philip Caputo, *Rumor of War* (New York: Ballantine, 1977), 103.
15. Lieutenant-General Hoang Phuong, "Several Lessons on Campaign Planning and Command Implementation During the Plei Me Campaign," (Hanoi: 1995); and Nguyen Huy Toan and Pham Quang Dinh, *The 304th Division*, vol. 2 (1990).
16. Joseph Galloway, "Ia Drang – The Battle That Convinced Ho Chi Minh He Could Win," *Vietnam Magazine* (October 18, 2010), 10.
17. Tom Mangold and John Penycate, *Tunnels of Cu Chi* (New York: Random House, 1985), 83.
18. Stuart Herrington, *Stalking the Vietcong: Inside Operation Phoenix: A Personal Account By Stuart Herrington* (New York: Presidio, 1997), 33–36.
19. Douglas Anderson, "Doc" in *Everything We Had: An Oral History of the Vietnam War*, ed. Al Santoli (New York: Random House, 1981), 70.
20. Rodney Baldra, "Dear Editor", June 1967, *Dear America*, 208.
21. Paul Kelly, "Dear Mom", July 15, 1969, *Dear America*, 109.
22. George Williams, "Dear Ma", April 1967, *Dear America*, 105.
23. Daniel Bailey, "Dear Mom", September 5, 1966, *Dear America*, 110–111.
24. Bruce McInnes, "Dear Mom", July 20, 1969, *Dear America*, 113.
25. In *The Best and the Brightest* (New York: Random House, 1969), 249–250, David Halberstam audaciously judged McNamara a "fool" for his refusal on earlier fact-finding missions to interrogate seriously information provided by military personnel or seriously seek out the views of civilian advisors, both of which might have forced him to question his sanguine appraisals of the state of things in country and in his influential recommendations to LBJ and his staff.
26. Moore's views on these issues were clearly articulated in what has become the standard book on the battle that he co-authored with Joseph L. Galloway, *We Were Soldiers Once . . . and Young.*
27. See McNamara's memorandums for the President of 30 November 1965 and 7 December addressing his "Military and Political Actions Recommended for South Vietnam," in *The Pentagon Papers, Gravel edition,* vol. 4: 308–309 [Document 262], 622–624 [Document 263].
28. As Andrew Preston has cogently argued, by the end of 1965 Bundy had become one of LBJ's most influential advisors. *The War Council: McGeorge Bundy, the NSC, and Vietnam* (Cambridge, MA: Harvard University Press, 2006), chapters 6 and 7.
29. Quoted in Robert K. Brigham's *Guerrilla Diplomacy: The NLF's Foreign Relations and the Vietnam War* (Ithaca, NY: Cornell University Press, 1999), 53. See also Lien-Hang T. Nguyen, *Hanoi's War: An International History of the War for Peace in Vietnam* (Chapel Hill, NC: The University of North Carolina Press, 2012), chapter two; and William J. Duiker, *Sacred War: Nationalism and Revolution In A Divided Vietnam* (New York: McGraw-Hill, 1995), 110–137.
30. Lyndon B. Johnson, "Remarks Upon Signing the 'Cold War GI Bill' [Veterans' Readjustment Benefits Act of 1966]," March 3, 1966.
31. For the complete article see, "Bunker Life: Loneliness, Mosquitoes and Viet Cong," in *Tropic Lightning News* 1, No. 5 (April 1, 1966), 2.

Chapter 6

1. Theodore T. Jagosz, Cpt Inf, U.S. Army, "Tribute to First Lieutenant Frank D'Amico, Bobcat Bravo 3-6," *5th Mechanized Infantry Regiment Association*, 2016.
2. "Bobcats 1966 The First Battalion (Mechanized) Fifth Infantry, Twenty-Fifth Infantry Division in the Vietnam War, 1966 – 1971," complied by 1st Battalion (Mechanized) 5th Infantry Society of Vietnam Combat Veterans, *5th Mechanized Infantry Regiment Association*, 2016, http://bobcat.ws/history1966.htm
3. Unknown Combatant, "Dear Parents", April 1970, as quoted by Andrew Carroll in *War Letters: Extraordinary Correspondence from American Wars* (New York: Washington Square Press, 2001), 425.
4. "Bobcats, The 1/5th (Mech) History," ed. Randy Keithcart and 1st Bn(M) 5th Infantry Society of Vietnam Combat Veterans, April 5, 1966.
5. For events on April 8, 1966, see "Bobcats 1966 The First Battalion (Mechanized) Fifth Infantry, Twenty-Fifth Infantry Division in the Vietnam War, 1966–1971."
6. Jagosz, "Tribute to First Lieutenant Frank D'Amico, Bobcat Bravo 3-6."
7. Ibid.
8. In a book with that title, published by Macmillan in 1973.
9. Quoted in Samuel Zaffiri, *Westmoreland: A Biography of William C. Westmoreland* (New York: Morrow, 1994), 106.
10. See, for example, James William Gibson, *The Perfect War: Technowar in Vietnam* (Boston: The Atlantic Monthly Press, 1986), 196–201.
11. Henry Graff quoting Robert McNamara, *The Tuesday Cabinet* (Englewood Cliffs, NJ: Prentice-Hall, 1970), 82.
12. See Kathleen Belew's forthcoming book *Bring the War Home: The White Power Movement and Paramilitary America* (Cambridge, MA: Harvard University Press, 2017).
13. Quoted in one of the many interviews of infantrymen included in Eric M. Bergerud's *Red Thunder: Tropic Lightning: The World of a Combat Division in Vietnam* (New York: Penguin, 1994), 147.
14. Nick Turse, *Kill Anything That Moves: The Real American War in Vietnam* (New York: Henry Holt, 2013), 69.
15. Herbert Y. Schandler, "U.S. Military Victory in Vietnam: A Dangerous Illusion," in Robert McNamara et.al., *Argument Without End: In Search of Answers to the Vietnam Tragedy* (New York: Public Affairs, 1999), 319.
16 Andrew Krepinevich Jr., *The Army and Vietnam* (Baltimore, MD: Johns Hopkins, 1986), 24.
17. David Kaiser, *American Tragedy: Kennedy, Johnson, and the Origins of the Vietnam War* (Cambridge, MA: Harvard University Press, 2000), 187, 308–309 (quoted passage).
18. The apt characterization of Vann's assessment is in Neil Sheehan's magisterial book, *A Bright Shining Lie: John Paul Vann and America in Vietnam* (New York: Random House, 1988), 540.
19. See Huntington, "The Bases of Accommodation," *Foreign Affairs* 46 (July 1968), 645–652.
20. Jonathan Schell, *The Village of Ben Suc (*New York: Random House, 1967*)*, 46-47.
21. Ronald V. Dellums, *The Dellums Committee Hearings on War Crimes in Vietnam: An Inquiry into Command Responsibility in Southeast Asia* (New York: Vintage Books, 1972), 72.
22. On American losses by Vietnamese booby traps and mines see, Lieutenant General Julian J. Ewell and Major General Ira A. Hunt, Jr, "Tactical Refinements and Innovation: Mines and Booby Traps," in *Sharpening the Combat Edge: The Use of Analysis to Reinforce Military Judgment* (Department of the Army, Washington, DC, 1975), 136–139; United States Army, "Booby Traps," Washington DC: Department of the Army, 1965, *Field Manual FM 5-31*, 132; Richard R. Murray and Kellye L. Fabian, "Compensating

the World's Landmine Victims: Legal and Anti-Personnel Landmine Producers," *Seton Hall Law Review* 33.2 (2002), 303–369; Human Rights Watch and the Vietnam Veterans America Foundation, "In Its Own Words: The U.S. Army and Antipersonnel Mines in the Korean and Vietnam Wars," *Human Rights Watch* 9 (1997): 7.

23. Jagosz, "Tribute to First Lieutenant Frank D'Amico, Bobcat Bravo 3–6."
24. Ibid.
25. Bobcats 1966 The First Battalion (Mechanized) Fifth Infantry, Twenty-Fifth Infantry Division in the Vietnam War, 1966–1971."
26. Jagosz, "Tribute to First Lieutenant Frank D'Amico, Bobcat Bravo 3-6."
27. Lieutenant Brian Sullivan, "Darling," March 2, 1969, as quoted by Bernard Edelman ed. *Dear America: Letters Home From Vietnam*, 131–132.
28. Lieutenant Marion Lee "Sandy" Kempner, "Dear Mummum and Muggins", August 9, 1966, *Dear America*, 207, and "Dear Aunt Fannie," Oct. 20, 1966, 138.
29. Cost per truck estimate from a U.S. Senate subcommittee report, quoted in Paul N. Edwards, *The Closed World: Computers and the Politics of Discourse in Cold War America* (Cambridge, MA: MIT Press, 1997), 4; The estimated amount of tonnage to kill an NVA soldier is from Michael Clodfelter, *Vietnam in Military Statistics* (Jefferson, NC: McFarland, 1995), 73.
30. Quoting Edwards, *Closed World*.
31. On the ineptitude of the Saigon Regime, see the fine overview in Ronald H. Spector, *After Tet: The Bloodiest Year in Vietnam* (New York: Vintage, 1993), chapter 5.
32. *A Viet Cong Memoir* (New York: Random House, 1985), 36.
33. Quoted phrasing from *Memoir*, 65.
34. Krepinevich, *Army and Vietnam*, 76–78, 132–133, 151–153, 220. Krepinevich's well-documented, detailed analysis has been essential for our overview of the deficiencies of both ARVN and American counterinsurgency operations from the mid-1950s through the fall of Saigon to communist forces.
35. Clodfelter, *Vietnam in Statistics*, 50, and Tom Mangold and John Penycate, *The Tunnels of Cu Chi*, 51
36. Shell, *Village of Ben Suc*, 19.
37. Michael Lee Lanning and Dan Craig, *Inside the VC and the NVA* (New York: Fawcett, 1992), 46.
38. Ibid., 51 and 46–50 ; Mangold and Pennycate, *Cu Chi*, 84, 127, 164–165, 196–197; Shell, ibid., 99; Krepinevich, *Army and Vietnam*, 25, 33,
39. Shell, *Village of Ben Suc*, 48, 54–60, 66–67.
40. *Things They Carried* (London: HarperCollins, 1990), 78–79.
41. Douglas Kinnard, *The War Managers* (Hanover, NH: University Press of New England, 1977), 69.
42. Schell, *Village of Ben Suc*, 103–104.
43. Turse, *Kill Anything That Moves*, 42–50.
44. (New York: Ballantine Books, 1977), 191.
45. Alain, Enthoven, "Memorandum for the Secretary of Defense, " May 4, 1967, *The Pentagon Papers, Gravel Edition* (Boston: Beacon, 1971), vol. 4, 461–462.
46. Both quoted passages by Eric Bergerud, in *Red Thunder*, 151–152.
47. Quoted in James R. Ebert, *A Life in a Year: The American Infantryman in Vietnam* (Novato, CA: Presidio, 1993), 382–383.
48. Cecil E. Curry, "Free Fire Zones," in Spencer Tucker, *The Encyclopedia of the Vietnam War: A Political, Social, and Military History* (New York: Oxford University Press, 2000), 140. For detailed accounts of the impact of US firepower unleashed on the peasant

population, see Krepinevich, *Army and Vietnam*, 203–205, and David Elliot, *The Vietnamese War: Revolution and Social Change in the Mekong Delta, 1930–1975* (Armonk, NY: M.E. Sharpe, 2007), chapter 15.

49. Oral interview with Vince Olsen in Ebert, *Life in a Year*, 381; also 364–365, 392.
50. Nick Turse, *Kill Anything That Moves*, chapters 2–4; Appy, *Working Class War*, 190–205; Martha Hess, *Then the Americans Came* (NY: Four Walls Eight Windows, 1993), 140–142, 151–153, 159, 192; and Ebert, *Life in a Year*, 364–365, 376, 392.
51. The incident, as related by Chee, is included in Harry Maurer's aptly titled *Strange Ground: An Oral History of Americans in Vietnam, 1945–1975* (NY: Avon, 1989), 359–360.
52. As Nick Turse found while conducting his painstaking research into the widespread abuses of Vietnamese civilians in the war: see above, *Kill Anything That Moves.*
53. See Michael Bilton and Kevin Sim, *Four Hours in My Lai* (New York: Penguin, 1992), especially 135–141.
54. "MACV Gives Advice On Vietnam Conduct," in *Tropic Lightning News* 1, No. 10 (May 6, 1966), 7.
55. "Big Hand Helps Vietnamese," in *Tropic Lightning News* 1, No. 9 (April 29, 1966), 3.
56. Unknown Combatant, "Dear Mom & Dad", Unknown Date, in *War Letters: Extraordinary Correspondence from American Wars*, ed. Andrew Carroll (New York: Washington Square Press, 2001), 424–425.
57. "Americans Offer Letter Support," in *Tropic Lightning News* 1, No. 8 (April 22, 1966), 2.
58. Robert W. Chandler, *War of Ideas: The US Propaganda Campaign in Vietnam* (Boulder, CO: Westview, 1981), 33, 135.
59. Robert E. Tschan, "Dear Dee (Wife)", 19 February 1968, quoted by Bill Adler, ed., in *Letters from Vietnam* (New York: Presidio, 2003), 46.
60. Lieutenant Colonel Edwin T. Cooke, "Combat Stress and Its Effects: Combat's Bloodless Casualties," in *US Army Psychiatry in the Vietnam War: New Challenges In Extended Counterinsurgency Warfare* (Washington, DC: Government Printing Office, 2015), 145–209.
61 Bob Leahy, "Dear Grandma", February 2, 1970, *Dear America*, 423.
62. James Simmen, "Dear Vern", May 10, 1968, *Dear America*, 178.
63. Kenneth Bagby, "Dear Folks," November 17, 1965, as quoted in *Letters from Vietnam: Voices of War* (NY: Praesidio, 2003), 42.
64. Delta Company, 3/21, 196th Light Infantry Brigade of the American Division, "Dear President Nixon," April 20, 1969, *Dear America*, 144.
65. Ibid.

Chapter 7

1 Philip Caputo, *A Rumor of War* (NY: Ballantine, 1977), 167.
2. Robert C. "Mike" Ransom, Jr., "Dear Mom and Dad", Date Unknown, *Dear America: Letters Home From Vietnam* (New York: W.W. Norton & Company, 1985), 181.
3. A Company was in front of B Company on the return trip. The ambush had cut A off from supporting B, and then the VC started to mortar Company A.
4. Theodore T. Jagosz, interview by Joseph Gilch, July 23, 2004.

Epilogue

1. Jim Sheeler, "Final Salute," *Rocky Mountain Times*, April 24, 2006, 1–24. Online edition available from the *American Society of News Editors, Missouri School of Journalism*; Eric Wester, Col. Todd Heisler, Maj. Steve Beck, and Bill [last name unknown], interview by Neil Conan, *Talk of the Nation*, "A Grim Task: Military Death Notification," NPR, May 29, 2006.

2. *Vietnam Conflict File* of the Defense Casualty Analysis System (DCAS), National Archives and Records Administration, April 29, 2008. An additional 1,201 "declared dead" are not included in our totals because it is not clear to us what this designation signifies.
3. The seminal account of one of these odysseys is Lewis B. Puller, Jr.'s *Fortunate Son* (New York: Bantam, 1993).
4. Robert J. Lifton, *Home from the War, Vietnam Veterans: Neither Victims nor Executioners* (New York: Simon and Schuster, 1973), 37, et. passim.
5. See, for example, Larry Heinemann, *Paco's Story* (New York: Farrar, Straus, Giroux, 1984). The disparity among the experiences and responses to the war of returnees is treated extensively by Myra MacPherson in *Long Time Passing: Vietnam and the Haunted Generation* (New York: Doubleday, 1984) and Ron Kovic, *Born on the Fourth of July* (New York: McGraw-Hill, 1976).
6. Tom Roberts, "A Conversation with Fr. Michael Doyle," *National Catholic Reporter*, December 8, 2009.
7. Nick Turse, *Kill Anything That Moves: The Real American War in Vietnam* (New York: Henry Holt, 2013), 13.
8. The most comprehensive accounts of this form of resistance against invading armies and oppressive regimes to date are Robert B. Asprey's, two-volume survey in *War in the Shadows: The Guerrilla in History* (Garden, City, NY: 1975), and Max Boot's more recent *Invisible Armies* (New York: Norton, 2013).
9. Michael Clodfelter, *Vietnam in Military Statistics: A History of the Indochina War, 1772–1991* (Jefferson, NC: McFarland, 1995), 225.
10. For a harrowing account of the suffering of those who managed to survive a napalm explosion, see Viet Than Nguyen, *The Sympathizer* (New York: Grove, 2015), 393–398.
11. Alain Jaubert, "Zapping the Viet Cong by Computer," *New Scientist* 30 (March, 1972), 685.
12. *United States House Subcommittee on Defense Appropriations*, 88th Congress, Session1, Part 1 (1964), 483–484.
13. Thomas Bodenheimer and George Roth, "Health and Death in Vietnam," in Barry Weisberg, ed., *Ecocide in Indochina: The Ecology of War* (San Francisco: Canfield, 1970), 163.
14. William F. Pepper, "The Children of Vietnam" reprinted from *Ramparts Magazine* in Weisberg, *Ecocide,* 99.
15. Neil Sheehan, *A Bright Shining Lie: John Paul Vann and America in Vietnam* (New York: Random House, 1989), 562.
16. Totals calculated by H. Westing, Department of Biology, Windham College, Putney, Vermont in Weisberg, ed., *Ecocide in Indochina*, 95.
17 Stephen Daggett, "Costs of Major US Wars," *CRS Report for Congress* (Washington, DC: Congressional Research Service, 2010), 2.
18. U.S.G. Sharp, *Pentagon Papers, Gravel Edition* (Boston: Beacon, 1971), volume 4, 39–40.
19. For the most balanced overview of Ho Chi Minh's efforts and wartime American-Viet Minh coordination see Marilyn Young, *The Vietnam Wars, 1945–1990* (New York: HarperCollins, 1991), chapters 1 and 2; and Archimedes Patti, *Why Viet Nam?: Prelude to America's Albatross* (Berkeley: University of California Press, 1982), chapter 6. For US rebuffs of Ho's overtures, Frederik Logevall, *Embers of War: The Fall of an Empire and the Making of America's Vietnam* (New York: Random House, 2012), 98–107, 220, 229–233.
20. Robert S. McNamara. *In Retrospect: The Tragedy and Lessons of Vietnam* (New York: Random House, 1995), xx.

Select Sources

Primary Sources - General

After-action reports, United States Army, First Battalion (Mechanized), Fifth Infantry Regiment, Twenty-Fifth Infantry Division, February 22–July 23, 1966.

Adler, Bill, ed. *Letters from Vietnam.* Novato, CA: Presidio, 2003.

Antti, Richard D. *The Landscape of My Memory.* Morrisville: NC: Rantti Creations, 2008.

Carroll, Andrew ed. *War Letters: Extraordinary Correspondence from American Wars.* New York: Washington Square Press, 2001.

Dutton, George *et. al.*, eds. *Sources of Vietnamese Tradition.* New York: Columbia University Press, 2012.

Edelman, Bernard. *Dear America: Letters Home from Vietnam.* New York: Norton, 1985.

Eisenhower, Dwight D. "Telephone Broadcast to the AFL-CIO Merger Meeting in New York City," December 5, 1955.

Gilch, James X. *Letters to George and Katherine Gilch.* (1–72) October 19, 1965–July 21, 1966.

Gilch, James X. *Letters to Gerry Shields.* (1–4).

Pentagon Papers. Senator Gravel Edition. Boston: Beacon, 1971.

United States Army. *The 25th's, 25th in Combat, Tropic Lightning 25th Infantry Division.* Doraville, GA: Albert Love Enterprises, 1966.

Oral Interviews

Gilch family members, particularly Jimmy's brothers, George and Joe, and sisters, Maureen, Kathleen, and Helen.

Lisa and Peggy Shields, and Louise Fasulo-Cosenz, January 8th and February 23rd, 2011.

Personal Correspondence

Captain Theodore T. Jagosz, "Correction and Post Script," July 18, 2004.

Captain Theodore T. Jagosz, "Second Platoon Combat," July 23, 2004.

Captain Theodore T. Jagosz, "Photos: 66054 Van Clief & VCPOW," July 31, 2004.

Captain Theodore T. Jagosz, "Tribute to First Lieutenant Frank D'Amico, *Bobcat Bravo 3-6*" June 10, 2010.

Randy Kethcart, ed., Second Platoon, Co. B, 1/5 Mech., Bobcats, The First Battalion (Mechanized) Fifth Infantry, "Twenty-Fifth Infantry Division in the Vietnam War, 1966-1971," July 2004.

Post–World War II American Society, 1945 through the 1960s

Bremer, Robert and Gary Reichard, eds. *Reshaping America: Society and Institutions, 1945–1960.* Columbus: Ohio State University Press, 1982.

Cohen, Lizabeth. *A Consumers' Republic: The Politics of Mass Consumption in Postwar America.* New York: Vintage Books, 2003.

Conant, James Bryant. *The Education of American Teachers.* New York: McGraw Hill, 1963.

Conant, James Bryant. "The University and the High School" *School and Society* (January 1965), pp. 52–55.

Galbraith, John K. *The Affluent Society.* New York: New American Library, 1958.

Halliwell, Martin. *American Culture in the 1950s.* Edinburgh: Edinburgh University Press, 2007.

Harrington, Michael. *The Other America: Poverty in the United States.* New York: Simon and Schuster, 1997.

Jamison, Andrew and Ron Eyerman. *Seeds of the Sixties.* Berkeley: University of California Press, 1994.

Keats, John. *The Insolent Chariots.* Philadelphia: J.B. Lippincott Company, 1958.

Leap, William. *The History of Runnemede New Jersey, 1626–1976.* Runnemede, NJ: self-published, 1981.

Lichter, Solomon *et al. The Drop-Outs: A Treatment Study of Intellectually Capable Students Who Drop Out of High School.* New York: Free Press, 1962.

Marc, David. *Demographic Vistas: Television in American Culture.* Philadelphia: University of Pennsylvania Press, 1984.

Medved, Michael and David Wallechinsky. *What Really Happened to the Class of 65?* New York: Random House, 1976.

Mehling, Harold. *The Great Time-Killer.* Cleveland, OH: World Publishing Company, 1962.

Monteith, Sharon. *American Culture of the 1960s.* Edinburgh: Edinburgh University Press, 2008.

O'Neill, William L. *American High: The Years of Confidence, 1945–1960.* New York: The Free Press, 1986.

Palladino, Grace. *Teenagers: An American History.* New York: Basic Books, 1996.

Potter, David M. *People of Plenty: Economic Abundance and the American Character.* Chicago: University of Chicago Press, 1954.

Reich, Robert B. *Aftershock: The Next Economy and America's Future.* New York: Vintage, 2011.

Robertson, Thomas. *The Malthusian Moment: Global Population Growth and the Birth of American Environmentalism.* New Brunswick, NJ: Rutgers University Press, 2012.

Roszak, Theodore. *The Making of a Counter Culture: Reflections on the Technocratic Society and Its Youthful Opposition.* New York: Doubleday and Company, 1969.

Strom, Robert D. "The School Dropout and The Family." *School and Society* (April 1964).

White, Donald W. *The American Century: The Rise and Decline of the United States as a World Power.* New Haven, CT: Yale University Press, 1996.

Wilson, Sloan. "Time to Close our Carnival" *Life Magazine* 44/12 (March, 1958), 36-45.

Early Vietnamese Resistance Movements and Vietnam during the French Colonial Era through the First Vietnamese War of Independence

Arnold, James R. *The First Domino: Eisenhower, the Military, and America's Intervention in Vietnam.* New York: William Morrow, 1991.

Biggs, David. *Quagmire: Nation-building and Nature in the Mekong Delta.* Seattle: University of Washington Press, 2010.

Bradley, Mark Philip. *Imagining Vietnam and America: The Making of Postcolonial Vietnam, 1919–1950*. Chapel Hill: University of North Carolina Press, 2000.

Bradley, Mark. "Making Sense of the French War: The Postcolonial Moment and the First Vietnam War, 1945–1954," in Lawrence and Logevall, eds., *The First Vietnam War*, 16–40.

Brocheux, Pierre. *Ho Chi Minh: A Biography*. New York: Cambridge University Press, 2007.

Buttinger, Joseph. *The Smaller Dragon: A Political History of Vietnam*. New York: Praeger, 1967.

Chesneux, Jean et. al., ed. *Tradition et Révolution au Vietnam*. Paris: Editions Anthropos, 1971.

Duiker, William J. *The Rise of Nationalism in Vietnam: 1900–1941*. Ithaca, NY: Cornell University Press, 1976.

Ennis, T. E. *French Policy and Developments in Indo-China*. Chicago: University of Chicago Press, 1936.

Hammer, Ellen. *The Struggle for Indochina, 1940–1955*. Stanford, CA: Stanford University Press, 1954.

Hoàng Văn Chí. *From Colonialism to Communism: A Case History of North Vietnam*. New York: Praeger, 1964.

Hodgkin, Thomas. *Vietnam: The Revolutionary Path*. New York: St. Martin's Press, 1981.

Huỳnh Kim Khánh. *Vietnamese Communism, 1925–1945*. Ithaca, NY: Cornell University Press, 1982.

Jackson, L.R. "The Vietnamese Revolution and the Montagnards," *Asian Studies* 9.5 (May, 1969), 313–330

Lacouture, Jean. *Ho Chi Minh: A Political Biography*. New York: Vintage, 1968.

Lawrence, Mark Atwood and Fredrik Logevall. *The First Vietnam War: Colonial Conflict and Cold War Crisis*. Cambridge, MA: Harvard University Press, 2007.

Lê Thanh Khôi. *Le Viêt Nam: Histoire et civilization*. Paris: Éditions de Minuit, 1955.

Logevall, Fredrik. *Embers of War: The Fall of an Empire and the Making of America's Vietnam*. New York: Random House, 2012.

Marr, David. *Vietnamese Anticolonialism, 1885–1925*. Berkeley: University of California Press, 1971.

Marr, David. *Vietnam 1945: The Quest for Power*. Berkeley: University of California Press, 1995.

McAlister, John T. Jr. and Paul Mus. *The Vietnamese and Their Revolution*. New York: Harper and Row, 1970.

Osborne, Milton E. *The French Presence in Cochin China and Cambodia: Rule and Response, 1859–1905*. Ithaca, NY: Cornell University Press, 1969.

Pham Cao Duong. *Vietnamese Peasants under French Domination, 1861–1945*. Berkeley, CA: Center for South and Southeast Asia Studies, 1985.

Quinn-Judge, Sophie. *Ho Chi Minh: The Missing Years, 1919–1941*. Berkeley, CA: University of California Press, 2002.

Roy, Jules. *The Battle of Dienbienphu*. Translated by Robert Baldick. New York: Harper and Row, 1965.

Ruscio, Alain. *La Guerre Française d'Indochine 1945–1954*. Brussels: Editions Complexe, 1992.

Sainteny, Jean. *Ho Chi Minh and His Vietnam: A Personal Memoir*. Translated by Herma Briffault. Chicago: Cowles, 1972.

Tai, Hue-Tam Ho. *Millenarianism and Peasant Politics in Vietnam*. Cambridge, MA: Harvard University Press, 1983.

Tai, Hue-Tam Ho. *Radicalism and the Origins of the Vietnamese Revolution*. Cambridge, MA: Harvard University Press, 1992.

Tønnesson, Stein. *Vietnam 1946: How the War Began*. Berkeley: University of California Press, 2010.

Truong Buu Lam. *Colonialism Experienced: Vietnamese Writings on Colonialism, 1900–1931*. Ann Arbor: The University of Michigan Press, 2000.

Truong Buu Lam. *Patterns of Vietnamese Response to Foreign Intervention, 1858–1900*. New Haven, CT: Yale Southeast Asian Studies Monograph Series, 1967.

Truong Nhu Tang. *A Viet Cong Memoir: An Inside Account of the Vietnam War and Its Aftermath*. New York: Vintage, 1985.

Werner, Jayne Susan. *Peasant Politics and Religious Sectarianism: Peasant and Priest in the Cao Dai in Viet Nam*. New Haven, CT: Yale Southeast Asian Series, 1981.

American Interventions from FDR through LBJ, the Diem Interregnum in South Vietnam, and the Renewal of the Vietnamese Wars of Independence

Anderson, David. *Trapped by Success: The Eisenhower Administration and the Vietnam War, 1953–61*. New York: Columbia University Press, 1991.

Berman, Larry. *Lyndon Johnson's War*. New York: Norton, 1989.

Blaufarb, Douglas S. *The Counterinsurgency Era: U.S. Doctrine and Performance, 1950 to the Present*. New York: Free Press, 1977.

Brigham, Robert K. *Guerrilla Diplomacy: The NLF's Foreign Relations and the Vietnam War*. Ithaca, NY: Cornell University Press, 1999.

Carter, James M. *Inventing Vietnam: The United States and State Building, 1954–1968*. New York: Cambridge University Press, 2008.

Dallek, Robert. *Flawed Giant: Lyndon Johnson and his Times, 1961–1973*. New York: Oxford University Press, 1998.

Devillers, Philippe. "La lutte pour la reunification du Vietnam entre 1954 et 1961," in *Tradition et révolution au Vietnam*, eds. Jean Chesneaux et Daniel Hemery. Paris: Editions Anthropos, 1971.

Gardner, Lloyd. *Approaching Vietnam: From World War II through Dienbienphu*. New York: W.W. Norton, 1988.

Gardner, Lloyd. *Pay Any Price: Lyndon Johnson and the Wars for Vietnam*. Chicago: Ivan R. Dee, 1995.

Halberstam, David. *The Best and the Brightest*. New York: Random, 1972.

Harrison, Benjamin T. and Christopher L. Mosher, "The Secret Diary of McNamara's Dove: The Long-Lost Story of John T. McNaughton's Opposition to the Vietnam War," *Diplomatic History* 5/3 (2011), 505–534.

Herring, George C. *America's Longest War: The United States and Vietnam, 1950–1975*. New York: McGraw-Hill, 1996.

Hunt, David. *Vietnam's Southern Revolution: From Peasant Insurrection to Total War*. Amherst, MA: University of Massachusetts Press, 2008.

Kaiser, David. *American Tragedy: Kennedy, Johnson, and the Origins of the Vietnam War*. Cambridge, MA: Harvard University Press, 2000.

Karnow, Stanley. *Vietnam: A History*. New York: Viking, 1983.

Kimball, Warren. *Forged in War: Roosevelt, Churchill, and the Second World War*. New York: Morrow, 1997.

Latham, Michael. *Modernization as Ideology: American Social Science and "Nation Building" in the Kennedy Era*. Chapel Hill: University of North Carolina Press, 2000.

Lawrence, Mark Atwood. *The Vietnam War: An International History in Documents.* New York: Oxford University Press, 2014.

Logevall, Fredrik. *Choosing War: The Lost Chance for Peace and the Escalation of the War in Vietnam.* Berkeley: University of California, 1999.

McNamara, Robert S. *In Retrospect: The Tragedy and Lessons of Vietnam.* New York: Vintage, 1995.

Miller, Edward. *Misalliance: Ngo Dinh Diem, The United States, and the Fate of South Vietnam.* Cambridge, MA: Harvard University Press, 2013.

Nashel, Jonathan. Edward Landsdale's Cold War. Amherst, MA: University of Massachusetts Press, 2005.

Nguyen, Lien-Hang T. *Hanoi's War: An International History of the War for Peace in Vietnam.* Chapel Hill: The University of North Carolina Press, 2012.

Preston, Andrew. The War Council: McGeorge Bundy, the NSC, and Vietnam. Cambridge, MA: Harvard University Press, 2006.

Shapley, Deborah. *Promise and Power: The Life and Times of Robert McNamara.* Boston: Little, Brown, 1993.

Tønnnesson, Stein. *The Vietnamese Revolution of 1945: Roosevelt, Ho Chi Minh, and de Gaulle in a World at War.* London: Sage, 1991.

Van De Mark, Brian, *Into the Quagmire: Lyndon Johnson and the Escalation of the Vietnam War.* New York: Oxford University Press, 1995.

Warner, Denis. *The Last Confucian: Vietnam, Southeast Asia, and the West.* Baltimore: Penguin, 1964.

Young, Marilyn. *The Vietnam Wars, 1945–1990.* New York: HarperCollins, 1991.

Vietnamese Guerrilla War and American Responses, 1965–1972

Adas, Michael. *Dominance by Design: Technological Imperatives and America's Civilizing Mission.* Cambridge, MA: Harvard University Press, 2006.

Appy, Christian G. *Working Class War: American Combat Soldiers and Vietnam.* Chapel Hill: University of North Carolina Press, 1993.

Bao Ninh. *The Sorrow of War: A Novel of North Vietnam.* Translated by Phan Thanh Hoa. New York: Pantheon, 1993.

Baker, Mark. *Nam: The Vietnam War in the Words of the Soldiers Who Fought There.* New York: Morrow, 1983.

Bergerud, Eric M. *The Dynamics of Defeat: The Vietnam War in Hau Nghia Province.* Boulder, CO; Westview, 1991.

Bergerud, Eric M. *Red Thunder, Tropic Lightning: The World of a Combat Division in Vietnam.* New York: Penguin, 1994.

Blaufarb, Douglas S. *The Counterinsurgency Era: U.S. Doctrine and Performance 1950 to the Present.* New York: Free Press, 1977.

Boudarel, Georges. "Essai sur la pensée militaire Vietnamienne," in Chesneux, ed., *Tradition et Révolution au Vietnam*, 460–495.

Bradley, Mark Philip. *Vietnam at War.* New York: Oxford University Press, 2012.

Brigham, Robert K. *ARVN: Life and Death in the South Vietnamese Army.* Lawrence: University of Kansas Press, 2006.

Brown, Malcolm. *The New Face of War.* Indianapolis: Bobbs-Merrill, 1965.

Callaway, Joseph W., Jr. *Mekong First Light.* New York: Ballantine, 2004.

Caputo, Philip, *A Rumor of War.* New York: Ballantine, 1977.

Chanoff, David and Doan Van Toai, *"Vietnam" A Portrait of Its People at War.* London: Tauris Parke, 2009.

Davidson, Phillip B. *Vietnam at War: The History, 1946–1975.* New York: Oxford University Press, 1988.

Duiker, William J. *Sacred War: Nationalism and Revolution in a Divided Vietnam.* New York: McGraw-Hill, 1995.

Duong Thu Huong. *Novel Without A Name.* Translated by Phan Huy Duong and Nina McPherson. New York: William Morrow, 1995.

Ebert, James R. *A Life in A Year: The American Infantryman in Vietnam.* New York: Ballantine, 1993.

Elliot, David W. P. *The Vietnamese War: Revolution and Social Change in the Mekong Delta, 1930–1975.* Armonk, New York: M.E. Sharpe, 2007.

Gibson, James William. *The Perfect War: Technowar in Vietnam.* Boston: Atlantic Monthly Press, 1986.

Hay, John H. Jr. *Vietnam Studies: Tactical and Material Innovations.* Washington, DC, Department of the Army, 1974.

Heinemann, Larry. *Close Quarters.* New York: Vintage, 2005.

Herr, Michael. *Dispatches.* New York: Avon, 1968.

Krepinevich, Andrew. *The Army and Vietnam.* Baltimore: Johns Hopkins University Press, 1986.

Lair, Meredith H. *Armed with Abundance: Consumerism and Soldiering in the Vietnam War.* Chapel Hill: The University of North Carolina, 2011. Mahnken, Thomas G. *Technology and the American Way of War since 1945.* New York: Columbia University Press, 2008.

Mangold, Tom and John Penycate. *The Tunnels of Cu Chi.* New York: Random House, 1985.

Maraniss, David. *They Marched Into Sunlight: War and Peace in Vietnam and America, October 1967.* New York: Simon and Schuster, 2003.

Marlantes, Karl. *Matterhorn.* New York: Atlantic Monthly Press, 2010.

Maurer, Harry. *Strange Ground: An Oral History of Americans in Vietnam, 1945–1975.* New York: Avon, 1989.

Moore, Harold G. and Joseph L. Galloway. *We Were Soldiers Once . . . and Young.* New York: Random House, 1992.

O'Brien, Tim. *The Things They Carried.* New York: Penguin, 1991.

Page, Tim. *Another Vietnam: Pictures of the War from the Other Side.* Edited by Doug Niven and Chris Riley. Washington, DC: National Geographic, 2002.

Pham Cuong. "Cu Chi, A Guerrilla Base," in *American Failure*, edited by Nguyen Khac Vien. Vietnamese Studies 20. Hanoi: Xunhasaba, 1968.

Pike, Douglas. *Viet Cong: The Organization and Techniques of the National Liberation Front of South Vietnam.* Cambridge, MA: MIT Press, 1966.

Prados, John. *The Blood Road: The Ho Chi Minh Trail and the Vietnam War.* Hoboken, NJ: Wiley, 1998.

Race, Jeffrey. *War Comes to Long An.* Berkeley, CA: University of California Press, 1972.

Sansom, Robert L. *The Economics of Insurgency in the Mekong Delta.* Cambridge, MA: MIT Press, 1970.

Santori, Al. *Everything We Had: An Oral History of the Vietnam War.* New York: Random House, 1981.

Sheehan, Neil. *A Bright Shining Lie: John Paul Vann and America in Vietnam.* New York: Random House, 1989.

Schell, Jonathan. *The Village of Ben Suc.* New York: Random House, 1967.

Spector, Ronald H. *After Tet: The Bloodiest Year in Vietnam.* New York: Vintage, 1993.

Starry, Donn A. *Mounted Combat in Vietnam* Washington, DC: Department of the Army, 1989.

Tanham, George K. *Communist Revolutionary Warfare: From the Vietminh to the Viet Cong.* New York: Praeger, 1967.

Turse, Nick. *Kill Anything That Moves: The Real American War in Vietnam.* New York: Henry Holt, 2013.

Westmoreland, William C. *A Soldier Reports.* New York: Doubleday, 1976.

Zaffiri, Samuel. *Westmoreland: A Biography of William C. Westmoreland.* New York: William Morrow, 1994.

Zumwalt, James G. *Bare Feet, Iron Will: Stories from the Other Side of Vietnam's Battlefields.* Jacksonville, FL: Fortis, 2010.

Fallout from a Misbegotten War: Runnemede (NJ), America, Vietnam, and the Global Cold War

Appy, Christian G. *American Reckoning: The Vietnam War and Our National Identity.* New York: Penguin, 2015.

Appy, Christian G. *Patriots: The Vietnam War Remembered From All Sides.* New York: Penguin, 2003.

Appy, Christian G. *American Reckoning: The Vietnam War and Out National Identity.* New York: Penguin, 2015.

Butler, Robert Olen. *A Good Scent From a Strange Mountain.* New York: Henry Holt, 1992.

Clodfelter, Mark. *The Limits of Air Power: The American Bombing of North Vietnam.* New York: The Free Press, 1989.

Clodfelter, Michael. *Vietnam In Military Statistics: A History of the Indochina Wars, 1772–1991.* Jefferson, NC: McFarland, 1995.

Ehrhart, W.D. *Unaccustomed Mercy: Soldier-Poets of the Vietnam War.* Lubbock, TX: Texas Tech University Press, 1989.

Heinemann, Larry. *Paco's Story.* New York: Farrar, Straus and Giroux, 1979.

Hess, Martha. *Then the Americans Came: Voices from Vietnam.* New York: Four Walls, Eight Windows, 1993.

Lewallen, John. *Ecology of Devastation: Indochina.* Baltimore: Penguin, 1971.

Lifton, Robert Jay. *Home From the War, Vietnam Veterans: Neither Victims Nor Executioners.* New York: Simon and Schuster, 1973.

MacPherson, Myra. *Long Time Passing: Vietnam & the Haunted Generation.* New York: Doubleday, 1984.

Neu, Charles ed. *After Vietnam: Legacies of a Lost War.* Baltimore: Johns Hopkins University Press, 2000.

Nielands, J.B. et. al. *Not Since the Romans Salted the Land.* Ithaca, NY: Glad Day, 1970.

Orians G.H. and E.W. Pfeiffer. "Ecological Effects of the War in Vietnam," *Science* 168 (May, 1970): 544–554.

Polner, Murray. *No More Victory Parades: The Return of the Vietnam Veteran.* New York: Holt, Reinhart & Winston, 1971.

Viet Thanh Nguyen. *The Sympathizer.* New York: Grove, 2015.

Weisberg. Barry, ed. *Ecocide in Indochina: The Ecology of War.* San Francisco, CA: Canfield, 1970.

Whiteside, T, ed. *Defoliation.* New York: Ballantine, 1970

Credits

Prologue

Page xiv: Lafoon, Robert C., Photographer Department of Defense. Department of the Army. Office of the Deputy Chief of Staff for Operations. U.S. Army Audiovisual Center. ca. 1974-5/15/1984. **xv:** "Tunnels" from Dien Cai Dau ©1988 by Yusef Komunyakaa. Published by Wesleyan University Press. Used by permission.

Chapter 1

Page 2: ClassicStock/Masterfile (top); Photo by Howard Sochurek/The LIFE Picture Collection/Getty Images (bottom). **6:** New Jersey Turnpike Photograph (XXX54300), 1950 Oct. 2, R.C. Maxwell Co. Records, Hartman Center for Sales, Advertising and Marketing History, David M. Rubenstein Rare Book and Manuscript Library, Duke University. **10:** Photo by ADN-Bildarchiv/ullstein bild via Getty Images. **11:** Vietnam National Museum of History. **13:** Letter from Ho Chi Minh to President Harry S. Truman, 02/28/1946 (National Archives Identifier: 305263). **19:** Photo by Collection Jean-Claude LABBE/Gamma-Rapho via Getty Images.

Chapter 2

Page 26: Photo by Hulton Archive/Getty Images (top); Photo by ullstein bild/ullstein bild via Getty Images (bottom). **30:** Courtesty OSS Society. **35:** Collection: Richard Nixon Foundation Collection of Audiovisual Materials, ca. 1926–ca. 1994. **40:** Photo by John Dominis/The LIFE Picture Collection/Getty Images.

Chapter 3

Page 54: Photo by George Rinhart/Corbis via Getty Images (top); Okamoto, Yoichi R. (Yoichi Robert), 1915–1985, Photographer (bottom). **58:** Department of Defense. Department of the Army. Office of the Deputy Chief of Staff for Operations. U.S. Army Audiovisual Center. ca. 1974-5/15/1984. **61:** LBJ Library photo by Cecil Stoughton. **63:** Library of Congress, Prints & Photographs Division, drawing by Edmund S. Valtman, [reproduction number, e.g., LC-USZ62-123456]. **64:** Gulf of Tonkin Resolution, as Introduced, S.J. Res. 189, 8/5/1964. National Archives Identifier 2127364. **83:** Photo by TASS via Getty Images. **84:** © Bao Hanh/Another Vietnam. **85:** Fifth Battalion The Royal Australian Regiment Association; Fifth Battalion The Royal Australian Regiment Association. **87:** Esprit Quarterly.

Chapter 4

Page 90: © Le Minh Truong/Another Vietnam (top); The Pan Am Historical Foundation (bottom). **102:** Photo courtesy of Larry "Doc" Butcher, Delta Company, 2nd Battalion, 14th Infantry Regiment. **104:** Photo: Robert Paragallo. **108:** Photo: Vincent Simonelli.

Chapter 5

Page 118: army. Mil (top); © Doan Cong Tinh/Another Vietnam (bottom). **121:** Psywarrior.com. **132:** © Nguyen Dinh Uu/Another Vietnam. **135:** Provided Courtesy of the Tropic Lightning Museum, U.S. Army. **140:** Bettman/Getty Images. **142:** Steve Stibbens ©1963, 2017 Stars and Stripes, All Rights Reserved. **144:** LC-DIG-ds-01310 (digital file from original negative) Repository: Library of Congress Prints and Photographs Division Washington, D.C. 20540 USA.

Chapter 6

Page 150: Photographs of American Military Activities, ca. 1918–ca. 1981 (top); © Le Chi Hai/Another Vietnam (bottom); **155:** General Photograph File of the U.S. Marine Corps, 1927–1981. **172:** AP Photo/Horst Faas. **174:** VA004542, Douglas Pike Photograph Collection, The Vietnam Center and Archive, Texas Tech University. **183:** psywarrior.com.

Chapter 7

Page 188: From the collection of Roger Pic.

Epilogue

Page 196: Department of Defense. Department of the Army National Archives 530619. **200:** Photo by © Tim Page/CORBIS/Corbis via Getty Images. **202:** National Archives 530626. **207:** Library of Congress Prints and Photographs Division.

Index